Regionalism in International Law

This publication is exceptional and original and gives a new global look at the importance and development of international regionalism in its relation to the development of general international law.

—JUDr. Josef Mrázek
Institute of State and Law
Academy of Sciences of Czech Republic
Prague

. . . Due to its original and thought-provoking content this publication opens new perspectives of analysis on the current problems of regionalism and its relation to current international law.

—Prof. JUDr. Ján Mazák, CSc.
Former Advocate General of ECJ
Law Faculty Košice-Slovakia

Regionalism in International Law evaluates regionalism in its various relationships and forms with respect to international law, as well as the importance and duties of international law with respect to the establishment and functioning of various forms of regional groups. A great deal of attention has been paid to regionalism from the global, political, economic and security aspects, but a complex evaluation of the impact it has had on international law, and vice versa, is still lacking. The main purpose of this volume is to eliminate this gap and present the latest state of knowledge on the topic.

This text will be of interest both to students at an advanced level, academics and reflective practitioners. It addresses the topics with regard to international law and regionalism and will be of interest to academics dealing with legal aspects of current regionalism and for the specialized courses in the faculties of law, as well as anyone studying diplomacy and international studies, international relations, regional integration law, EU law, international law and international relations.

Ján Klučka is Professor of International Law at Pavol Jozef Šafárik University, Košice, Slovakia.

Routledge Research in International Law

For a full list of titles in this series, visit www.routledge.com/Routledge-Research-in-International-Law/book-series/INTNLLAW

Available:

The Rule of Law in the United Nations Security Council Decision-Making Process
Turning the Focus Inwards
Sherif Elgebeily

Universal Jurisdiction in International Criminal Law
The Debate and the Battle for Hegemony
Aisling O'Sullivan

The Right to Democracy in International Law
Between Procedure, Substance and the Philosophy of John Rawls
Khalifa A Alfadhel

Latin America and the International Court of Justice
Contributions to International Law
Edited by Paula Wojcikiewicz Almeida and Jean-Marc Sorel

Fragmentation vs the Constitutionalisation of International Law
A Practical Inquiry
Edited by Andrzej Jakubowski and Karolina Wierczyńska

Legal Accountability and Britain's Wars, 2000–2015
Peter Rowe

Means of Transportation and Registration of Nationality
Transportation Registered by International Organizations
Vincent P. Cogliati-Bantz

Regionalism in International Law
Ján Klučka

Regionalism in International Law

Ján Klučka

Routledge
Taylor & Francis Group
LONDON AND NEW YORK

First published 2018
by Routledge

2 Park Square, Milton Park, Abingdon, Oxfordshire OX14 4RN
52 Vanderbilt Avenue, New York, NY 10017

Routledge is an imprint of the Taylor & Francis Group, an informa business

First issued in paperback 2019

Library of Congress Cataloging-in-Publication Data
Names: Klučka, Ján, author.
Title: Regionalism in international law / Jâan Kluécka.
Description: Abingdon, Oxon ; New York, NY : Routledge, 2018. |
Series: Routledge research in international law | Includes bibliographical references and index.
Identifiers: LCCN 2017039766 | ISBN 9781138064959 (hardback) |
ISBN 9781351661508 (epub) | ISBN 9781351661492 (adobe) |
ISBN 9781351661485 (mobipocket)
Subjects: LCSH: Regionalism (International organization)
Classification: LCC KZ1273 .K573 2018 | DDC 341.24—dc23
LC record available at https://lccn.loc.gov/2017039766

ISBN: 978-1-138-06495-9 (hbk)
ISBN: 978-0-367-88870-1 (pbk)

Typeset in Galliard
by Apex CoVantage, LLC

Contents

Preface

The main reason for choosing the topic of the present monograph *Regionalism and International Law* was to evaluate regionalism in its various relationships and forms with respect to international law, and also to consider the importance and duties of international law with respect to the establishment and functioning of various forms of regional groupings.

It should be pointed out that even though a lot of attention has been so far paid to regionalism from the historical, political, economic, security and other similar aspects, a more concentrated evaluation of the impact it has had on international law, and *vice versa*, is still lacking. The efforts of the present monograph are to partially eliminate this gap. The monograph is divided into the eight chapters dealing with the specific aspects of regionalism in relation to international law.

After giving a brief insight into how regionalism has developed, its content and terminology, the monograph studies in more detail individual types of regionalism in the forms of old and new regionalism, as well as treaty and institutional regionalism, their specifications and different aspects of their relations to contemporary international law.

Attention is paid also to a specific institutional and treaty phenomenon of current regionalism: the impact the European Union has on making it stable and developed by means of both factual measures and a system of measures regulated by international treaties. This concerns the treaties concluded between the European Union and the international organizations, groups of states or states themselves. In this respect the issue of interregionalism, or the interregionalism treaty, is being analysed from the viewpoint of its specifications and contributions to general international law. A more detailed analysis is concentrated on two specific aspects of the activities of regional organizations, namely to guarantee the uniform interpretations and application of regional treaties through the specific proceedings of their judicial and non-judicial bodies and the regional systems of the protection of human rights. The final chapter concerns the codification of international law because of the need to unify the legal regulation of relationships which the regional organizations currently enter into, and the evaluation of the possible impact of initial activities and the application of international law rules through regional organizations and their judicial bodies within the context of the so-called fragmentation of international law.

Without claiming in any respect to have presented an exhaustive and comprehensive analysis of all aspects of the existing relations between regionalism and international law, the author assumes that he has in principle managed to identify the main points of the contacts between regionalism and international law, their mutual impact and the contribution of various forms of regionalism with respect to general international law and *vice versa*. In this regard the present monograph is intended to provide a concise introduction into the area of regionalism and international law as well as the point of departure for more advanced study and next research of this topic.

About the Author

Prof. JUDr. Ján Klučka, CSc., Professor of International Law at Law Faculty, University P.J.Šafárik, Košice (Slovakia). Former judge of Slovak Constitutional Court (1993–2004), Former Judge of the European Court of Justice (2004–2009), Member of the Venice Commission for Democracy through Law (1993–2004), Member of the Slovak National Group at Permanent Court of Arbitration (since 1993). Author of more than 100 articles and studies in Slovakia and abroad dealing with various topics of public international law (international air and space law, international law on human rights, environmental law and European law). A number of expertises on constitutional justice issues have been elaborated within the Venice Commission for Democracy through Law. Author of textbooks on public and private international law as well as European law.

Abbreviations of the Regional Organizations and Interregional Groupings

ACMW	ASEAN Committee of Migrant Workers
ACWI	ASEAN Commission on the Rights of Women and Children
AEC	African Economic Community
AICHR	Intergovernmental Commission on Human Rights
APEC	Asian Pacific Economic Cooperation
ASEAN	Association of Southeast Asian Nations
ASEM	Asia European Meeting
AU	African Union
CAT	Committee against Torture
CEDAW	Committee on the Elimination of Discrimination against Women
CEMAC	Central African Economic and Monetary Community
CENTO	Central Treaty Organisation
CER	Australia-New Zealand Closer Economic Relations
CERD	Committee on the Elimination of Racial Discrimination
CESCR	Committee on Economic Social and Cultural Rights
CFA	African Financial Community France
CIS	Commonwealth of Independent States
CMW	Committee on the Protection of the Rights of all Migrant Workers and Members of their Families
CoE	Council of Europe
COMECON	Council of Mutual Economic Cooperation
COMESA	Common Market for Eastern and Southern Africa
CRC	Committee of the Rights of the Child
EAC	East African Community
EC	European Communities
ECCAS	Economic Community of Central African States
ECOWAS	Economic Community of West African States
ECSR	European Committee of Human Rights
EEA	European Economic Area
EEC	European Economic Community
EFTA	European Free Trade Association
EU	European Union

FEALAC	Forum for East Asia-Latin America Cooperation
GATT	General Agreement on Tariff and Trade
GCC	Gulf Cooperation Council
GEF	Global Environmental Facility
HRC	Human Rights Committee
IBRD	International Bank for Reconstruction and Development
ICAO	International Civil Aviation Organisation
IGAD	Intergovernmental Authority on Development (East Africa)
IMF	International Monetary Fund
IOR-ARC	The Indian Ocean Rim Association
LAS	League of Arab States
MERCOSUR	Mercado Común del Sur
NAFTA	North American Free Trade Agreement
NATO	North Atlantic Treaty Organisation
OAU	Organisation of African Unity
OPEC	Organisation of Petroleum Exporting Countries
PARLACEN	Central America Parliament
PIF	Pacific Islands Forum
OHADA	Organization for the Harmonization of Business Law in Africa
SAARC	South Asia Association for Regional Cooperation
SACU	South African Customs Union
SADC	Southern African Development Community
SEATO	South-East Asia Treaty Organisation
SICA	Central American Integration System
UNO	United Nations Organisation
WAEMU	West African and Monetary Union
WTO	World Trade Organisation

Abbreviations of the Regional Courts and Tribunals

ACHR	African Court on Human and Peoples' Rights
ATJ	Andean Tribunal of Justice
BCJ	Benelux Court of Justice
CAJC	Central American Court of Justice
CCJ	Caribbean Court of Justice
CCJA/OHADA	Organization for the Harmonization of Business Law in Africa—Common Court of Justice and Arbitration
CEMAC	Central African Economic and Monetary Community Court of Justice
COMESA	Eastern and Southern Africa Common Market Court of Justice
EACJ	East African Community Court of Justice
ECCIS	Economic Court of the Commonwealth of Independent States
ECJ	European Court of Justice
ECOWAS/CCJ	European Community of West African States Court of Justice
ECSC	Eastern Caribbean Supreme Court
ECtHR	European Court of Human Rights
IACtHR	Inter-American Court of Human Rights
SADCT	Southern African Development Community Tribunal
UEMOA/CJ	West African Economic and Monetary Union Court of Justice

Other Abbreviations

DEVAW	Declaration on the Elimination of Violence against Women
ECHR	European Convention on Human Rights and Fundamental Freedoms
GEPs	Group of Eminent Persons
FTA	Free Trade Agreement
FTAA	Free Trade Area of the Americas
ICBT	Informal Cross Border Trade
NGO	Non Governmental Organisation
PRC	People's Republic of China
TFEU	Treaty on the Functioning of the European Union
UNAIDS	The Joint United Nations Programme on HIV/AIDS
VCLT	Vienna Convention on the Law of Treaties

1 International Organizations as New Subjects of International Law and Its Institutionalization

States, as basic subjects of international law, have played an important role regarding the regulation of international relations for a long time, forming international customs and creating bilateral or multilateral treaties. But with the Industrial Revolution in the 19th century came a significant challenge to the system. Over a relatively short period of time, new types of human activity crossing the borders of individual states started in the areas of industry (steel, coal, metals and mining), transport (international sea, railway and air) and telecommunication (telephone and telegraph). The needs of economic development, and related technical advances, started to put pressure both on new domestic and international regulations with respect to a whole set of specific and so far unknown areas of human activities that crossed the borders of individual states and urgently required international cooperation.

The customs and treaties legal regulation was no longer satisfactory for managing such developments and the states started to enter into multilateral treaties, which gradually contributed to the establishment of the first international intergovernmental organizations, known *as international administrative unions*, established in the second half of the 19th century. These were the first international organizations of a non-political nature whose existence was based on the needs of huge cross-border economic growth. It included, the International Telegraph Union (1865), Universal Post Union (1874), International Metric Union (1875), International Union for the Protection of Industrial Property (1883), International Union for the Protection of Submarine Cables (1884), International Union for the Publication of Customs Tariffs (1890), International Union of Railways (1886), Union of Geodesy (1886) and the Radiotelegraph Union (1906).

International administrative unions were regulatory and they introduced unified, internationally agreed standards of a technical nature and, hence, made it easier for international trade and communication to develop. Their establishment was highly significant from the point of view of international law because the states for the first time applied a "constitutive" feature of their sovereignty, the application of which gave a rise to the establishment of new entities of international law in the form of international intergovernmental agencies.[1]

The same rules applied to the establishment of those agencies (hereinafter referred to as international agencies) are also applied today when establishing modern international organizations. In particular, it concerns the derived and restricted international subjectivity, which gave rise to the principle of speciality under which each international organization has a determined object and purpose for its activities.[2] This is achieved on a legal basis of international law, internal legal order of organization or a combination of both through an organization's organs and within their competence. Similar to current international law, traditional international law dealt neither with horizontal relations among such organizations nor with their superiority and subordination, although, as today, the process of their establishment was not planned or otherwise coordinated.

In this historical context, the nascent institutionalism of international law provided the international community with answers to the challenges of the era by means of permanent international institutions being established since it was not possible to deal with them by way of non-institutionalized instruments of international law.[3] These are the grounds, which are still used today, for the establishment of international organizations either of a regional or universal nature.

Hence, the establishment of an international organization is always a unique combination of economic, political and historical factors on the basis of which the states in a particular region, or on wider geographical basis, are positive about the need to create a stable cooperative international grouping. It is, however, difficult to find regularity or a plan in the process of their establishment, since it is a response by the international community to a specific and particular need within a given historical era.

The growing need for permanent and coordinated cooperation regarding new relations between states gave rise to the first permanent international institutions; and despite structural and other changes made during the 20th century, some international administrative unions (in their initial or amended institutionalized form)[4] have survived until the current time, which proves their practical use and worthiness to the current international community. This development continued throughout the 20th century and saw a growing number of international organizations as well as the extension of their activities followed by specialization.

These circumstances gradually had an impact on general international law, which was reflected in the need for new rules of a general nature that would regulate the specific aspects of their activities.[5] The growing vastness, as well as complexity of international relations meant that more and more areas previously managed by the states were now entrusted to international organizations regarded as not only useful, but as an irreplaceable part of the current architecture of international community and international law.[6] According to H. Mosler: "the increasing number of organizations have come to play such an important and permanent part in international relations that now form a kind of superstructure over and above the society of States".[7]

To complete the picture, we can state that the institutionalization of international law in the second half of the 20th century tended also to be significant in the areas of peaceful settlements of international disputes through a growing number of international judicial bodies: international law judicialisation. This trend, too, was reflected in general international law within the framework of its possible fragmentation.[8]

Finally, international non-governmental organizations, NGOs, represented a specific category of institutionalization. They were not subject to international law, yet they had a permanent and growing impact on some of its areas.

Notes

1. For more details see at least: Reinch, P.S.: International Unions and their Administration. In: *American Journal of International Law*, Vol. I, No. 3, 1907, pp. 579–623.
2. As given by the Advisory Opinion of the ICJ concerning Interpretation of the Agreement of 25 March 1951 between the WHO and Egypt: "*International organizations are governed by the principle of speciality that is to say they are invested by the states that create them with powers, the limits of which are a function of the common interest whose promotion those states entrust to them*". See: I.C.J. Reports 1980, p. 78, para. 25.
3. For its current characteristics see: Klabbers, J.: *An Introduction to International Institutional Law*. Cambridge: Cambridge University Press, 2009, p. 396.
4. While the Universal Postal Union (UPU) and the International Labour Organisation (ILO) did not undergo significant institutionalized changes in the 20th century, the International Telegraph Union (together with the International Radiotelegraph Union) was replaced by the International Telecommunication Union in 1932. The international administrative unions tend to be called international organizations approximately from the second half of the last century.
5. Growing number of international intergovernmental organizations as a new "segment" of international relations and international law gave rise to many questions of international legal nature, beyond their scope, requiring rules of general international law (rules regulating their treaty-making power, issues of responsibility for international wrongful acts, issues referring to their privilege and immunity, representation of member states and non-member states in international organizations and their immunity). Many of them became the subject of the International Law Commission's codification in the 1970s and 1980s.
6. Currently there are more than 900 intergovernmental regional and universal organizations.
7. Mosler, H.: The International Society as Legal Community. In: *Collected Courses of the Hague Academy of International Law*, Vol. 140, No. IV, 1974, p. 189.
8. Regarding the institutionalization of international law, see: Ruffert, M., Walter, C.H.: *Institutionalised International Law*. Lon don: Hart Publishing, 2014.

2 Place and Position of International Organizations Within the International Law System

Although the beginning of the first international agencies at the turn of the 20th century was rather spontaneous and there was limited cooperation, there were certain attempts by the first international political organizations to control and/or supervise them.

The first such attempt took place after the League of Nations was established in 1919 even though its constituent instrument (the Covenant of the League of Nations) did not include any specific competence regarding the economic and social areas. The League of Nations, however, wanted to carry out, at least indirectly, the coordination of activities and supervision of international administrative unions in economic and social areas. Article 24 of the Covenant of the League of Nations stated that all international bureaux already established by previous collective treaties should be placed under the direction of the League of Nations if the parties to such treaties consented, and so should be placed any such bureaux to be established in the future.

A practical reason for such a competence was mainly to cover the supervision over funding issues. This provision of the Covenant, however, failed to be met in practice, and international administrative unions carried out their activities independently the whole time the League of Nations existed, until 1946.[1]

We can assume that this provision of the Covenant was the first, although not the most favourable, attempt by an international organization of a political nature to supervise the activities of specialized international organizations of a non-political nature.

Further opportunities to supervise or coordinate activities of international organizations occurred after the Second World War, after the United Nations (hereinafter referred to as the UN) was established in 1945, when the trend regarding new international organizations gained a wide scope.[2] Unlike the League of Nations, the UN was charged not only to protect the international peace and security by means of collective measures, but also to deal with issues related to economic and social areas. The founding fathers of the Charter explicitly admit the connection between the maintenance of international peace on the one side and the stability of economy and economic development of states on the other.

Article 1 of the UN Charter (Purposes and Principles) states that the purposes of the United Nations are to maintain international peace and security by means of effective collective measures, to achieve international cooperation by means of solving international problems of an economic, social, cultural or humanitarian character, as well as to be a centre for harmonizing the actions of nations in the achievement of these common ends.[3] Such an approach by the UN ensures that international peace and security is maintained by international sanctions, as well as by enhancing such economic, social and other relations between its member states which would not give causes for breach of international peace and security. This approach reflected the historical experience of the international community confirming that wars broke out not only because of military or strategic reasons, but also because of economic and social ones.

Article 55 of the UN Charter states that the UN shall promote solutions of economic, social, health and other related problems, as well as international culture and educational cooperation, and all its members pledge themselves to take action, jointly or separately, to cooperate with the Organization for the achievement of these purposes. The purposes may, according to the Charter, be achieved in two ways.

The first is based on the creation of their own authorities, or the UN institutions that fulfil duties directly with respect to economic and social areas. The Economic and Social Council as one of the main organs of the UN (hereinafter referred to as the Council) plays a significant role in this approach, since it makes or initiates studies and reports with respect to international economic, social, cultural, health and related matters and makes recommendations with respect to any such matters to the General Assembly of the UN, or to the members of the UN (Article 62 of the UN Charter). The Council may prepare draft conventions for submission to the General Assembly, with respect to matters falling within its competence and it may call international conference on such matters. The General Assembly of the UN also initiates studies and makes recommendations for promotion of international cooperation in the economic, social, cultural and health areas. The Council is also authorized to create other organs or institutions that may help fulfil the duties of the UN in the economic and social area, which is part of this process.[4]

The second method for fulfilment of the UN duties in the economic and social field is through its cooperation with specific international agencies where the UN is represented by the Council. According to Article 57 of the UN Charter, the various specialized agencies established by intergovernmental agreements for the purposes of fulfilling extensive international tasks in the economic, social, cultural and educational areas, in the area of public health and related areas shall be brought into relationship with the UN on the basis of the agreements concluded with the Council. Each such agreement lays down conditions under which the international agency shall be brought into relationship with the UN and is subject to the approval of the General Assembly of the United Nations. Such agencies thus brought into relationship with the UN are referred to as the UN specialized agencies.

Not every international agency able to conclude an international agreement may become a UN specialized agency. A basic condition is that it must be able to participate in carrying out the obligations of the UN as defined in Article 55 of the Charter,[5] and even if such condition is met, a significant position and power in economic and social areas is required. Article 57 of the Charter says that the international agency aspiring to the post of a specialized agency of the UN must be defined for the purposes of carrying out extensive international tasks in economic, social and other areas.

Taking into account this condition, the economic and social agencies of regional or local nature are excluded from the cooperation with the UN. Provided that the international agency meets these conditions, the agreement may be signed with the Council and it is entitled to coordinate specialized agencies by means of consultations and recommendations. To be informed, the Council shall take appropriate steps to obtain regular reports from the agencies, as well as reports on the steps taken to give effect to its recommendations. The Council may also make arrangements for the specialized agencies to participate, without vote, in its deliberations and for their representatives to participate in deliberations of the specialized agencies. Both state parties agree to enter into close financial relations including concluding the relevant financial agreements.

Post-war practice confirms that some administrative unions are still participating within this system, as well as new international agencies established after the Second World War. Initially, administrative unions transformed into international specialized agencies, including the World Postal Union (since 1948), the International Telecommunication Union (since 1949) and the International Labour Organization (established in 1919). In 1946, the lattermost became the first specialized agency of the UN.

The first new specialized agency of the UN established after the Second World War was the Food and Agriculture Organization of the United Nations in 1945 and it became the first post-war specialized agency in 1946. Among other specialized agencies established after the Second World War, it is worth mentioning the International Monetary Fund, established in 1945 (it has been a specialized agency since 1947); the International Bank for Reconstruction and Development (IBRD), established in 1945 (it has been a specialized agency since 1947); the International Civil Aviation Organization (ICAO), established in 1947 (it has been a specialized agency since 1948); the World Health Organization (WHO), established in 1946 (it has been a specialized agency since 1948); the World Meteorological Organization (WMO), established in 1947 (it has been a specialized agency since 1948); the Intergovernmental Maritime Consultative Organization, established in 1948 (it has been a specialized agency since 1959) and others.[6]

Even though the specialized agencies are not formally part of the UN, they enjoy certain advantages offered by its system, as in the right to request advisory opinions of the International Court of Justice on legal questions arising within the scope of their activities in accordance with Article 86 of the

UN Charter. Unlike the League of Nations, the UN created a treaty system through its Economic and Social Council within which the specific international intergovernmental agencies contribute to achieve its goals in economic and social cooperation.

In addition to the international specialized agencies of the UN, there are also international organizations which are related to the UN (the UN-related organizations) and more independent than specialized agencies, for example the World Trade Organization (WTO), where its constituent instrument enables it to conclude international agreements with other international organizations without any privilege of the UN. Even though the WTO is not connected with the Economic and Social Council of the UN, it coordinates its activities through annual sessions of older representatives of the Bretton Wood institutions.[7]

Another example is the International Atomic Energy Agency (IAEA) established upon the resolution of the General Assembly of the UN of 1955 and by approval of its Statute at a special conference in New York in 1956. In 1957, the IAEA signed an agreement on cooperation with the UN according to which it acts under the auspices of two organs: the United Nations General Assembly and the United Nations Security Council. Even though it cannot be regarded as a UN specialized agency, it cooperates closely with the UN.

With the exception of the above outlined UN system, the post-war development of regionalism failed to provide more extensive cooperation among regional organizations and universal organizations of a political nature. The only relevant exception includes those regional organizations which the United Nations Security Council counts on when carrying out its functions under Chapter VII of the UN Charter (see below). As a result, a prevailing form of cooperation is carried out at the level of and between regional organizations through the system of so-called interregional relations, or interregionalism (see below).

Notes

1. Full wording of the Covenant of the League of Nations. Available at: www.iilj.org/wp-content/uploads/2016/08/The-Covenant-of-the-League-of-Nations.pdf; Literature in this connection states that: "Article 24 has built a luxurious hotel but the guests have not yet arrived". In The Spectator Archives, May 17, 1929 (The League of Nations), p. 14.
2. In 1945–1949 962 organizations existed (100 governmental and 862 non-governmental).
3. Full wording of the UN Charter. Available at: https://treaties.un.org/doc/Publication/CTC/uncharter.pdf
4. For the purposes of fulfilling its task, the Economic and Social Council of the UN created five regional economic commissions: for Europe, Asia and the Far East, Latin America, Africa and Western Asia. Upon the UN General Assembly Resolution No. 2205 of 1966, the UN Commission on International Trade Law (UNCITRAL) was recognized, the UN Conference on Trade and Development (UNCTAD) was established in 1964, the UN Development Programme in 1966, and others.

5. Because of this criterion, intergovernmental organizations of, for example, a military or defence nature, might not have the option to apply for a post of a specialized agency of the UN.
6. Currently there are 17 specialized agencies, where the UN World Tourism Organization (UNWTO), established in 1974, gained the post of the specialized agency as the last one.
7. Moreover, the WTO also has a specific agreement on cooperation with the UN: Arrangements for Effective Cooperation with Other Intergovernmental Organizations-Relations between the WTO and United Nations. Available at: www.wto.org/english/thewto_e/coher_e/wto_un_e.htm

3 Regionalism and International Law

The regional organizations, or more free groupings of states having a more or less institutional nature, represent a significant part of institutionalism in international law. Such developments in the 19th century can be seen in the international river commissions[1] or the martial alliances of states.

Various regional groupings continued to develop also at the beginning of the 20th century. This period was at first typical for the cooperation between the states by means of bilateral trade agreements with various institutional structures,[2] e.g. in the form of customs unions.[3]

Even though this system was interrupted by the First World War, various trade blocks and bilateral trade agreements continued also in the post-war period, though having a more protectionist character due to the post-war economic crisis and political rivalry between the countries.

The period after the Second World War brought stronger treaties and an institutional understanding of regionalism (becoming more distinctive in the second half of the 20th century) together with the development of general international law. This could especially be seen in economic and trade organizations such as the European Economic Community, the European Free Trade Association and the Council for Mutual Economic Assistance, which developed under the multilateral trade systems of the GATT, and later the WTO. These influenced the development of different trade-oriented regional cooperation, such as free trade areas, customs union, common market and economic union but in the context of the Cold War, mainly within regional organizations. One may agree with the view that: "since the end of the World War II in 1945, numerous sophisticated regional organizations come into existence, thereby manifesting a new major trend called regionalism that today has a large influence on cooperation among states".[4]

An important area being discussed after the Second World War concerned the role of regionalism within the area of international peace and security which was meant to be guaranteed by the collective sanction system of the UN Charter. The debates over the post-war international system of peace and security and its priorities at the conference held in San Francisco included views on the importance and task of universalism and regionalism, mainly with respect to competences the United Nations Security Council and cooperation between the countries in the economic area.

Even if it was acknowledged that the universal system of collective reaction is necessary (as the best guarantee for maintaining international peace and security), at the same time the member states agreed that they should be able to regulate issues regarding security, economy and politics also at regional level, as proved by the previous experience of the Latin American continent.

After comprehensive discussions, the founders of UN Charter accepted the concept of regionalism; even if the institutional and legal system of the UN Charter gives preference to a universal mechanism in matters regarding maintenance of international peace and security the UN Charter entrusted the regional organs with functions to maintain international peace and security, to achieve a pacific settlement of local disputes (Article 51–54 of the UN Charter). Accepted regional doctrines of peace ". . . were based on the claim that geographic neighbourhood have a better understanding of local problems and were better placed to provide help than a distant UN". The efforts of the "regionalists" during the San Francisco conference (Latin American countries, Arab League countries) finally led to the compromise "whereby regional groups were given a specific role in maintaining international peace and security".[5]

However, relations between universalism and regionalism regulated by the UN Charter failed to develop due to the Cold War and bipolar world, and the military regional alliance systems. Because of this, revitalization and the development of regionalism took place only after the Cold War at the end of the 1980s and beginning of the 1990s.[6]

With respect to its nature and scope of competence, the regional organizations did not become a part of the UN system in the form of its specialized agencies having an autonomous position within the international community.

Another feature typical of post-war development at the beginning of the 1960s was the formation of regional organizations within and among developing countries as a reaction to decolonization. The next wave came after the Cold War and represented a reaction to the transitory times and the need for globalization. Regionalism and regional organization in the second half of the 20th century thus became geographically more spread, their number rose, and despite some drawbacks they represented a significant and irreplaceable segment within international relations having a specific impact on general international law and international relations.[7] According to legal writing: "legal relations between states are more and more governed not by general international law or by bilateral treaty provisions, but by multilateral treaties, constitutions of international organizations".[8]

With regards to the dramatic entry of regionalism into the international community in the second half of the 20th century, there were debates over the impact it had on the Westphalian system of the international community, a system which counted on the exclusive position of states. According to the Westphalian principle of absolute sovereignty of states, dominant at the beginning of the 20th century, the international community was strongly convinced that: "autonomous decision-making authority of sovereign states should not be weakened because of activities carried out by international institutions",[9] fully respecting: ". . . the primacy of the territorial states as political player at a global level, their autonomy in managing their matters within recognized international borders . . . and absence of strong regional and global institutions".[10]

This system of the exclusive position of states started to emerge during the 20th century *inter alia* as a result of universal and regional intergovernmental organizations having their own international legal subjectivity which was different to the subjectivity of the member states, and creating their own system of legal rules. This reflected not just the exclusive will of the states but the international organizations' own interests and purposes. Similar to sovereign states, many international organizations kept close relations with the states and other international organizations (including those that governed the rules of international law), had their own constitutions in the form of constituent instruments and their own systems for peaceful settlements of disputes, including judicial bodies.[11]

As a result, the current international order may not be regarded as a continuation of the traditional Westphalian system of the international community because it consists of different subjects and various legal branches: environmental protection, trade law, humanitarian law, etc. These recognize the rights and obligations of non-governmental entities on the international scene and within which the legal acts and decisions of international organizations do not require the consent of the states.

Notes

1. Maybe the oldest (and still existing) regional organization is the Central Commission for the Navigation of the Rhine, established in Europe during the 1815 Congress in Vienna. Its main task is to regulate cross-boundary transport of goods along the river Rhine.
2. Literature states that the Great Britain concluded such trade agreements with 64 countries, Germany with 30 countries and France with 22 countries. See: Irwin, D.A.: Multilateral and Bilateral Trade Policies in the World Trading System: An Historical Perspective. In: Melo de, J., Panagariya, A. (eds.): *New Dimension in Regional Integration*. New York: Cambridge University Press, 1993, p. 97.
3. The first Customs Unions include those established by Austria in 1850, Switzerland in 1848, Denmark in 1853 and Italy in 1860. The Southern African Customs Union (1910) represented the world's first regional organization to regulate common customs control. For more details see: Mansfield, E.D., Milner, H.V.: The New Wave of Regionalism. In: *International Organizations*, Vol. 53, No. 3, 1999, p. 596.
4. Fanenbruck, C.H., Meisner, L.: Supranational Courts as Engines for Regional Integration? A Comparative Study of the Southern African Development Community Tribunal, the European Court of Justice and the Andean Court of Justice. In: *KFG Working Paper Series* (The Transformative Power of Europe), No. 66, 2015, FUB, p. 6. Available at: www.polsoz.fu-berlin.de/en/v/transformeurope/publications/working_paper/wp/wp66/WP-66-Fanenbruck_Meissner_WEB.pdf

5. Acharya, A.: Comparative Regionalism: A Field Whose Time Has Come? In: Fioramonti, L. (ed.): *Regionalism in a Changing World: Comparative Perspective in the New Global Order*. London and New York: Routledge, 2012, p. 6.
6. As given by the Report of the Secretary-General's High-Level Panel on Threats, Challenges and Change from 2004: A more secure world: Our Shared Responsibility: "Recent experience has demonstrated that regional organizations can be a vital part of the multilateral system. Their efforts need not contradict UN efforts nor do they absolve the UN its primary responsibilities for peace and security". In: Report of the Secretary-General's High-Level Panel on Threats, Challenges and Change From 2004: A More Secure World: Our Shared Responsibility United Nations, 2004, p. 85. Available at: https://documents-dds-ny.un.org/doc/UNDOC/GEN/N04/602/31/PDF/N0460231.pdf?OpenElement
7. See: Fawcet, L., Hurrell, A.: *Regionalism in World Politics: Regional Organizations and International Order*. Oxford: Oxford University Press, 1995, 342 p.
8. Tomuschat, C.: International Courts and Tribunals With Regionally Restricted and/or Specialized Jurisdiction. In: *Judicial Settlement of International Disputes: International Court of Justice, Other Courts and Tribunals, Arbitration and Conciliation: An International Symposium*. Berlin: Springer, 1987, p. 401.
9. Osiander, A.: *The States System of Europe, 1640–1990: Peacemaking and the Conditions of International Stability*. Oxford: Clarendon Press, 1994, p. 3.
10. Falk, R.: The Post-Westphalia Enigma. In: Hettne, B., Odén, B. (eds.): *Global Governance in the 21st Century: Alternative Perspective on World Order*. Stockholm: Almkvist & Wiksell, 2002, p. 154. Available at: www.academia.edu/1638977/Global_Governance_in_the_21st_Century_Alternative_Perspectives_on_World_Order
11. As stated by A. Acharya: "Regionalism is becoming and facing the pressure to become more 'intrusive' and less sovereignty-bound in the sense of going against the norms of non-interference and non-intervention that had underpinned the Westphalian international system". In Acharya, A.: Regionalism and Emerging (Intrusive) World Order: Sovereignty, Autonomy, Identity. In: *Paper for Conference on "After the Global Crisis: What Next for Regionalism?"*. Toronto: University of Warvick, 1999, p. 1. Available at: www2.warwick.ac.uk/fac/soc/csgr/events/conferences/1999_conferences/3rdannualconference/papers/acharya.pdf

4 Old and New Regionalism

4.1. Old Regionalism

It should be pointed out at the outset that the concept of regionalism does not represent a new phenomenon in human history. As a political project regionalism ". . . cuts through various epochs of human history as forms of cooperation across political borders largely pre-date the establishment of modern states and the very concept of nation".[1] The roots of regionalism are therefore historically deep and the study of so called ancient regionalism confirms its various forms, subjects and objectives depending upon the set of various specific external and internal factors in a concrete historical epoch. This essential "flexible" feature is typical also for the historically recent "waves" of regionalism during 20th century.

When assessing regionalism in the second half of the last century, a prevailing opinion in the literature was that there are two main types: the post-war old ("first generation") regionalism followed by the wave of new ("second generation") regionalism after the Cold War ended.[2] The two regionalisms can be characterized by the old regionalism, which started at the time of bipolar division of the world, i.e. from the end of the Second World War until the 1980s, and a new regionalism which started as a consequence of its demise at the beginning of the 1990s and the needs of a changing and globalizing multipolar world.[3]

A concept of old regionalism contained features of a bipolar world imitating the position of the two leading powers, as well as basic characteristics of the Cold War policy. Consequently, it is referred to as hegemony regionalism, where the initiators, or "external" (supraregional) hegemonic leaders of regional groups were the USA and the USSR—NATO, CENTO, SEATO, Warsaw Treaty Organization whose aim was to ensure regional security against external attacks (security regionalism) through military systems of collective defence.

Old regionalism was not of an open nature; it was internally oriented, designed for its members only and it was oriented towards the military and economic areas; in the case of the latter, it usually had a protectionist character. Its members were only the states, while the scope of their activities within the regional organization was affected by the bipolar world and policy of the

Cold War. As a result, the regional organizations of this era were understood as territorial, military and economic structures controlled by the states, representing a sphere of influence of their founding superpowers.

Even though the old regionalism was generally not successful because the Cold War ended, with the CENTO, SEATO, Warsaw Treaty Organization and COMECON ceasing to exist, some regional organizations continued to exist and were able to adapt to the regional and global challenges resulting from globalization.

The nature of the Cold War meant that the spread of old regionalism was restricted because it was aimed at the political, military and security needs of the superpowers of that time. Therefore, from this point it cannot be regarded as an autonomous and independent segment of international relations of that time. This illustrates the fact that along with the end of superpowers and the bipolar world, the regional organizations of old regionalism steadily ceased to exist, too.

4.2. New Regionalism

The end of the Cold War at the turn of the 1990s marked the chance for a new and modern concept of regionalism. The structures of new regionalism, established after the Cold War, and without the decisive influence of former superpowers, were built from the bottom up, meaning from the level of participating states, where also non-governmental entities function as potential initiators and participants.[4] From this point new regionalism may be regarded as a multilateral and multidimensional process of regional integration, including economic, political, social and cultural aspects not only among the states themselves, but also among states and other non-governmental entities. Unlike old regionalism, new regionalism emerges at the time of intensive economic contacts between the states and the existence of multilateral organizational structures (GATT/WTO) aimed at helping the states organize their business relationships.

Unlike old regionalism, new regionalism is therefore open to the global needs and challenges of the international community with the aim to strengthen mutual cooperation between countries and to remove any obstructions in economic and other areas, too.

Due to globalization introducing new challenges, the states more often create regional organizations because global problems cross the borders of states and need international cooperation. The uneven development of global trends is, however, reflected in the different levels and forms of development of regionalism with respect to economic, political and social fields in different parts of the world. In such a sense the regionalism is still an uneven phenomenon because regional organizations are particularly prominent in Europe, Africa and the Americas. It is also in these regions that the number of regional organization membership per country (*regional intensity*) is the highest.

Because there were no world hegemonic leaders with specific needs, the object of new regionalism gradually extends and includes not only traditional security and economic fields, but also the environmental, social policy and financial areas, migration, etc. It should be therefore noted that: "New regionalism is based on the idea that one cannot isolate trade and economy from the rest of the society: integration can also imply non-economic matters such a justice, security, culture".[5]

While the old regionalism dealt exclusively with relations between the states, new regionalism (regarded as an inherent part of globalization, structural transformation and overall economic liberalization) involves the non-governmental entities on various levels working completely or partially beyond the formal institutional structures governed by the state.[6] From the viewpoint of new regionalism, their cooperation might have various informal forms, e.g. micro regions, or cross-border regions having different effects on the traditional structures.[7]

New regionalism in its overall context might be therefore understood as a continual process of changes that started after the end of Cold War on different levels: at the level of states (the macro regions), at the interregional level (between and/or among regional structures established by the states) and at the subregional, or micro-regional level of non-governmental entities.[8]

The reasons for establishing such regional groupings represent not only military, security, economic or other interests connected traditionally with the states and their foreign policy (even though they continue to exist also in new regionalism), but also areas in which different non-governmental entities—such as supranational corporations, non-governmental organizations, professional groups and social groups involved or local communities—play an increasingly more important role. Their areas of interests include mainly international trade and finance, the protection of the environment, and the humanitarian and social fields in states which slowly lose their exclusive and monopoly position.[9]

Regional trends in these areas can be seen through the establishment of specific subregional and micro-regional groups (regions) that border the states and thus create cross-border regional groups. Within this new regionalism, macro-regional and subregional processes develop with their own dynamics of growth, as well as with mutual dialogues and cooperation which their entities may become involved in.[10] On the other hand, traditional regional organizations created by the states enter into relations of mutual cooperation within interregionalism.

External global challenges and problems are obviously not the only reasons for the establishment of the regional groups within new regionalism. The reasons for establishing regional groups differ in different parts of world. Member states might have economic, environmental, cultural or other reasons, including the protection of their own economic or development models, cultural identity against pressure from the outside, or to be an instrument for solving long-term problems between neighbouring states. The new regionalism represented an instrument for eliminating isolation that the developing countries found themselves in after the bipolar world ceased to exist as well as an instrument against the marginalization of their economies, the possibilities to participate in international integration processes and global market or to gain international financial aid for the purposes of domestic economy development. The states under the former USSR sphere of influence regarded the new regionalism as a way to overcome the economic and security vacuum they found themselves in after the COMECON stopped to exist and the Warsaw Treaty was terminated.

Even though its beginnings are traced back to Europe, new regionalism currently has a worldwide character as it covers both developing and developed countries across almost all the continents, and many non-governmental entities within a worldwide scale.[11] Regarding its scope and dynamics of development, new regionalism represents a significant factor of influence on international relations and international law, and in specific areas a prevailing form of cooperation between the states.[12]

Another significant feature also includes the democratic character it has, since the regional organizations require their member states, prior to joining them, to carry out democratic reforms respecting rule of law, the political plurality of one's domestic political system, the protection of human rights and minorities, together with market economy reforms.

Relations between regional groups (interregionalism) also requires compliance with the basic principles of democracy and international law. From this view, the regional groups of new regionalism make a contribution to the democratization of international law and compliance with the rule of law principle. Their legal system goes beyond the framework of a particular regional organization, creating, in its complexity, not only a democratic, legal environment of a regional organization suitable for future fruitful cooperation of member states, but enhance the trend of making the current international law democratic and the rule of law respected. Upon application of the regional sanction mechanism in case of failure to comply with them during the period of membership in a regional organization, the guarantees in regional contexts become both enforceable and real.

Although the development of new regionalism demonstrates the growing trend and a stronger mutual cooperation between various entities at different levels, it also proves that there is no single worldwide model of new regionalism. There are currently various models of new regionalism applied in different regions depending on their historical development, local democratic traditions and conditions or other political specificities of future members, attitudes toward state sovereignty, the needs to respect social and cultural particularities or other relevant circumstances.[13] From the above we can infer that new regionalism is not a direct and uniform process, but it operates differently within various parts of the world, being constantly influenced by a number of external, global and regional factors as well as being subject to internal factors.

The irreplaceable role of international law was common for both types of regionalism because the states, upon applying its rules, formed regional organizations and they followed them when carrying out their activities. This basic constitutive international legal framework is, however, within the legislative competences of regional organizations completed with their own legal orders with differing rigidity. The task and importance of the latter for development of regional cooperation depend on the specifications of regional organizations in various parts of the world.

The largest regional group currently consists of regional organizations of economic character. Their rising occurrence is due to the fact that regional cooperation usually took place among states with similar political systems, the same basic economic rules and comparable development priorities. As confirmed in practice, having complied with the defined conditions this type of regional organization is more homogeneous than universal organizations; thus the member states may empower them with more competences in order to carry out their tasks.

Depending on how compatible the political and economic systems of member states are, a situation might occur in which the regional economic organization goes beyond the traditional international intergovernmental organization and becomes the "supranational" international entity whose decisions are binding directly for member states. To make the picture complete, the member states protect the nature of these organizations by regulating the conditions for third states to join them, where joining depends on specific political and economic conditions that should be complied with.

As we mentioned earlier, new regionalism affects general international law in many ways, where further development in this area is not possible to avoid. It's worth mentioning that regional and other organizations during the post-war period gave grounds for setting the international law rules which the Commission of International Law (hereinafter as ILC) codified in the last quarter of the 20th century.[14] These reduce the number of states in specific areas of international law-making by substituting them with their own organs, make entering into international agreements easier and bring their own instruments for settlements of international disputes. It is worth noting that regional values, standards and principles or behaviour governed by international agreements and concluded between various regional groups become subject within the interregional cooperation.

Regional groups of a non-governmental nature established within new regionalism are not governed internationally, and it is either the legal order of the regional organization—the EU and its Europe of regions—the regulations of domestic law of the member states or the "soft" regulations that are the basis for such regional groups.

Notes

1. Fioramonti, L.: The Evolution of Supranational Regionalism: From Top-Down Regulatory Governance to Sustainability Regions? In: *UNU-CRIS Working Paper*, W-2014/2, p.7.
2. Imperial regionalism is also mentioned in connection with the first wave of regionalism in the 1930s of the 20th century based on the idea of aggressive nationalism of fascist states. The aim was to make Germany and Japan regional leaders within their pan-European and pan-Asian expansionist projects.

3. As stated by F. Söderbaum and A. Sbragia: "Whereas old regionalism in the 1950s and 1960s has been dominated by the bipolar Cold War structure with nation states as the uncontested primary actors, new regionalism since the end of the 1980s needs to be related by the current transformation of the world, especially globalisation". See: Söderbaum, F., Sbragia, A.: EU Studies and the "New Regionalism": What Can Be Gained From Dialogue? In: *Journal of European Integration*, Vol. 32, No. 6, 2010, p. 571.
4. Hettne, B.: Globalization and the New Regionalism: The Second Great Transformation. In: Hettne, B., Inotai, A., Sunkel, O. (eds.): *Globalism and the New Regionalism*. New York: St. Martin Press, 1999, p. 2.
5. Van Langenhove, L.: Regionalism as a Political Vision. In: *UNU-CRIS Occasional Paper*, No. O-2005/15. Paper Has Been Presented at the International Conference: "New Regionalism From Global and European Perspective", Prague, 2005.
6. For more informations: Hettne, B.: The New Regionalism Revisited. In: Söderbaum, F., Shaw, T. (eds.): *Theories of New Regionalism (A Palgrave Macmillan Reader)*. Basingstoke, UK: Palgrave Macmillan, 2003, p. 24. Also: Mansfeld, Milner, *supra* n. 18, pp. 589–672.
7. As stated by P. De Lombaerde, F. Söderbaum, L. Van Langenhove and F. Baert: "The tendency to see a pluralism of regional scales and regional actors has led to an increasing pluralism of definitions, scales and spaces-mega-, macro-meso-, sub- and microregions—all of which are intertwined with globalisation, interregionalism and national spaces". In De Lombaerde, P., Söderbaum, F., Van Langenhove, L., Baert, F.: The Problems of Comparison in Comparative Regionalism. In: *Jean Monet/Robert Schuman Paper Series*, Vol. 9, No. 7, April 2009, p. 10.
8. As stated by R. Väyrynen: ". . . since the late 1980s sub-regional and micro-regional organizations have become more common, for example the Baltic Council of Ministers, the Visegrad Group, the Shanghai Group and Mercosur. This trend is in part a response to the fragmentation of the great power blocs, especially in Eastern Europe and Central Asia but it also reflects the need to react to the pressures created by economic globalization through local means". In: Väyrynen, R.: Regionalism: Old and New. In: *International Studies Review*, Vol. 5, No. 1, 2003, p. 26.
9. As stated by M. Teló: "New Regionalism can be seen as an attempt by states to react by strengthening regional control when traditional centralized national sovereignty no longer functions and to bargain collectively with extra regional partners". In Teló, M.: Introduction: Globalization, New Regionalism and the Role of the EU. In: Teló, M. (ed.): *European Union and New Regionalism: Regional Actors and Global Governance in a Post-Hegemonic Era*. Aldershot: Ashgate Publishing, 2007, p. 7.
10. See at least: De Lombaerde, P.: How to "Connect" Micro-Regions With Macro-Regions? A Note. In: *Perspectives on Federalism*, Vol. 2, No. 3, 2010, pp. E29–E37.
11. A former UN Secretary B. B. Ghâli pointed out that it no longer represents: ". . . resurgent spheres of influence but a healthy complement to internationalism". Ghali, B.B.: *An Agenda for Democratisation*. New York: UN, 1996, p. 33.
12. As stated by L. Fawcett: "the post-Cold War expansion of regionalism across different regions and issue areas had a powerful impact on its status in international relations and international law". In Fawcett, L.: The History and Concept of Regionalism. In: *UNU-CRIS Working Paper*, W-2013/5, p. 9.
13. As stated by S. Fabrini: "Regionalism is considered one, if non predominant, form of inter-governmental cooperation pursued in different areas of

the world. Such regionalism is based on important differences between the nature, scope, decision making style, compliance mechanism, structures and international status of the different regional organizations". In Fabrini, S.: European Regionalism in Comparative Perspective: Features and Limits of the New Medievals Approach to World Order. In: *Paper Submitted at the 3rd Pan Helenic Conference on International Political Economy*, University of Athens, May 16–18, 2008, p. 5. Available at: http://aei.pitt.edu/14996/1/EurReg.pdf

14. In some details see: *The Work of the International Law Commission*, 8th Edition, Vol. I. New York: UN, 2012, pp. 154–161.

5 Treaty and Institutional Regionalism

5.1. Treaty Regionalism

From the viewpoint of international law, we can speak about treaty (non-institutional) regionalism represented by international treaties concluded among the states in concrete regions. An analysis of these treaties confirms that the decisive reason for their conclusion may differ from region to region. A traditional reason related to a certain group of states and their interest in a certain region is the specific geographical element.

The main impulse for regional regulation is the degree to which the involved states used it, connected with the need to regulate certain aspects of such use by international law. Regional treaties of this type obviously regulate a common legal regime of this geographical element as well as the rights and obligations of state parties. Examples of this type include the treaties on regional rivers and lakes, or on geographically restricted parts of environment (Convention on the Navigation Regime on the Danube, protection of environment in the Baltic Sea, Black Sea, Arctic, in the Amazon pool, regional environment biotope, transboundary lakes, etc.). The frequency of this type of legal regulation is not usually very high because it depends on an existing commonly shared geographical element and on the willingness of the states to regulate their activities related to this element by international treaty. Regarding the specification and geographic extent of a certain natural (geographical) element, the states might want to conclude international treaties crossing the regional frame. As an example one can mention the protection of air[1] or the ozone layer.[2]

Another aspect typical of treaty regionalism includes the geographical proximity (neighbourhood) of the states within a particular region. Regional treaty-making is in this case enhanced by their common historical roots, cultural, religious or other similarities, or the level of economic and political homogeneity of states that has been reached. As examples we can mention the regional treaties on free trade zones, customs unions, regional treaty on the free movement of goods and persons, regional agreements on human rights protection, on common defence, etc. The practice proves that this geographical element can also represent a significant impulse for the establishment of the regional organization within the system of institutional regionalism.

In addition to the mentioned geographic elements in the period of new regionalism, the strong interests of the states constitute also a significant impulse for establishment of the regional groups. Regional treaties and structures of such character cross the traditional frame of the old "protectionist" model of regionalism, since they represent a reaction of the involved entities for the purposes of globalizing the international community. As mentioned earlier, such entities are not only the states; there are also the supranational economic groups (corporations), non-governmental organizations, various interest groups, etc.

The International Law Commission in its Report on the fragmentation of international law, 2003, states: "while previously the geographical regions acting 'behind' the international law represented the driving power, now there are specific interests that are globally diverse: business interests, global groups (lobbies), associations of the environment or human rights protection, and such trend has recently become intensive".[3] Such regional trends and structures tend to be called functional, where the basis for them might include a substantial economic segment (production systems, oil drilling and transportation, coordination related to oil trading, air services), elements in the area of environment (e.g. acid rain, Amazon rainforest, ozone layer), culture (cultural identity of certain communities), language identity of members of a region (France and its former Western African territories) when reducing and/or suppressing the geographical element.[4] The treaties of this nature are based on the cooperation of the involved entities in order to achieve a common objective regardless of the intensity of geographical element.

However, it should be pointed out that no matter what the common interests are or what the geographical closeness is, in reality if there are serious disagreements in political, religious, cultural or other areas among the states, the establishment of close, regional cooperation or grouping is not possible (e.g. Iran/Iraq, Israel/Palestine, India/Pakistan, PRC/Japan, etc.).

5.2. Institutional Regionalism

Institutional regionalism is traditionally represented through international intergovernmental organizations of regional character established predominantly on the basis of international treaties for the purposes of fulfilling the tasks within the agreed field. As already mentioned, organizations of this type are usually established by the states having close geographical relations (neighbouring states), where their common elements regarding history, economy, religion, etc., help them make decisions to establish their organization. The definition of this kind of regionalism underlines that it is about a "restricted number of states mutually connected with geographical relations and certain level of dependence on each other",[5] the result of which is the "establishment of international intergovernmental groups on the regional basis".[6]

A trend prevailing in the second half of the 20th century suggests that regionalism is presented through its various institutional forms which are reflected in a growing number of international organizations of regional character and in extending the scope of their activities.

As a result, they play a more and more important role, starting cooperation with other regional organizations within the system of interregionalism[7] as well as with the organizations of universal character, and non-member states, too. It is generally recognized that both international universal organizations and international regional organizations have their own legal subjectivity different to the legal subjectivity of member states expressly regulated in their constituent instruments.[8]

In this respect it is worth noting that the traditional model of institutional regionalism in which the regional objectives are satisfied according to a specific legal basis, within the agreed institutional frame and within fixed competences of a regional organization's bodies, begin to be subject to certain challenges and changes.

More complicated problems that the regional organizations face in a globalized world require a more complete reaction also by means of various non-formal, flexible and open systems of regional cooperation (*the open, or networked regionalism*) between the regional organization and non-governmental entities such as supranational economic groups and corporations, non-governmental organizations, representatives of civil community and the interest and professional groups. Such mixed traditional and non-traditional regional groups are currently typical of some regional structures in Asia and Africa and it might have *pro futuro* impact on European integration groups as well.

An expression of this more open trend is the membership diversification within traditional inter-governmental organizations resulting in the creation of the hybrid institutional regionalism, which the ASEAN is also heading towards.[9] It exists because there is a strong belief that such mixed membership of regional organization might help to impact more effectively on the problems of a concrete region by enabling various non-governmental entities to actively participate within the process of their solutions. Further development undoubtedly shows to what extent globalized international relations and various regional models can modify traditional institutional structures of new regionalism, as well as the role international law will play in the process of its establishment and proper functioning.

This is the main reason why regional organizations as significant representatives of current institutional regionalism will be the subject to further more detailed study.

5.2.1. Territorial Scope of the Competences of Regional Organizations

A legal regime that the member states of a regional organization created tends to be geographically determined by the state territories of its members because it is there that the organization is entitled to carry out its competencies. In regards to the international treaties concluded between the international organization and the states, or other international organizations this is expressly stipulated in Article 29 of the Vienna Convention on the Law of Treaties between States and International Organizations or between International Organizations of 1986.[10]

However, regional legislation shows that various "elements" of a legal regime of an international organization, as well as its treaties sometimes (and under specific conditions) may cross the scope of its geographical dimension. According to its constituent instrument, the member states of a concrete regional organization may extend the application of a regional standard to the third (external) territory with whom they have specific relations.[11]

In addition to outside the geographical scope that the legal regime of a regional organization may have, some of them might use their capacities outside the defined geographical dimension. It is especially the case of regional organizations carrying out their activities in the maintenance of international peace and security. Chapter VIII of the UN Charter expressly counts on regional organs being used for the purposes of international sanctions under the authorization of the UN Security Council. Their growing involvement can be marked from the beginning of 1990s within the UN peacekeeping missions (Blue Helmets) and also the system of "Responsibility to Protect".[12]

There are two main reasons for the increasing participation of regional bodies in the area of international peace and security; the first represents a failure of traditional enforcement actions of member states carried out under Chapter VII of UN Charter, and the second the considerable financial costs of such actions. The regional organizations (or their armed forces) currently carrying out their activities outside the geographical dimension of its "maternal" organization are typically being engaged in regional conflicts in which the states with a weak or disintegrated state structure are involved.[13] Recent figures also show that there are more peacekeeping operations that the UN is engaged in together with the armed forces of regional organizations.[14] Regional organizations herewith cross their purely regional scope, since they engage in the protection of values recognized by the international community as a whole, i.e. protection of international peace and security. It should be however noted that not all regional organizations are able to comply with the tasks issuing from the need to protect international peace and security.[15]

5.2.2. The "Term" of Regional Organizations

In practice, the states intend to establish international organizations of a permanent character, so it is rather exceptional to have a limited term of validity for a constituent instrument of regional organization.[16] If international organizations properly fulfil their duties and are useful for their member states, there is obviously no relevant reason to consider their termination, or dissolution. On the contrary, the organizations that are viewed as successful attract the attention of other states which, in turn, try to join them with a view to benefiting from membership, or eventually copying their institutional structure in the process of establishing new organizations. The reasons for dissolution of international organizations may represent the occurring changes in (and unfavourable) external, or internal relations considerably different from those that existed at the time of their establishment, as well as their unsuccessful activities. When such circumstances are taken into account, the member states of the organization usually regulate the methods and voting conditions regarding dissolution of organizations in their constituent act.[17]

A specific reason connected to the increasing number of international organizations is that they become dissolved because the subject matter of their activities is replaced with a new, or more modern, international organization which is expected to better fulfil its original tasks. In such a case the rights, as well as moveable and immovable assets, are transferred to a new organization within the scope of succession of international organizations.[18] The growing number of regional organizations, however, currently proves the fact of how useful, and irreplaceable, they are in some areas.

5.2.3. The Regional Organizations' Scope of Activities

Similarly to other subjects of international law, regional organizations are not established in a legal and factual vacuum and their establishment depends not only on the will of member states and their needs, but also external circumstances have an influence on this process.

In different periods they can revive organizations of a regional character which might be temporarily out of operation or their programme might be subject to change or amendments. Therefore, different periods might show regional organizations that are being replaced or amended by a new and different wave with a different purpose. As was already mentioned, at the time of the bipolar world, the regional organizations were typical for having a protectionist character economically and/or militarily, while new regionalism has brought an extension to their scope of activities, reflecting the needs of globalization.

The current period also brings various challenges to regional organizations' scope of activities. Such challenges might include the peace and security threats through international terrorism.[19] Because such threats after the Cold War have rather a local or regional character, it is obvious that the relevant reaction itself is of regional character, too. This trend is visible mainly across the African continent where various regional groups, initially having a purely economic character, gradually completed their organizational structures and capacities so that they were able to respond to a local (regional) threat of international peace and security, as well as to react effectively to the call of the UN Security Council.[20] The extension of regional competences in such a sense may be also identified on the European continent in the shape of the EU.

Because of the increasingly globalised world, new challenges and problems of global nature have to be confronted. One can share the view that: "in the modern world no organization can serve the people it represents unless it reforms itself to cope with new global challenges".[21] These challenges obviously require the formulation of a long-term policy for regional organizations reflecting external factual and political changes. They need as well to determine the priorities for organizations and procedures of their practical implementation, an analysis of their impact on the institutional structure of an organization, the financial and material aspects, etc. New evolving policies of regional organizations reflecting environmental changes have been started within the ASEAN (ASEAN Agreement on Disaster Management and Emergency Responses), AU (African Strategy on Climatic Change), ECOWAS (ECOWAS Policy for Disaster Risk Reduction), etc.

The practice of both universal and regional organizations shows that international organizations regularly set up so-called groups of eminent persons or group of wise men (GEP)[22] to address these challenges. This obviously results in reports with relevant analysis and/or recommendations for the regional organizations.[23]

Taking into account the frequency of their occurrence during recent times, the still increasing geographic scope of their contemporary activities (relevant regional organizations nearly around all the world), the high level and complexity of their reports and the attention and practical application of their conclusions by the organs of the organizations, it seems appropriate to analyse the role and contribution of GEP to contemporary institutional regionalism in a more detailed manner.[24]

Considering the significant external factors to the establishment of regional organizations, we can say that current institutional regionalism is typical in not only its uneven geographical spread and changing importance in different periods but also for its importance in various areas of international law.

There are some areas of international law where institutional regionalism thrives through various regional structures (international protection of human rights, international trade law and protection of environment) and areas where institutional regionalism is still lacking. The development in the second half of the 20th century also proves that there are areas where institutional regionalism flourishes and forms its stable and vital role. It includes mainly international peace and security, international protection of human rights, international trade and economy and regional systems for settlements of international disputes. As regards to the lattermost, it is worth mentioning that regional systems for settlements of disputes obviously do not represent an autonomous kind of regionalism, since they are usually "attached" to the regional organizations as one of their organs for peaceful settlements of disputes.

Finally, it should be pointed out that institutional regionalism fails to be evenly spread because of its geographical aspect and because the regional groups in individual geographical areas differ in their institutional structure, legal regulation (their own legal order), sanction system and system of peaceful settlement of disputes—as well as in respect to conditions for third states to join the regional organization, opportunities for non-governmental entities to join the regional group, etc.

Practical application confirms that some regional organizations established outside Europe picked the European Union as a certain referential model for their institutional and legal arrangements, attractive not just for its results in the field of economy, but also because it is an effective instrument for eliminating historical discrepancies among the member states (France, Germany) and for creating a common regional space of security, stability and welfare for all people living in the member states.[25] Such efforts are however confronted with the fact that legal standards, principles or institutional structures of the European model are not automatically transposable into a different political and economic environment in which they are confronted with bigger or smaller local problems.[26]

Finally, the most crucial issue of this effort is whether the regional organization wants to remain at the level of the traditional intergovernmental model or it prefers a supranational model of cooperation which has an impact on the sovereignty of the member states (as in the EU).

5.2.4. Membership in the Regional Organizations

The history of universal and regional organizations shows that they had been for a long time established exclusively by the states and only the states could become their members. Such a "monopoly" regarding the membership of international organizations lasted until the 1980s. We can assume that such homogeneity of membership was natural, because only states became the basic and exclusive subjects of international law. Along with the rising number of international organizations in the second half of the 20th century and the impact new regionalism had, this approach started gradually to change because the membership in regional organizations is of interest not only to the states, but also to other differing international organizations and entities.

One of the first reactions of international law regarding this trend is the draft of the International Law Commission on Responsibility of International Organizations. A draft of articles on Responsibility of International Organizations (hereinafter as Draft) of 2011 pursuant to Article 2 (a) refers to the international organization which shall mean: "the organisation established upon a treaty or other document that is governed by international law and has its own international personality. In addition to the states, also the other entities might become members".[27]

Unlike previous drafts made by the ILC regarding international organizations, this definition refers not only to international organizations with exclusive membership of states but also to those whose membership is, in addition to the states, available also to other international organizations or non-governmental entities.[28] Diversification of international organization membership might be regarded as one of the new regionalism specifications.

A comment made by the ILC regarding Article 2 of the Draft about the definition underlines that inclusion of non-governmental entities within the international organization members reflects the significant trend which prefers mixed membership in order to achieve more efficient cooperation in certain areas. The international law doctrine refers to it as the functional trend, which believes that not only the states, but also other entities (entities of domestic law, non-governmental organizations, supranational communities or other international organizations), different from the states, can successfully carry out their functions.[29]

At the same time, practice confirms that depending on the nature of a non-governmental entity, the type of membership of an international organization might differ (e.g. affiliated member, extraordinary member, etc.) Problems related to the legal and practical application of this trend, however, might occur on the part of the "receiving" international organization when its constituent instrument does not allow membership to entities different from that of the states. A similar problem might apply to parties interested in membership provided that their constituent instruments (international treaty on establishment of international organization) do not consider such an option. In the context of international law, such a trend might be regarded as one of the aspects for the increasing importance that the non-governmental entities have on the international legal order; its impact is restricted not only to issues and institutes of general international law, but it penetrates into the areas that form the subject of activities carried out by universal and regional international organizations.

The above-mentioned element of functionality can be identified also when the international organization enters into agreement with another organization in order to fulfil its tasks without becoming its member. As an example of such a "treaty's functionality" one can mention the specialized agencies of the UN referred to in Articles 57 and 63 of the UN Charter.[30]

Another issue connected with membership in a regional organization is what the optimal number of members is and what criterion is decisive for the fixing of this number. We have already mentioned the geographical criteria under which the establishment of a regional organization consisting of subjects from a certain geographical area is possible. The choicc of relevant membership rules in practice influence the number of states in concrete regional organization and the depth of cooperation among them. These models are not definitive and can vary during the "life" of the concrete organization.

Another question is whether the purposes of a regional group can be fulfilled by such states regardless of their economic development, mutual complementarity of their economies, etc. It is to be noted that heterogeneity among the states in the regional organizations is extremely important for successful regional cooperation, and the building of joint political and other institutions for development of economic integration.

The experience of integration groups across developing areas shows that differing levels of economies within their member states or differences in their orientation (e.g. economies aimed at export versus those aimed at import) tend to impede good functionality. This contrasts to the more favourable outcome whereby a small or smaller number of members comply with a full extent with the economic or other projects of an organization and where their number may increase if other members gradually reach the required economic level and ability. The practice confirms that regional organizations can use differentiated (multi-speed) integration as a specific reaction to the different levels of heterogeneity among their member states resulting *inter alia* from the fact that states became members of the organization at different times. Multi-speed integration has been used within the EU vis-á-vis new member states and will be much discussed as one of the potential courses of the EU after Brexit, later in 2017. The Rome Declaration of 27 member states of the EU adopted on March 25, 2017 at the 60th anniversary of the Rome Treaties points out that: "We will act together, at different paces and intensity where necessary while moving in the same direction as we have done in the past, in line with the Treaties and keeping the door open to those who want join later".[31]

Some elements of multi-speed integration may be identified in Asia (ASEAN) and Africa (NEPAD).[32] Multi-speed integration enables intensifying new forms of cooperation within a regional organization, without the necessity to wait for all member states to be prepared for this. Although the states which are not prepared to cooperate remain outside, they still remain members of the organization and at the appropriate moment can join the concrete multi-speed project. It should be noted that if all regional states are not members of the regional organization, the position of multiple levels of association may define their relationship vis-á-vis a concrete organization.

5.2.5. Democracy and Rule of Law as Conditions of Membership in Regional Organizations

Constituent instruments of international organizations regularly laid down conditions with which the states concerned are obliged to comply in order to become members. A traditional and lasting condition is that applicants for membership in the international intergovernmental organization are naturally the states, and for a long time attention was paid especially to their financial or material eligibility, to fulfil obligations arising from the membership, regardless of their political regime and legal order character.

From around the second half of the last century, these conditions start to involve also the character of a governing political regime and the democratic principles of the legal order related to the future member state, which is gradually reflected, even when having different formulations and details, in constituent instruments of various regional organizations.[33] Regional organizations also increasingly seek to strengthen constitutional governance in their member states by developing a regulatory framework[34] that rejects and sanctions attempts to remain in power unconstitutionally, particularly unconstitutional transfer of powers. The practice confirms that regional organizations play a critical role in the formulation of a normative framework in supporting their member states to strengthen democratic and accountable institutions, and in facilitating rule-based cooperation and peaceful settlements of disputes between member states. In so doing they contribute to the implementation of Chapter VIII of the Charter of the United Nations.[35] Generally speaking one can say that regionalism thrives better in a democratic environment, even though it may not be regarded as the sole guarantee of democracy of the member states within the regional organization.

In a wider context, the respect for democratic principles of the governing political regime and legal order, being the conditions for the member state to join the regional organization and for its membership, can be viewed as a specific contribution of the regional organizations to respect the rule of law in current international law.[36]

In the situation where the principle of democracy and rule of law is violated from and within the member state, the international organization is entitled to impose sanctions anticipated by the constituent instrument. In this case the violation of democratic principles inside the member state becomes the subject to sanctions imposed by the regional organization even though there are no, or not necessarily any, grounds for sanctions being imposed by the general international law. In this context, the presence of sanctions of the regional organization represent one of the guarantees for the purposes of compliance with the principles of a rule of law within its member state, as well as of the democratic legal environment within the regional organization itself. The absence of such sanctions may cause problems and unexpected tension within the regional organization.[37]

5.2.6. Guarantees for the Due Performance of Regional Organizations

The states aiming to establish a regional organization naturally wish that it is able to perform duties laid down in its constituent instrument which are beneficial and helpful for the member states and also help to promote their international cooperation. From the time the first international organizations were established in the course of the 19th century (international administrative unions), their member states believed that relevant factual and legal conditions were necessary for their proper functioning. The legal area was to ensure the international organization and its representatives were independent from the bodies of the host state and member states through the system of immunities and privileges.

Until the end of the Second World War, their founders used a model of the diplomatic immunities and privileges granted to diplomatic representatives of states within the bilateral relationship. This period was typical for two specifications: the diplomatic immunities and privileges granted within the international organization had a treaty and not customary character, and until the second half of the 1940s they were granted by virtue of bilateral agreements between the host state and the international organization (the *headquarters agreements*). In such a way, the international organizations were inspired mainly by the League of Nations and the International Labour Organization.

Another feature was that diplomatic immunities and privileges were granted in a more or less unified way, regardless of the character and scope of the international organization's activities.[38]

The situation in this area changed after the Second World War. Even though the international organizations and their representatives were entitled to enjoy privileges and immunities, a unified diplomatic level for the provision (of the said) has been eliminated, and there is a new approach under which their scope is individual and depends on specific needs of the international organizations necessary for the proper accomplishment of their tasks (the principle of functional need).[39]

Another legal condition necessary for the proper functioning of the regional organizations is that their legal orders are to be regulated with respect to the internal legal orders of member states. This means, fundamentally, that there should be no option for the member states of an international organization to avoid the fulfilment of their obligations arising out of their membership by referring to their legal orders and thus complicating or paralysing the activities of the organization.

It should be pointed out that with respect to obligations of the member states under the constituent acts, we can apply Article 27 of the Vienna Convention on the Law of Treaties of 1969 under which the state parties may not invoke the provisions of its internal law as justification for its failure to perform the treaty obligation. Pursuant to Article 5 of the Vienna Convention, this rule applies to any treaty which is either the constituent instrument of an international organization or to any other treaty adopted within the framework of the international organization.

Some regional organizations have their own legal orders which are, however, not uniform, but differ in the nature of legal rules and level of details. The regional legal regulations confirms that the legal orders usually consists of two parts: the organization internal order, composed of procedural, administrative and financial rules which ensure the "service" function necessary for proper functioning of the organization, and the substantial rules which regulate the behaviour of the member states and organs of the organization in the area forming the scope of their activities. The regulative rules can have the character of either an international treaty or of their own rules created within the organization by their organs for the performance of its functions. Such legal orders are individual and "fit" each international organization, therefore they are not transferable automatically from one organization to the other. In order to prevent their abuse by the bodies of the organization the control system is obviously established by: "checks and balance within the structure of international organization sometimes in the form of judicial organ, which will then monitor the activities of the organization's organs and their compliance with the constituent treaty and general norms and principles of international law".[40] The tendency to specialization has even led to a whole new class of international organizations established through a decision of their "maternal" organization, for example, Global Environment Facility[41] and UNAIDS.[42] Such "sub-delegation" and "sub-specialization" obviously diminish the control of the members of the original organization over these "derivative" organizations.[43] This, however, has no impact on various features that they have in common, for example, from the viewpoint of their institutional arrangement.[44]

If the international organization has its own legal order (e.g. the EU) there raises the need to resolve its relationship towards the internal legal orders of the member states. It happens in situations when the content of the rule of legal order applicable within the international organization is either the same or similar to the rule of the domestic legal order of the member states, while they themselves might differ from each other. Because the Vienna Convention of 1969 may not be applied to their relationships (it is not the relationship between the international treaty and the internal law of state), it is necessary to apply either the relevant rule of the legal order of the organization reflecting the principles of efficiency and functionality of the international organization or on the stable practice of their organs. In any case, the basic idea of this relationship is that no member state of an organization is entitled to refer to its domestic legal order in order to avoid complying with their obligations arising from the legal order of the international organization.[45]

5.3. Prevention, Dispute and Sanction Mechanisms of the International Organizations

No matter how perfect the legal order of the regional organization might be, its efficiency will not be sufficient unless monitored and supervised by their organs. International organizations, having their own systems for monitoring and supervising the fulfilment of obligations from their member states, show their differences from each other from the viewpoint of procedural, administrative, quality and strictness of outputs adopted after completing the supervision. Financial organizations possess one of the best systems of supervision because it is in their interest to provide the member states with financial debts strictly in accordance with agreements and exclusively for the goals agreed in these agreements. The International Bank for Reconstruction and Development (IBRD) or the International Monetary Fund (IMF) may serve as examples of international organizations having effective supervising mechanisms. The regional economic organizations also have a system of monitoring and supervision that is well elaborated and effective, since the efficiency of their activities depends on the efficiency of these mechanisms. A leading role among them is given to the European Union, even though other international organizations have acquired their own experience in this area, too. The EU (and some African economic organizations following the EU model) mechanism for supervision, consists of two phases: an administrative, including preliminary investigations, reconciliation and adoption of reasonable opinion; and the judicial, including proceedings before the regional international court. The administrative part of proceedings is usually concentrated in the hands of an executive body of an organization (the European Commission within the EU), or of a political or executive body, as in the case of the African Economic Community (AEC) and the Economic Community of Central African States (ECCAS), and in the executive and administrative body in case of the Economic Community of West African States (ECOWAS). The parliamentary organs can also be in charge of specific supervising functions, for example, the European Parliament.

The benefits of the administrative systems of supervision lie in the fact that many offences committed by the states are not intentional, but they are caused by an insufficient understanding of their obligations as a result of a wrong interpretation, or mistake made in communication at the national level, or within the organization. As a result, many mistakes, omissions or vague interpretations can be explained already at the first, preliminary discussions with no need to take any court action.[46]

5.3.1. Settlement of Disputes in International Organizations

Not even the existence of a supervising and monitoring system can prevent disputes arising between the member states and an organization, between the member states themselves or between the organs of an organization. The reason for, and the object of, disputes can be a different interpretation or application of the organization's legal order or constituent treaty, its practical activities, including financial matters, application of sanctions and many other problems. The number of disputes in international organizations varies, though we can say that it is rather higher in active organizations with a wider scope of competences. Experience within the international organizations in this area confirms that the parties of a dispute in the first stage try to avoid more formal administrative and judicial means and seek less formal procedures, such as meetings, investigations and consultation. This is also the main reason why international organizations devote special attention to consultations and meetings in their constituent instruments, for example, the Organisation for Economic Co-operation and Development (OECD), the Association of Southeast Asian Nations (ASEAN), etc.

Similarly to international law, the international organizations consider meetings and consultations of disputing parties as the most natural and accessible forum, and they are therefore the most frequent instrument for the settlement of mutual disputes because, unlike formalized administrative, arbitration and judicial instruments, these means are more discreet and the parties keep more control without the interference of a third party.

Another way to deal with disputes is through the highest executive organs of the organization, which adopts a binding and final decision without the option to ask another organ to participate in the dispute. The advantage here lies in their promptness, as well as the procedural and administrative concentration of the proceeding in front of just one organ.

However, there might be a problem with the qualified evaluation of the dispute, followed by the credibility of the decision that has been adopted.

Some organizations may for the purposes of dealing with disputes set up quasi arbitration organs, the use of which brings various advantages. Regarding its qualification, such organs provide a qualified analysis of the dispute by means of which the preparation stage is shorter, and the flexible procedure might bring compromise without having the executive organ of the organization make a final decision. Experience proves that the quasi arbitration organs are successful as they are able to enjoy the confidence of the parties and allow them to participate in order to agree to a compromise.

Its establishment is anticipated in the constituent instruments of the International Monetary Fund (IMF),the Organisation of the Petroleum Exporting Countries (OPEC), etc. An important contribution for the settlement of disputes arising within the international organizations are international courts, the existence of which is presumed in constituent instruments of many of them. The best known include the Court of Justice of the European Union, European Court of Human Rights of the Council of Europe, the Court of Justice of the Andean Community, the Court of Justice of the African Economic Community, the Tribunal of the Economic Community of West African States (ECOWAS), the Court of Justice of the Economic Community of Central African States (ECCAS), the Economic Court of the Commonwealth of Independent States (CIS)—former members of the USSR and others.[47]

Similarly in the settlement of disputes before the international judicial organs of general competences, the parties in a dispute can turn to the specialized courts of the international organizations after having used all the moderate and less painful methods of settlement. It is understandable because having to refer the case to the judicial organs, the parties lose their control over the dispute. Consequently, the member states of international organizations do not seek the services of international courts very often, the European Court of Justice and the Court of Justice of the Andean Community being the exceptions.[48]

From this brief overview one can infer that the regional organizations have their own judicial and non-judicial systems of proceedings for settlement of disputes which might arise among their member states, or the member states and the organization itself. As we mentioned earlier, such proceedings fully respect the principle of specialization of international organizations, since their bodies deal with disputes concerning only the activities of the organization and its member states laid down in its constituent instrument.

5.3.2. Sanction Regimes of International Organizations

As with states, the international organizations also have their own sanction regimes which are applicable to the member states for failure to carry out obligations arising from their membership. Even though they differ from the sanctions of the states, they have some features in common.

Firstly, the organizations are entitled to apply them as a last possible remedy (*ultima ratio*) after having applied a softer coercive approach in order to make them comply with their obligations of membership. Similar to sanctions applied among states, when applying sanctions to international organizations a principle of proportionality and temporariness must be respected as well. Unlike individual sanctions applied by the states, the sanctions of international organizations have a centralized form with a greater political and moral importance, thus creating more pressure on the member state. Because they are usually adopted on the decision of the organization's body, they must be well reasoned and applied only if the unlawful behaviour or acts of the member state is duly confirmed. In this respect they differ from the individual countermeasures of the states in general international law, because the conditions for their application are subject to the individual assessment of a concerned state. On the other hand, it is possible to identify some common features through the system of collective sanctions of the UN (the decision of the Security Council, collective assessment of the conditions for application of the international sanctions).

The application of sanctions may, however, be prevented due to the existence of specific circumstances of factual character even if the legal conditions to apply them have been met. There might occur a situation in which the sanctions are to be imposed on the organization's member state(s) who makes significant contributions to the budget and, therefore, the sanctions would cause more harm to the organization than to the concerned members. Another circumstance is that the relevant organ of the organizations might not be willing to adopt a collective decision on sanctions for political reasons.

Provided that the conditions for imposing the sanctions are met and the organizations are set to adopt them, the method (details) and scope of their legal regulation laid down in their constituent instruments are of high importance. Some organizations did not explicitly regulate their sanction system therefore no such provisions referring to sanctions are included in the constituent instruments. In this case it is possible to either refer to the implied powers of an organization or to explicitly complete the provisions of the statute regarding the sanctions. It is generally recognized that the second option should have preference in practice because any such intervention into the membership rights of member states should be expressly laid down in the constituent instruments. Even though some international organizations lack regulations with respect to their sanctions, there are others that have it and regulate different kinds of sanctions. They are, however, not used very frequently, since simply the existence and threat of sanctions has a preventive function against a state who is intending not to comply with obligations arising from its membership within the international organization. Experience shows that international organizations prefer those means of dealing with disputes arising between the organizations and its member states that exclude sanctions. In the wider context, it is a reflection of a general trend under which these enforcement measures are not currently used for settlement with disputes.

To suspend the member state's voting rights is a relatively "soft" sanction used within organs of organization and its regulation can be found in the constituent instruments of both the universal and regional organizations. Regarding the first group, we can mention the United Nations Organization (UN).[49] This sanction is also stipulated in the constituent instruments of some regional organizations.[50] It is usually used when the international organization reacts to a member state failing to pay contributions into the organization's budget, and it is actually applied when the constituent act of an organization either determines the due date for making contributions, or other conditions related to the payment thereof.[51] It is fair to say that sanctions to enforce financial discipline of members are important mainly for the organizations that suffer from constant resource instability.

In addition to the suspension of voting rights, the member states can be subject to other administrative sanctions that restrict their further rights arising from membership. Among them one can mention the denial of access of states to meetings held by the organs of an organization, disallowing proposals for their own candidates for vacant positions, disallowing their participation in the representative bodies of an organization, etc.

To impose sanctions on the member state is just one side of a coin. Other member states complying with their obligations might acquire special entitlements against the member state which is under the regional "sanction regime". The organs of an international organization might authorize them to suspend their obligations towards the state in question, the result of which is that the effect of administrative sanctions is "multiplied" and, at the same time, the economic impact of sanctions is greater (for example, the GATT).

The most substantial sanctions of an administrative nature are to suspend the membership or to exclude the member state from the international organization. In both cases these sanctions of an extraordinary nature are taken only in cases of apparent, long-term and serious breaches of obligations following from their membership. In this circumstance, such a member state is no longer acceptable for the organization since it represents a permanent problem and does not contribute effectively to fulfilling their obligations. Because of their extraordinary nature, such sanctions are usually not regulated by constituent instruments of international organizations.[52] The suspension or exclusion of member states are drastic measures and obviously require a high level of consent among the member states of the organization. Whatever their scope and nature is, it is notable that international organizations, both universal and regional, have their own sanction systems in order to guarantee the proper fulfilment of obligations of their member states.

However: "sanctions mean very different things to different regional organizations, both in terms of political content and formal process".[53] This different approach confirms the practice of the African Union automatically imposing sanction against unconstitutional changes of governments in its member states,[54] Arab League sanction against Libya and Syria (2011) as a reaction to internal armed conflict within their borders. The exemption represents the ASEAN with the lack of its own sanction mechanism in case of regional rules breached by its member states. Finally some regional organizations have a specific sanction system applied in the case of non-compliance of member states with the valid judgments of a regional judicial institution. Examples include the European Court of Human Rights,[55] Inter-American Court of Human Rights[56] and European Court of Justice.[57]

Therefore, the result of analysis carried out three objectives to be pursued by the system of regional sanctions namely to ensure the proper institutional functioning of the regional organizations, the guarantees of the constitutional and democratic nature of the member states and effective implementation of the judgments of regional courts.

5.4. Supranational and Intergovernmental Model of Regional Organizations

Depending on the will to respect above said conditions, the establishment of regional organizations is currently marked by two basic approaches: the intergovernmental and the supranational model. It is worth noting that an effective system of regional organizations is not sovereignty-neutral because member states must choose between two regional models, namely, fully respecting their sovereignty, and/or transferring some parts of their sovereignty in favour of regional organization. For the intergovernmental approach, it is typical that the member states continue with full sovereignty, while established regional organs only prepare and carry out their agreed common projects. In contrast, the supranational approach means the member states have decided to transfer some parts of their sovereignty through, and within, the organs of regional organization. To be more detailed, the constituent acts of regional organizations have traditionally been formed of international intergovernmental treaties, having two principal aspects. The first comprises their "creative" dimension, because on the basis of the agreed will of the states, parties' constituent acts establish a new subject of international law. The second one fixes the institutional structure of regional organization, the scope and nature of the competences of its bodies, rights and obligations of member states and the like. For this "traditional" intergovernmental approach to regionalism there is a typical horizontal structure which positions states on "one axis" as sovereign and equal actors.

Intergovernmentalism is based on the dominant position of states, which remain the primary actors in the area of policy making, while regional organization only represents a legal and institutional platform for different interaction among them. Regional organizations of intergovernmental character are constantly controlled by the governments of the member states, and all negotiations within organizations are also carried out exclusively at the level of representatives of the member states. The different outcomes of these negotiations are more acceptable in such a horizontal structure because the member states effectively carry out the control pending all procedures preceding their adoption.

One of the legal consequences of the intergovernmental nature of regional organization lies in the fact that (and in contradiction to supranational organizations) the decisions of regional organizations have no force of law within national legal systems of member states and generally do not confer any rights on individuals. The states establishing intergovernmental regional organizations therefore wish to satisfy their own interests and to achieve their national goals. The practice, however, confirms that under specific circumstances, an intergovernmental organization can transform into an organization with supranational elements. As regards the character of reaching decisions, the intergovernmentalist approach prefers decision-making by unanimity, while the supranationalist approach supports majority voting.

Unlike the intergovernmental model, the supranational process of regionalism starts with the delegation of some powers (competences) by the member states to a regional organization which, acting independently, (without the participation of the member states' representatives) obtains the supranational character. The supranational nature of regional organization is determined by the measure of sovereignty that has been transferred to such organization by its member states. In such a way these powers are "internationalised" because they are transferred from the national to the international level with the consent of all member states. With the establishment of supranational organizations acting on the basis of delegation of powers, the horizontal (intergovernmental) system transforms into the vertical and supranational. Such delegated powers authorize the supranational institutions to act independently of member states, take binding decisions, and are responsible for the supervision and implementation of such decisions and constitute a separate legal order of organization.

In this general context the talk is about so-called normative and decisional supranationalism; the normative supranationalism is based on the policy and legal acts of the organization which have direct effects on the member states and are superior to their domestic legal orders, and member states are preempted from enacting contradictory legislation. Decisional supranationalism relates to the autonomy of regional institutions with respect to policy formulation and the decision-making process. At the core of this autonomy is the majority voting system. Majority voting system ensures that as long as the voting requirement is satisfied, member states are bound by a decision, whether or not they support it. Essentially, supranationalism implies the existence of an organization capable of exercising authoritative powers over its member states. This is the point where the supranational organizations are different from intergovernmental institutions since the latter are merely forums for interstate cooperation.[58] However, this does not mean that member states of a regional organization are totally excluded from the decision-making process; they remain together with supranational institutions privileged players in the integration process.[59]

The practice of supranational organizations confirms that they usually comprise both elements of supranational and intergovernmental nature in their systems of governance because they are considered as important for their proper functioning. The EU may be used as a typical example, having both types of supranational organs: the European Parliament and Court of Justice, and the intergovernmentally organized European Council and Council of Ministers.

The EU example confirms that specific legal rules and principles are created within the supranational integration grouping, having priority over the internal legal orders of the member states. In this respect, the EU significantly differs from regional organizations of an intergovernmental nature. Not only is its own legal order typical for the EU, but also autonomous common institutions (organs) are entitled to propose and adopt supranational legal rules in order to deepen and promote the integration process.[60]

The majority of regional organizations within the developing world still remain at the intergovernmental level, since their member states are not willing to share some parts of their sovereignty with a regional group despite the often proclaimed efforts for deeper integration. Many states in Asia and Africa still consider membership in regional organizations as an instrument to reinforce their sovereignty (the sovereignty-reinforced regionalism), which sharply contradicts the obligation to transfer part of their sovereignty for the benefit of the regional group. The usual argument for this approach is that they have been fighting strongly for their sovereignty and independence and this is why it is without logic to transfer part of their sovereignty to regional groups. From their point of view it seems impossible not to reinforce but, on the contrary, to restrict their sovereignty, which is a feature characteristic of supranational regional organizations. Even though the original reasons for the establishment of integration groups have been in the meantime changed, the reluctance of countries in the developing world to create supranational models for integration is long-lasting (ASEAN, APEC, MERCOSUR, NAFTA). As a consequence, current regional organizations in Asia and Africa deal only with issues reflecting the more or less common will of their member states, without having any of their own "positive" agenda for the regional group itself. Such purpose of integration within the developing world obviously puts no pressure on building an effective regional institutional structure. It should be therefore pointed out that, in the light of the relative "youth" of states in the African region (decolonization being a very recent historical process), it is not surprising to find that leaders in many countries are reluctant to yield their prerogative to regional institutions. Therefore a gap can be found between pronouncement made at the heads of state level and the translation of those pronouncements into practical implementation requiring an actual surrender of sovereignty. These problems highlight the obvious fact that the regional organization in Africa ought to be primarily intergovernmental with a minimum of supranational aspirations.[61]

Another reason for the lack of such structures is that weaker states within the integration groups worry that through them only the economic or political interests of the stronger states would be promoted. Any kind of "leadership" by a strong country within a regional group without relevant legal guarantees against its abuse can undermine the consensus, which as a basic principle is regarded as an essential condition for its effective functioning. For instance, the ASEAN, a successful Asian regional group, illustrates that despite efforts being made to institutionally improve the integration mechanism[62] and to build a more stable institutional structure (the ASEAN Charter of 2008), its intergovernmental character, and absence of a supranational organ, are still present. This approach reflects the basic principles it is based on, namely to respect the sovereignty and not to intervene in the internal affairs of the member states[63] and to make decisions based on consensus reached upon previous diplomatic consultations, thus reinforcing the principles of pragmatism, flexibility and non-formality within the relationships among the members. The talk is about so-called networked regionalism because: "Openness consultation and coordination are the main external and internal characteristics of networked processes. There should also be a multitude of actors and agents in such a network".[64] In the larger context it is worth noting that member states of ASEAN still support the traditional Westphalian concept of state sovereignty and also other big countries of the Asian continent (China, India and Russia) object to any efforts to redefine this traditional concept of sovereignty.

In the above context, literature usually refers to the "ASEAN way", or the "Asian way" of integration.[65] In reality it is based on agreements between the member states formulated generally at the level of political elites and diplomatic representatives, on the preference of personal ties and the absence of enforcement measures, etc. As a result, the ASEAN represents a model of regional groupings enhancing the sovereignty of their member states. It serves the member states *inter alia* as a means of dealing with territorial or other disputes which are a heritage of their colonial history.

Another characteristic is the huge difference in economy between the richest and poorest member states, which prevents their closer economic cooperation and creation of common regional agenda, as well as a deeper regional institutional structure.[66] Within the Asian way of integration, the founders however do not consider the absence of a stable, institutional structure of regional institutions as its weakness, but as part of an effort to promote the flexibility of integration processes and exploitation of the options of cooperation in a flexible manner without a legally unbinding character. In a wider context ASEAN might be considered as an Asian version of "open" regionalism, rejecting the European "strict" model of regionalism that is based on free and pragmatic integration without legally binding decisions made by the integration organs. For these reasons, the European integration model is currently not considered as an example to be followed by Asian integration groups.

African regionalism was formed at the beginning on the anti-imperialistic orientation of its members, and was grounded in the ideology of pan-Africanism (as an ideology aimed at uniting all black people on a racial basis) with the aim of protecting the sovereignty of new states having been established on the ruins of the old colonial world. It was based on non-intervention in the internal affairs of member states, and such a trend has lasted till the present time.

In the main, the national interests of the most influential states are promoted in already existing regional structures, and in many cases regionalism has become for heads of states a "hostage" for influence.

African regionalism is usually characterized as without common values because the differences in colonial heritage (and related problems), uneven economic and political development in member states and in various regional groupings, and the nationalism and incompatibility between the economic and political priorities, prevent it from being fully developed. Both the small range of domestic markets and economies and the low volume of official trade contracts stunt the development of African regionalism. The aforesaid also implies the absence of real political will to act for the benefit of integration, which is proved by the fact that regional rhetoric lacks practical implementation measures (COMESA, ECOWAS, SADC) defined in their constituent instruments to be the necessary conditions for proper functioning of such groups.

As we already mentioned, a common feature of both the supranational and the intergovernmental approaches towards regional integration is the irreplaceable role of international law, whose importance and purpose however differ in both cases. The only exception is the approach of the African continent in individual parts where international trade cooperation grows dynamically within the informal cross-border trade (ICBT) as an inherent part of the black and/or second economy and without the relevant domestic or regional regulation and effective control of state bodies.[67] This system is very important for the African economy because it contributes to its growth, job creation and food security for the majority of the region's population. Some 43 percent of Africans are involved in this form of commercial activity, with women representing the large majority with 75 percent of the sector. ICBT characteristically involves by-passing border posts, concealment of goods, under-reporting false qualifications, under- involving and other similar tricks. In addition to seeking to evade taxes or fees imposed by governments, traders also try to avoid administrative formalities in areas such as health, agriculture, security and immigration, which are perceived as costly, complex and time-consuming.[68]

ICBT has its own history across Africa, rooted deeply in colonial times. Furthermore, literature implies that with respect to its extent and dynamics, ICBT alone actually represents the real African economy.[69] Such a process is sometimes called "regionalization", without having to establish any formal bureaucratic and institutional regional structures (regionalization without regionalism).

The ICBT in essence represents a *sui generis* transfer of one of the principles of new regionalism, which is the creation of informal regional structures from below within specific African conditions. There are various reasons why it still growing, including: the inability of official regional structures to reflect economic changes connected with globalization, insufficient transport and logistic infrastructure necessary for international trade exchange, a tenuous network of bank and financial institutions and problems with getting loans, attempts to evade high taxes and different fees, growing corruption and bureaucracy of state bodies and at the borders and finally low level and failures of domestic economies.

It seems that some of the African regional organizations live in their own abstract world, more or less separated from economic reality, not counting on the informal second economy because of their grandiose plans and aims for a better African economy.[70] The exception which, however, proves this approach is currently COMESA implementing a "simplified trade regime initiative" which aims to bring ICBT within the formal trading system, as well as extending the benefits of the free trade area to small traders".[71] As a logical result of these trends: ". . . nobody knows how much informal and unrecorded trade takes place across national borders in Africa. Partly this is because borders are not firmly under control but there is also an element of corruption at play".[72]

A current issue is how to deal with the problem of the second (black) economy and how to involve legislative and other measures in order to draw the second economy into efforts to enhance and promote African regionalism. This problem is very urgent because of the negative impact it has on regional structures: it prevents them from functioning well, disrupts economic stability and the financial and administrative capability of the concerned states. Consequently, the national economies start to become fragmented along local ethnic, religious and communal lines and the possibility of the conflicts inside or among the states are more probable.

Some regional projects have been inspired by the experience of the EU model, mainly in the area of institutional structure. The following main organs copying the EU model are characteristic for regional organizations within the institutional area: the Commission or Secretariat (administrative and legal questions and internal life of organization), the Council (executive nature, consisting of heads of states or ministers), the regional Parliamentary Assembly (elected deputies, legislative issues), the regional Court of Justice (nominated judges, judicial settlement of disputes) and possibly other organs depending on scope and complexity of the regional agenda, for example, economic and social issues, regional central or development banks, etc.

However, in reality such organs do not strictly copy the European supranational model of competences of these bodies because the need to respect the sovereignty of member states is always taken into account. For instance, the establishment of regional commissions (after the European Commission model) makes it impossible to propose regional legislation; regional sanctions, imposed due to breach of regional rules, are subject to the unanimous consent of the member states. Within some regional organizations the directly applied legal norms as regulations and directives (AU, CEMAC, COMESA, ECOWAS, EAC) have to be approved by the relevant authority composed of the representatives of member states (Assembly of heads of states and governments, etc.).[73]

In this respect, there were also more ambitious integration projects following Europe in developing countries, but not corresponding to the economic and political reality of their member states. In such cases there is an essential lesson to be learnt from European integration, saying that the selection of different institutional levels and structural systems depends fully on specific economic characteristics and the real political ambitions of each region. We can encounter such an overestimation of the European integration model in areas of Africa and Latin America[74] (Andean Community). Ambitious projects like these usually assume that if some regional institutes were working well within European integration, naturally they would work well under different conditions and in different parts of the world.

To say that European integration is reminiscent of "skeet shooting" is thus a just description, since the current situation within the European integration is the result of the previous long development within the economic, political, institutional or other areas, and still continues to the present day. Therefore, the rules applied within the European model in the 1960s and 1970s might still be applicable for purposes of regional integration development in the developing world, but the current rules reflecting the actual higher level of economic integration and institutional complexity are not so.

A brief analysis of the EU model implies that conditions necessary for the success of a regional project vary and represent a complex of political, economic and legal factors specific to a particular region and depending on each other, based on mutual dynamics. Even though (for this reason) they cannot be applied automatically outside a particular region, the regional groupings in various parts of the world and at various stages/phases of their integration process aspire to it as a model proven in practice.

A main obstacle preventing the developing regional groups from coming closer to the European model is the difference in understanding the importance of sovereignty of member states within the integration process as well as the role of regional organs in making the integration process more developed and deepened. Due to historical, political and different economic conditions, the regional groupings within the developing world are not willing to assign a more important role to the regional groups and their organs in furthering the development and deepening of the integration process. They specifically worry about their sovereignty becoming weaker by transferring part of it to organs of a regional group, as well as having their own agenda separate to the member states. Regional practice confirms the existence of other elements having a negative impact on the development of supranationalism, including: non-implementation of key supranational measures, the chaotic proliferation of regional organizations resulting in double membership of states, political instability of member states and their democratic deficit, hegemonic position of strong member states within regional organization and the like.

For these reasons, the prevailing model of regional integration groups within the developing world is still a model of intergovernmental character, with an agenda at such a level and scope accepted by all member states. It should be, however, pointed out that the tendency to copy certain elements of supranationalism can be recently identified within regional groupings of the developing world (e.g. African continent—see below).

Unlike the European model, governed and institutionalized in every detail by law as: "a rule-based model with a multiplicity of institutions"[75] Asian and African regionalism currently prefer more liberal and informal models reflecting some principles of new regionalism. They include informal international networks and regimes of trade and cooperation between various types and groups of regional subjects, so without the states having a dominant position. In Asia it is a consequence of a different philosophy of the so-called Asian way of "open" regionalism, while in Africa, structures of informal cross-border trade do not form an accepted or proper part of the official regionalism. The regional African organizations show no real interest in making such informal groups integrated and cooperative with their activities and, on the contrary, some of their member states profit from trade and economic activities of the ICBT for their own needs.

5.4.1. Supranational Elements Within Some Regional Organizations of the Developing World (Example of Africa)

Unlike the well-functioning supranational system of the EU, different supranational attempts within regional organizations in the developing world have appeared in the meantime. As regards to ECOWAS, since its rise in 1975 it has had an intergovernmental nature, and some elements of supranational nature have been inserted into its structure and legal order later (mainly on the recommendation of the Committee of Eminent Persons in 1990) into the revised Treaty of ECOWAS 1993.[76] The supranationalism elements within ECOWAS consists of vesting more powers and competences into their bodies in order to reinforce their position vis á vis member states. Within such institutional transformation its Authority (in 2006) approved the transformation of the Executive Secretariat into a nine-member Commission. Their decisions taken at the Community level are directly enforceable in the member states without the necessity of their previous formal consent. Confronted with the problems of international security, ECOWAS puts in place a supranational security mechanism consisting of Mediation and Security Council, Defence and Security Commission and Council of Elders. The Mediation and Security Council is made up of the 10 members and decisions are made by a two-thirds majority of six members.

In respect of the OHADA should be pointed out that it represents one of the successful attempt at supranationalism on the African continent. In a sense, it is a good example of the initiative aimed at harmonizing specific legal standards. It works on the basis of the OHADA Treaty of 1993[77] and its main goal is to accelerate economic development and foreign investments in member states through the provision of a secure judicial environment. An important supranational element of the OHADA Treaty represents the provisions stipulating that its Uniform Acts (adopted by the Council Ministers—Article 3) are immediately applicable in the domestic legal order of member states having direct effects (Article 9 of the OHADA Treaty).One of the strongest supranational institutions is the OHADA Common Court of Justice and

Arbitration, having two main functions with respect to OHADA legal order, namely, an arbitration centre and a Supreme Court for judgments delivered by a national Courts of Appeal. It is fair to say that the successful implementation of the harmonization of business is largely attributable to this independent and reliable Court of Justice.

Some supranational elements may be identified also in constituent acts of some other African subregional bodies. Concerning WAEMU, established in 1994,[78] its objectives include the harmonization of laws, the creation of a common market and the convergence of the macroeconomic and economic policies of member states (Article 4 of the WAEMU Treaty 1994). Its Article 4 states that WAEMU's statutes are superior to the legal order of member states, and institutional aspects of supranationalism are represented by the Central Bank of States of West Africa solely responsible for issuing currency on the territory of member states and common monetary policy. Similar conclusions also concern CEMAC[79] because it aims to create a common market, harmonized laws and sectoral policies, and promote the convergence of the macroeconomic policies of member states. The strong supranational position has its Bank of Central African States responsible for issuing CFA francs and to control the monetary policy. Both these organizations created structures for monitoring and ensuring compliance with the monetary policies of member states. Further elements of the supranationalism have been inserted also in the SACU and EAC.[80] These organizations confirm that despite different obstacles and local specificities, some elements of normative and decisional supranationalism are today clearly identifiable in the African subregional architecture.[81]

As regards to the persisting obstacles of supranationalism, the absence of a political will of member states to reinforce the ability and competences of regional organizations through transferring the elements of their sovereignty to organizations represents an influential factor in a lot of unsuccessful regional projects in the developing world. It is not suggested that political will is the only requirement for a successful regional integration project, but it certainly helps firm up the foundation on which stable cooperation may be built. Regional practice confirms the existence of other elements having a still negative impact on the development of supranationalism, including: the weak institutional machinery of regional organizations, non-implementation of key supranational measures, the lack of relevant funds, the chaotic proliferation of regional organizations resulting in double membership of states, political instability of member states and their democratic deficit, hegemonic position of strong member states within regional organizations, the negative impact of armed conflicts and the like.[82]

5.5. Impact of the European Union on Current Regionalism

Even though the regional organizations establish their member states freely and they are independent of each other and without any subordination, it does not mean that they do not cooperate mutually (including cooperation regulated by the rules of international law) and that they in certain cases do not try to copy the successful and long-existing functioning regional models. While a perfect integration model may be lacking, a lot of the regional organizations in the developing world consider the EU model as an exceptionally suitable *point of reference*, and also as an alternative to the economic integration model promoted by the USA. The advantages and impact of EU model on regionalism in developing countries have become relatively often the subject of doctrinal analysis.[83]

The founders of regional organizations across the developing world sometimes think that copying and applying certain segments of the EU model might help them achieve their own integration projects faster, more easily and better.[84] Since the beginning of the 1960s a number of regions around the work copied Europe's approach to regional economic integration, omitting, however, its legal mechanisms.

Another inspiring aspect of the EU model of economic integration lies in its perceived beneficial impact on the larger areas of international peace and security, connected to the long-term political and economic stability within the integration organization.[85] The EU model of integration, first seen in the EEC and originally of a purely economic character, was able to effectively overcome the historical post-war animosity between the member states (France and Germany) and for its members to gradually build in areas: "of peace, security, political and economic stability, promoting democracy, rule of law and human rights protection".[86] It is worth noting that a principal impulse for West European integration was the political motive of avoiding the next war in Europe based on the idea of economic integration as a main tool to secure future European peace and stability. In this respect, European integration, despite having some weak periods, represents a thriving example of regional integration (and inspiration) that is worth following by developing countries.[87] The European Union's ability to manage conflicts among their member states is therefore " . . . proffered to developing countries. This is particularly influential in the African context owing to that region's historical and existing links to Europe via trade, investment and development assistance".[88] For the sake of completeness it should be however stressed that only the future reveals if this affirmative "image" of the European model will be negatively affected by, among other things: the euro-financial crisis, the problems to manage the debt of EU member states (e.g. Greece), the continuing immigration crisis and the departure of the United Kingdom from the EU.

Some principles on which the EU model is founded can be, under certain circumstances, also applied to regional organizations outside Europe, as they imply a well-functioning regional system verified by long-term practice. The main problems are, however, that the real legal and factual conditions and circumstances under which the regional organizations outside Europe are established, the political and economic differences among their future member states and the different approaches to the main goals of organizations all limit the real application of such EU principles.

In this context it is worth noting that the establishment of each regional organization is always a unique, political, legal and economical process, the results of which are that there are various types of regional groups with different levels of integration. Such different types are a logical consequence of varying economic, political, historical or other conditions in different parts of the world. They therefore differ in their membership, institutional and legal nature, structure, content and aims, and also in how successful they are in applying the experiences and principles of the EU model to their own conditions.

In this regard, the EU serves as an institutional model with a specific program which the regional organizations in the developing world more or less take into account, depending on their specifications and real possibilities.

Experience, however, does not exclude the assumption that current regionalism should have different forms, without the influence of the European integration model. The EU in practice does not restrict itself to a passive role, but within its external and mainly interregional relationships, uses various active means and methods. In such a sense the EU today actively affects the development of regionalism across the world through the promotion of its integration approach, acquired experiences, standards, norms, institutional structures and legal principles and values on which it is based. Such means include financial and technical aid, conclusion of agreements for purposes of promoting business relations (FTA—Free Trade Agreements), exchange of experiences, standardization of procedures in areas of banking and business, etc. From the acquired experiences of the European model it is possible to deduce various conditions necessary to be met if the regional organizations want to succeed.

The basic condition to establish regional organization supposes the common interest of the future members that is strong enough for such establishment and proper functioning. As mentioned earlier, such interest might depend on geographical proximity (neighbouring), a common geographical element (international river, cross-border lake, inland sea, desert, rainforest, cross-border biotope, etc.) or other such serious interests that need permanent institutional cooperation between the states. The existence of these conditions should not be either underestimated or overestimated. As current experience confirms, some suitable conditions are not sufficient enough for the purposes of a common integration project, providing there are long-lasting problems of a political, religious, cultural or of another character among future member states. The European experience shows that a critical element necessary for obtaining political willingness crucial for the establishment and development of the EC was the historical reconciliation between France and Germany, built over the years through mutual political cooperation among the leading representatives of those countries,[89] together with favourable circumstances developed during the post-war arrangement of Europe.[90] It should be therefore pointed out that the integration project requires, in addition to intensive and specific integration interest, a certain level of politically accepted standards of relationships with no conflicts among future members in order to be successful—a so-called "clear table" of mutual relationships.

Geographic areas where efforts made by states to settle long-term conflicts were insufficient (despite attempts to establish regional integration groups) have the opposite outcome. For instance in Asia, it is in the near future hard to expect intensive regional development without historical reconciliation between Japan and Korea, India and Pakistan, Israel and Palestine, Iran and Iraq, Japan and China, etc.

Every regional project requires not only the strong, but persistent will of its founders, who are able to confront temporary, unfavourable conditions, and, depending on an integration model, also to transfer a part of sovereignty in favour of a regional organization. Initial enthusiasm is not sufficient for its establishment, as it loses momentum after a certain time as a consequence of the failure to reach the anticipated results.

In the case of European integration, it is an integration process which has taken more than 60 years during which the political willingness has lasted, despite various problems and difficulties, no matter what the governments were. Even though we can observe various periods of stagnation in the integration process of Europe, they were replaced by shorter, yet more intensive reformative stages resulting in the conclusion of international treaties which moved the integration development forward (the Single European Act of 1986, the Maastricht Treaty of 1992, the Treaty of Amsterdam of 1997, the Treaty of Lisbon of 2007).

The absence of a lasting political will is apparent within African regional organizations which were established in great numbers after the former colonies became independent at the beginning of 1960s. Their efficiency is, however, weak and their lifetime, in some cases, is short. In the majority of cases they represent only a rhetorical integration, especially in the case of ambitious political leaders' projects, and unrealistic goals resulting in their termination or inactivity.

The African continent is currently a "cacophony" of various organizations and initiatives in pursuit of the same or similar aims, but making no efforts to cooperate and coordinate activities mutually. Another typical attribute of African integration groupings is: "the overlapping membership among the states, in various regional groups, resulting in efficiency being reduced and chaos increased, and the non-transparency of the African continent integration map".[91] This results in duplication, non-productive competition between the members and the organs of various regional organizations, poor use of time and energy and the imposition of increasing financial obligations and higher bureaucracy on its members.

Such competing regionalism is reflected not only in relationships among various regional groups, but also in their internal structures, and it relates to efforts to get, for example, external financial aid (e.g. from the EU), extension of political influence, as well as other forms of regional cooperation and policy, etc. Literature states that out of 53 African countries, 26 of them are members of two regional organizations, 19 are members of three, two countries (the Democratic Republic of Congo and Swaziland) are members of four organizations and only six countries are members of just one regional group.[92] Institutional "pell-mell" is increasing also due to the relationships between regional organizations and the African Union, which seeks a certain coordination of regional activities on the African continent. But it is confronted with various institutional structures, different financial sponsors and interests, and also with a reluctance, great and small, to join a common institutional structure covering the African continent.[93]

Nevertheless, the African Union has succeeded in having various regional groups participating in activities ensuring international peace and security in Africa (ECOWAS, SADC, ECCAS, COMESA, EAC). It is however worth noting that this situation of African regionalism which is today not able to enjoy all profits resulting from functioning regionalism is not immutable. Increasing integration and growing influence of external global trade and others factors will put the pressure on the member states of regional organizations either to reduce their numbers to a reasonable level or to dissolve some of them because "the increasing integration and cooperation in economic and legislative areas will eventually lead to two regional blocs: one covering West and Central Africa and one spanning across Eastern and Southern Africa".[94]

A similar situation is on the Latin America continent, the regionalism of which is still segmented and decentralized and where its four waves have emerged of "many coexisting and competing projects with fuzzy boundaries (regions inflation). The multiple number of regional organizations emptied them—and the very concept of integration of real content".[95] In the same time the prevailing practice of overlapping regionalism logically results in the outcome that "every country belongs to more than one regional organization is potentially subject to double loyalty and norm conflict".[96] This situation logically causes problems concerning the compatibility of economic and other priorities of member states with respect to the specific goals and purposes of different regional organizations, their real capability to comply simultaneously with specific obligations issuing from legal orders of regional organizations, financial implications of multiple membership, etc. A common minimum denominator is therefore still lacking in Latin America to unite their countries around a single integration project.

Respecting the rule of law and democracy among its members, the EU model reflects this principle as a necessity for granting stability and irreversibility of the integration process. Such a condition is within the context of regional groupings needed to ensure proper functioning of regional organs and institutions, and from the economical point, enhance the atmosphere of trust essential for long-term and extensive investments.[97] The benefits that EU membership offers to their members thus depends on creating basic democratic institutions and principles with respect to their political systems and domestic legal orders. Consequently, regionalism and democracy are processes depending on and strengthening each other. The aforesaid is confirmed also with respect to Central and Eastern European states, which, prior to joining the EU, were obliged to comply with the need to be and to state they were functioning democracies based on the rule of law and a market economy, as was earlier the case with Greece, Spain and Portugal.

This condition is, however, hard to accept across the developing world because of the nature of the political and ideological character of states and the different orientation of their domestic and foreign policies. The majority of states were established during the post-war process of decolonization; their political developments took different directions and they remained at different levels of economic development. It is then not feasible to expect them to join the integration groupings with their market economies functioning well and pluralistic political systems respecting the human rights and rule of law. ASEAN, for instance, comprises two democratic members (Indonesia, Philippines), two "soft" authoritarian members (Malaysia and Singapore) and the remaining members have non-democratic regimes. Even if the democratic system is not a necessary precondition to become a member of a each regional group in the developing world, it is, however, true that regionalism thrives in states which respect principles of the rule of law and human rights, but not in those which are politically unstable, with no representation organs and with autocratic regimes.

Notes

1. The Kyoto Protocol to the frame Convention on Climate Change of 1997. Available at: www.kyotoprotocol.com/resource/kpeng.pdf
2. The Vienna Convention on the Protection of the Ozone Layer of 1985. Available at: http://ozone.unep.org/sites/ozone/files/Publications/Handbooks/VC-Handbook-2016-English.pdf
3. An essential fact is: "convergence of interests values and political objectives of states" resulting in the so-called functional differentiation of international law. As a result: "Regionalism (today) loses its specificity as a problem and should be rather dealt with in connection of the functional diversification of the international society in general . . .". In: Report of the Study Group of ILC: Fragmentation of International Law: Difficulties Arising From the Diversification and Expansion of International Law (A/CN.4/L.682), p. 204, 209. Available at: http://untreaty.un.org/ilc/documentation/english/a_cn4_l682.pdf
4. As stated by Väyrynen, R: ". . . functional conceptualizations of region emanate from the interplay of subnational and transnational economic, environmental and cultural processes that the states are only partially able to control". In Väyrynen, *supra* n. 36, p. 27.
5. Nye, J.S. (ed.): *International Regionalism: Readings.* Boston, MA: Little, Brown & Co., 1968, p. xii.
6. Archer, C.: *International Organizations.* London: Routledge, 1992, p. 12.
7. It might be the bilateral interregionalism which is typical for various forms of cooperation between two regional groups. A typical example from the beginning of 1970s includes the relations between the EU and ASEAN. Depending on orientation and subject of activities regarding regional organizations, the interregional cooperation among more regional organizations or other entities might not be excluded (multi-regionalism, or trans-regionalism).
8. International legal subjectivity of the EU was finally (and formarly) confirmed by the Lisbon Treaty of 2009, and in 2007 in case of ASEAN.

9. See at least: Conference on Networked Regionalism Versus Institutional Regionalism (Singapore 6-8/12, 2009), p. 13. Available at: www.eucentre.sg/wp-content/uploads/2013/06/RegionalismConf-Dec2009.pdf
10. Not yet in validity. In: Watts, A. (ed.): *The International Law Commission 1949–1998*, Vol. II. Oxford: Oxford University Press, 1999, p. 874.
11. Article 56 of the Convention for the Protection of Human Rights and Fundamental Freedoms of 1950 states that any State Party may extend its applicability to "all or any of the territories for whose international relations it is responsible". This method of extending the geographical scope of the application of a regional treaty beyond the territories of its original member states is, however, on the decline since the number of territories for which the member states are responsible is still decreasing.
12. Basic principles of the "Responsibility to protect" have been included in Article 4 h) of the Constitutive Act of the African Union yet before their approval and publication in the Outcome Document of the UN World Summit in 2005.
13. For example, engagement of NATO in Afghanistan and in the waters of the Somalian coast, engagement of the EU forces in Southern Europe and Congo, etc.
14. The Centre for International Cooperation states that armed forces of the regional organizations were engaged in almost half out of 40 peacekeeping missions taking place in 2010. Cited from: Fawcett, *supra* n. 40, p. 13.
15. As ICJ has stated: ". . . the Lake Chad Basin Commission is an international organization exercising its powers within a specific geographical area, that it does not however have as its purpose the settlement at a regional level of matters relating to the maintenance of international peace and security and thus does not fall under Chapter VIII of the Charter". In Land and Maritime Boundary Between Cameroun and Nigeria, Judgment of the ICJ, I.C.J. Reports 1998, pp. 306–307, para. 65.
16. The European Coal and Steel Treaty (18 April 1951), Article 97: "The Treaty is concluded for the period of 50 years after entering into force". The Belgium-Luxembourg Economic Union Treaty was initially concluded for the period of 50 years, but its validity has been repeatedly extended (last time in 2002).
17. The Southeast Asia Treaty Organization (SEATO), whose constituent pact was concluded without any time restriction was dissolved in 1977; the Organisation for Economic Co-operation and Development (OECD) replaced the Organisation for European Economic Co-operation (OEEC) established in 1948; the Council for Mutual Economic Assistance established in 1949 was dissolved upon a special Protocol in 1991, and others. The constituent acts of International Bank for Reconstruction and Development, International Monetary Fund, European Bank for Reconstruction and Development include provisions regulating conditions and voting concerning their dissolution.
18. A special resolution of the League of Nations adopted by its Assembly on 18 April 1946 where a decision was made on its dissolution because the UN was established for the same purpose. On the same day, the Permanent Court of International Justice was also dissolved. Practical questions regarding UN succession in relation to the former League of Nations' moveable and immovable property, including bibliotheca and archive, were dealt with resolutions of the UN General Assembly during its first meeting in 1946. The European Space Agency, established in 1973, replaced the European Space Research Organisation and the European Launcher Development Organisation (ELDO), etc.
19. As stated by Fawcett, L.: "Reflecting the presence of newer security threats, strategies to combat terrorism have been added to the existing convention

in the EU (has it own antiterrorist capacity) and OAS as well as other groupings". In: Fawcett, L.: Exploring Regional Domains: A Comparative History of Regionalism. In: *International Affairs*, Vol. 80, No. 3, 2004, p. 440.

20. Among the best-equipped African regional organizations are ECOWAS and SADC, but such structures can be found also in IGAD, ECCAS, (CEN-SAD), COMESA, Arab Maghreb Union (AMU), East African Community (EAC), etc.
21. Remarks by Sir Roland Sanders, Member of Commonwealth Eminent Persons Group to Caribbean Regional Civil Society Consultation, Guyana June 28, 2011, p. 1.
22. There is no generally recognized definition of the GEP. One of the simplest states that: "It is a group of prominent individuals appointed by an organization to investigate a particular issue", while another refers to GEP as "An unofficial or quasi-official advisory group consisting of influential figures from varied backgrounds. Such a group may be employed to advise a state or international organization on a particular problem and disband when its task is completed". See: Berridge, G., Lloyd, L.: *The Palgrave Macmillan Dictionary of Diplomacy*. London, UK: Palgrave Macmillan, 2012, p. 135–136.
23. Project Europe 2000 (Challenges and Opportunities) – Report to the EU European Council By the Reflection Group on the Future of the EU 2030, May 2010.

    Common Purpose—Towards a More Effective OSCE. Final Report of the Panel of Eminent Persons, June 2005.

    We the Peoples: Civil Society, the UN and Global Governance. Report of the Panel of Eminent Persons on UN—Civil Society Relations, June 2004.

    A New Global Partnership—The Report of the High Level Panel of Eminent Persons on the post-2015 UN Development Agenda, 2013.

    The African Union—Panel of the Wise: Strengthening Relations With Similar Regional Mechanism, 2012.
24. A more detailed evaluation of their role and contribution to the development of institutional regionalism exceeds the scope of this monograph.
25. As stated by Hettne, B.: "European regionalism is the trigger of global regionalisation at least in two different ways: one positive (promoting regionalism), the other negative (provoking regionalism)". In: Hettne, B., Inotai, A.: The New Regionalism: Implications for the Global Development and International Security. In: *UN University: The Research for Action*, UN, 1994, p. 10. Available at: www.wider.unu.edu/sites/default/files/RFA14.pdf
26. For example, the external tariffs as part of the European common market have been confronted with an unwillingness to put it into practice in other economic areas. The political field faced the problems of accepting the principle of the so-called divided sovereignty of the member states, the unanimous consent of the member states when deciding on regional sanctions, the exclusive competence of the organization's bodies in proposing regional legislation, etc. Considering the institutional area, seemingly the simplest is the situation where the basic organs of the EU institutional system, having considered the regional specifications, can be accepted within other regional groupings. Inspired by the EU Court of Justice, there are currently 11 regional organizations that established judicial authorities of similar kind. See, f.e: Lenz, T.: External Influences on Regionalism: Studying EU Diffusion and Its Limits. *E-International Relations*, 2013. Available at: www.e-ir.info/2013/07/17/external-influences-on-regionalism-studying-eu-diffusion-and-its-limits/
27. Responsibility of International Organizations (Doc.A/66/10). Available at: http://untreaty.un.org/ilc/reports/2011/2011report.htm

28. The European Community became the member of the International Food and Agriculture Organization (FAO), whose constituent act was in 1991 amended in order to enable membership to other regional economic organizations.
    The World Tourism Organization has, in addition to the states as a full members, also "groups of territories" as extraordinary members, and international intergovernmental and non-governmental organizations as affiliated members.
    The Arab States Broadcasting Union (ASBU) has, in addition to the states as full members, also "broadcasting unions" of member states.
    The Arctic Council established upon the Ottawa Declaration in 1996 has six states that are permanent members, six international organizations representing the people of Arctic as permanent members, plus 12 states, nine intergovernmental and 11 non-governmental organizations acting as observers.
29. As stated by L.B. De Chazournes: "Non-state actors including *inter alia* individuals, non-governmental organizations, foundations, scientific associations and the private sectors play an increasingly important role in the life of international organizations". In De Chazournes, L.B.: Changing Roles of International Organizations: Global Administrative Law and the Interplay of Legitimacies. In: *International Organizations Law Review*, Vol. 6, 2009, p. 656.
30. Similar problems can be observed in the case when an international organization wants to become a contracting party to the international convention in which its state parties anticipate only the participation of the states (efforts of the EU to join the Convention for the Protection of Human Rights and Fundamental Freedoms).
31. The Rome Declaration—Declaration of the Leaders of 27 Member States and of the European Council, the European Parliament and the European Commission. Available at: www.consilium.europa.eu/en/press/press-releases/2017/03/25-rome-declaration/
32. The New Partnership for Africa's Development, 2001.
33. Article 3 of the Statute of the Council of Europe of 1949 states that: "Every member of the Council of Europe must accept the principles of the rule of law and of the enjoyment by all persons within its jurisdiction of human rights and fundamental freedoms . . .".
    Article 2 of the North Atlantic Treaty of 1949: "The Parties will contribute toward the further development of peaceful and friendly international relations by strengthening their free institutions . . .".
    Article 2 of the Lisbon Treaty states that: "The Union is founded on the values of respect for human dignity, freedom, democracy, and respect for human rights, including pluralism, non-discrimination, tolerance, justice, solidarity and equality between women and men, and the rights of persons belonging to minorities. These values are common to the Member States. . .".
34. The African Union has developed normative standards ranging from the Algiers Declaration on Unconstitutional Changes of Government of 1999 to the African Charter on Democracy, Elections and Governance; the Organization of American States is guided by the Inter-American Democratic Charter of 2007, etc.
35. Rule of Law and Constitution Building: The Role of Regional Organizations. International Institute for Democracy and Electoral Assistance, Stockholm, 2014, p. 3. Available at: www.idea.int/sites/default/files/publications/rule-of-law-and-constitution-building.pdf
36. "The rule of Law is one of the values the regional organizations are founded on, together with maintenance of human dignity, freedom, democracy, equality and human rights". See: Elbert, L.: Regionalism and International Organizations. In: Klucka, J., Elbert, L. (eds.): *Regionalism and Its Contribution*

to General International Law. Kosice: P.J. Šafarik University in Košice, 2015, p. 123.

37. A situation in the EC in 2000, when R. Haider was in power after the election in Austria, in 2012–2013 the European Commission appealed to Hungary to redress non-democratic amendments to the Constitution, especially the legal position of the Constitutional Court, minority laws, position of the Central Bank, etc.
38. Diplomatic immunities and privileges were granted to the International Commission of Congo (1888), the Central Commission for Navigation on the Rhine and to the Permanent Court of Arbitration (1907), the International Prize Court (1907), the Permanent Court of International Justice (1921), the League of Nations (1921), etc.

    For more details see at least: Kunz, J.L.: Privileges and Immunities of International Organizations. In: *American Journal of International Law*, Vol. 41, No. 4, 1947, pp. 828–862.
39. "The organizations have been granted such legal capacity as will permit them to accomplish their purposes and functions as to permit them to remain as free as possible from national interference or control". See: Fedder, E.H.: The Functional Basis of International Privileges and Immunities: A New Concept in International Law and Organizations. In: *American University Law Review*, Vol. 9, 1960, p. 63.
40. Wouters, J., De Man, P.: International Organizations as Law-Makers. In: *Leuven Centre for Global Governance Studies*, Working Paper No. 21, 2009, p. 13. Available at: https://ghum.kuleuven.be/ggs/publications/working_papers/new_series/wp21-30/wp21.pdf
41. Created by World Bank together with EBDT and UNEP.
42. Created by UNICEF, UNDP, UNFPA, UNESCO, WHO, World Bank.
43. Wouters, De Man, *supra* n. 85, p. 23.
44. A traditional institutional "triad" of the international organizations organs consists of the Assembly having general powers and joining all the member states, the Council as an executive body of the organization and the Secretariat dealing with administrative tasks and functioning of the organization.
45. Regulation of this kind of relationship can be expressed by virtue of obligations that the EU member states have towards EU regulations and/or directives and their effects in their domestic legal orders.
46. For more details concerning settlements of disputes and sanctions regime of economic organizations. See: Voitovich, S.A.: *International Economic Organizations in the International Legal Process*. London: Martinus Nijhoff Publishers, 1995, p. 114 and subsequent.
47. "International Economic Courts follow two basic models. The GATT/WTO model has compulsory jurisdiction and only states can initiate a non-compliance suit and only disputes governments care about are adjudicated. Regional system that adopt the WTO model often also adopt its panel system of dispute settlements which allows governments to first try consultation followed by a more arbitration style of disputes adjudication before any appeal to more a legalized appellate body. Next is ECJ model, which has a supranational Commission that monitors state compliance and brings non-compliance cases to supranational court, a preliminary ruling mechanism that allows private litigants to raise cases in national courts which can be referred to the supranational court and system of administrative and constitutional review that allows states, community institutions and private litigants to challenge community acts in front of the supranational court". See: Alter, K.J.: The New International Courts. In: *iCourts Working Paper Series*, No. 2, 2013, pp. 25–26. Available at: http://jura.ku.dk/icourts/research-resources/working-papers/

48. As stated by Y. Shany: ". . . international courts such as the ECJ and WTO promote the goals of their overreaching regimes, but at the same time help to maintain, under changing circumstances, the political economic and legal equilibrium that states reasonably expected to hold among them when joining a specific co-operative regime". See: Shany, Y.: No Longer a Weak Department of Power? Reflections on the Emergence of a New International Judiciary. In: *The European Journal of International Law*, Vol. 20, No. 1, 2009, p. 82.
49. In 1989, the voting rights for Cambodia in FAO were suspended for failure to pay its membership fees.
50. Art. 7 Section 3 of the Treaty of European Union stipulates that the Council "may suspend certain rights deriving from the application of the Treaties to the member state in question, including the voting rights of its representatives in the Council".

    Art. 19 A of the Statute of the IAEA: a member of the Agency shall have no vote (if a member is late in the payment of its membership contributions), or privileges and membership rights might be suspended (Art. 19 B—in case of persistent violation of the provision of the Statute).

    Art. 15 of the Pact of the League of Arab states that the state which is not fulfilling the obligations resulting from the Pact may be excluded by a decision taken by a unanimous vote of all the states (except the state referred to). The League of Arab States decided in February 2011 on suspension of membership of Syria and on economic sanctions. It was for the first time that a member state has been excluded because of actions against its people within its own borders.

    Art. 9 of the Statute of the Council of Europe states that the suspension of the right of representation of a member state in the Committee of Ministers and on the Consultative Assembly (failure to fulfil its financial obligations), Art. 8—suspension of the right of representation on the Committee of Ministers (serious violation of the Statute) with a possible option of membership to be ceased.
51. Article 23 para.1 of the Constitutive Act of the African Union states that the Assembly of member states shall determine the appropriate sanctions to be imposed on any member state that defaults in the payment of its contributions to the budget of the Union in the following manner: denial of the right to speak at meetings, to vote, to present candidates for any position or post within Union or to benefit from any activity or commitments therefrom.
52. As the exception which proves the rule, we can mention the constituent instrument of the International Coffee Agreement of 1983 (Article 66), or the International Agreement on Olive Oil of 1986 (Article 58).
53. Hellquist, E.: Regional Organizations and Sanctions Against Members: Explaining the Different Trajectories of the African Union, the League of Arab States and the Association of Southeast Asian Nations. In: *KFG Working Paper Series* (The Transformative Power of Europe), No. 59, 2014, p. 5, 9. Available at: http://userpage.fu-berlin.de/kfgeu/kfgwp/wpseries/WorkingPaperKFG_59.pdf
54. Among another examples one can mention Pakistan and Fiji suspended from the Councils of the Commonwealth in 1999 and 2000 following unconstitutional changes in governments.
55. For more details see: The Execution of Judgments of the ECHR. Human Rights File No. 19, Council of Europe Publishing, 2008.
56. For more details see: Tan, M.: Member State Compliance With the Judgments of the Inter-American Court of Human Rights. In: *International Journal of Legal Information*, Vol. 33, No. 3, 2005, Available at: http://scholarship.law.cornell.edu/ijli/vol33/iss3/4

57. For more details see: Oving, A.K.: The Effectiveness of the Enforcement Procedure in the European Community, Lund, 2008. Available at: http://lup.lub.lu.se/luur/download?func=downloadFile&recordOId=1563347&fileOId=1566255
58. For more details see: Weiler, J.: The Community System: The Dual Character of Supranationalism. In: *Yearbook of European Law*, Vol. 1, No. 1, 1981, pp. 267–306.
59. Weiler, J.: *The Constitution of Europe: Do the New Clothes Have an Emperor? And Other Essays on European Integration*. Cambridge: Cambridge University Press, 1999, p. 273.
60. "At the same time the regional organizations having institutional regimes comprising independent-norm setting authority: 'are a vehicle for deterritorialization in international law.' Thus deterritorialization occurs when an organization has the power to enact norms within a normative regime of which they are an institutional component". See: Brölmann, C.: Deterritorialization in International Law: Moving Away From the Divide Between National and International Law. In: Nijman, J., Nollkaemper, A. (eds.): *New Perspectives on the Divide Between National and International Law*. Oxford: Oxford University Press, 2007, p. 94.
61. Draper, P.: Breaking Free From Europe: Why Africa Needs Another Model of Regional Integration? In: Fioramonti, L. (ed.): *Regionalism in a Changing World: Comparative Perspective in the New Global Order*. London and New York: Routledge, 2013, p. 73.
62. The Asian crisis (1997–1998) led to intensified efforts by the East Asians to look into more formal economic integration as opposed to the more loose and informal economic interdependence that had existed for years. See: Yeo, L.H.: Institutional Regionalism Versus Networked Regionalism: Europe and Asia Compared. In: *International Politics*, Vol. 47, No. 3/4, 2010, p. 326.
63. This principle has its own historical origin whereas: "ASEAN's focus on sovereignty reflects its members' historical experiences with Western and Japanese colonialism. The commitment to sovereignty and non-intervention also reflects the concern of regional states that had interfered in each other's affairs in the past, and understood that if their fragile efforts at state-building were to be effective, they needed to cooperate with one another". See: Narine, S.: Asia, ASEAN and the Question of Sovereignty: The Persistence of Non-Intervention in the Asia Pacific. In: Beeson, M., Stubbs, R. (eds.): *Routledge Handbook of Asian Regionalism*. New York: Routledge, 2012, p. 155.
64. Yeo, *supra* n. 107, p. 333.
65. ". . . the European Union is often showcased as a successful model of institutional regionalism where integration is more formal and legalistic and achieved through endowing specific institutions with decision-making power to shape the behaviour of member states. In contrast, region building in Asia seems to operate on a different logic with an emphasis on open-ended networked regionalism where cooperation is achieved through informal networks and with less emphasis on institutionalisation". In *Conference on Networked Regionalism Versus Institutional Regionalism: Managing Complexities in Regional Cooperation and Global Governance*. Singapore, 6–8th December 2009, p. 2. Available at: www.uni-due.de/~hy0387/fileadmin/resource/Singapore_Conf_2009-12.pdf
66. As stated by E.D. Mansfield and H.V. Milner: ". . . network character of Asian states and their emphasis on consensus building and the convergence between public and private spheres in domestic politics differentiate them from European countries and render them less likely to develop regional institution". Mansfield, Milner, *supra* n. 18, p. 618.

67. See at least: Afrika, J.-G.K., Ajumbo, G.: Informal Cross Border Trade in Africa: Implications and Policy Recommendations. In: *Africa Economic Brief*, Vol. 3, No. 10, 2012. Available at: www.afdb.org/fileadmin/uploads/afdb/Documents/Publications/Economic%20Brief%20-%20Informal%20Cross%20Border%20Trade%20in%20Africa%20Implications%20and%20Policy%20Recommendations%20-%20Volume%203.pdf
68. Njiwa, D.: Tackling Informal Cross-Border Trade in Southern Africa. In: *Bridges Africa*, Vol. 2, No. 1, 2013, pp. 1–2.
69. Ndiaye, T.: "There is often the suggestion in the literature that the informal/parallel economy including ICBT is Africa's 'Real' Economy". In Ndiaye, T.: Case Story on Gender Dimension of Aid for Trade, ITC, UNIFEM, New York, p. 2. Available at: www.intracen.org/uploadedFiles/intracenorg/Content/About_ITC/Where_are_we_working/Multi-country_programmes/Women_and_trade/Women%20Informal%20Traders%20Transcending%20African%20Borders.pdf
70. As stated by M. Bøås: "If regional organisation is to play a real role in African economies it has to be embedded into the African context and this is the context of second economy". See: Bøås, M.: Regions and Regionalisation: A Heretic's View. In: *Regionalism and Regional Integration in Africa*. Uppsala: Nordiska Afrikainstitutet, 2001, Discussion Paper 11, p. 35. Available at: www.files.ethz.ch/isn/102627/11.pdf
71. Njiwa, *supra* n. 113.
72. Draper, *supra* n. 106, p. 77.
73. Killander, M.: Legal Harmonisation in Africa: Taking Stock and Moving Forward. In: Fioramonti, L. (ed.): *Regionalism in a Changing World: Comparative Perspective in the New Global Order*. London and New York: Routledge, 2013, p. 88.
74. As stated by Ch. Clapham: "Any set of prescriptions for integration which does not start from an appraisal of the political and economic structure of African states is built on sand". See: Clapham, C.: Review Article Africa's International Relations. In: *African Affairs*, Vol. 86, No. 345, October 1987, pp. 578–579.
75. "European experience shows that ambitious projects . . . will only succeed if they are strictly based on the law and if the respect for and the reliable implementation of the law throughout the region in the daily economic life is secured by strong institutions and efficient mechanisms of law enforcement and legal protection. European experience indicates that the supranational way (where the geo-regional way is directly binding in the member states) is the most if not only efficient way". Schmitz, T.: The ASEAN Economic Community and the Rule of Law, 2014. Available at: http://home.lu.lv/~tschmit1/Downloads/BDHK-Workshop_15-12-2014_Schmitz.pdf
76. ECOWAS-Revised Treaty of the Economic Community of West African States. Available at: www.ecowas.int/wp-content/uploads/2015/01/Revised-treaty.pdf
77. OHADA Treaty on the Establishment of the Organisation for the Harmonization of Business Law in Africa, 1993. Available at: www.ohada.org/index.php/en/ohada-reference-texts/treaty-carrying-revision-of-the-treaty-concerning-the-harmonization-of-the-business-law-in-africa (French version available).
78. WAEMU-Treaty on the West African Economic and Monetary Union, 1994. Available at: www.wipo.int/wipolex/en/other_treaties/details.jsp?treaty_id=313
79. CEMAC Treaty: Central African Economic and Monetary Community, 1994 (Revised 2008). Available at: www.internationaldemocracywatch.org/attachments/173_CEMAC%20Treaty%20(French).pdf
80. East African Community Treaty (1967 EAC Treaty). Available at: www.eac.int/sites/default/files/docs/treaty_eac_amended-2006_1999.pdf

81. As regards as current overview of the supranationalism in Africa see: Fagbayibo, B.: Common Problems Affecting Supranational Attempts in Africa: An Analytical Overview. In: *Potchefstroom Electronic Law Journal*, Vol. 16, No. 1, 2013, pp. 1–67.
82. "As long as the landscape of African integration is defined by the existence of multiple regional economic communities with overlapping and replicated membership integration will remain mirage". See: Fagbayibo, *supra* n. 127, p. 53.
83. Revauger, J.-P.: Regional Integration in the Commonwealth Caribbean and the Impact of the European Union. In: *The Round Table: The Commonwealth Journal of International Affairs*, Vol. 97, No. 399, 2008, pp. 857–869.

    Berkofsky, A.: Comparing EU and Asian Integration Processes: The EU a Role Model for Asia? European Policy Centre (EPC), 2002. Available at: www.epc.eu/documents/uploads/606968147_EPC%20Issue%20Paper%2023%20EU%20Asian%20Integration.pdf

    Lenz, *supra* n. 70, p. 5.

    Jetschke, A., Murray, P.: Diffusing Regional Integration: The EU and Southeast Asia. In: *West European Politics*, Vol. 35, No. 1, 2012, pp. 174–191.

    Börzel, T.A., Risse, T.: Diffusing (Inter-) Regionalism: The EU as a Model of Regional Integration. In: *KFG Working Paper Series* (The Transformative Power of Europe), No. 7, 2009, p. 23. Available at: http://userpage.fu-berlin.de/kfgeu/kfgwp/wpseries/WorkingPaperKFG_7.pdf
84. The only exception is the Asian integration experience which, with respect to having different philosophy and specifications, regards the European integration model as not suitable.
85. As stated by M. Teló: ". . . the success story of the manner in which the European Union copes with both traditional internal conflicts and national diversities by transforming states' functions and structures plays an important role as a reference (neither as a model nor as a counter-model) for new regionalism elsewhere". For more details: Teló, *supra* n. 37.
86. As stated by F. Rueda-Junquera: "The experience has shown how economic integration has been used as a direct means to achieve economic objectives and as an indirect means to deal with non-economic objectives of great significance in the European Construction such as the pacification after the second World War and the gradual political integration overcoming destructive nationalism". See: Rueda-Junquera, F.: European Integration Model: Lessons for the Central American Common Market. In: *Jean Monnet/Robert Schuman Paper Series*, Vol. 6, No. 4, 2006, p. 12. Available at: www6.miami.edu/eucenter/ruedafinal.pdf
87. The European Union was awarded the Nobel Prize in 2012: "For more than 60 years it has been contributing to peace, reconciliation, democracy, and human rights in Europe".
88. Draper, *supra* n. 106, p. 70.
89. As stated by L. Kühnhardt: "The rationale for European integration was the idea of reconciliation based on a gradually emerging common rule of law". In: Kühnhardt, L.: African Regional Integration and the Role of the European Union, p. 21. Available at: www.files.ethz.ch/isn/55859/Africa_Reg_Integration.pdf
90. As stated by P. Fabbrini: "European Integration in the second half of the century was a response to the trauma of the first half. Its success was dependent on the security side, by the military protection of NATO and on the economic side by the formation and enlargement of a common market aimed to generate and diffuse economic growth. It would be wrong to see the origins and extension of the European regionalism simply as a result of economic pressures". See: Fabbrini, *supra* n. 41, p. 9.

91. As stated by L. Kühnhardt: "Africa has to move from efforts to understand the chaotic world of overlapping memberships in regional groupings, to an analytical frame that is trying to make sense of region building in Africa through the prism of concentric circles. Africa has to re-design its region building map along the notion of concentric circles". In: Kühnhardt, *supra* n. 135, p. 17.
92. Franke, B.K.: Competing Regionalism in Africa and the Continent's Emerging Security Architecture. In: *African Studies Quarterly*, Vol. 9, No. 3, 2007, p. 5.
93. Eight regional economic organizations have been formally recognized by the African Union, which is the supreme organization on the continent: Arab Magreb Union (AMU), The Community of Sahel-Saharan States (CEN-SAD), the Common Market of Eastern and Southern Africa (COMESA), the East African Community (EAC), the Economic Community of Central African States (ECCAS), the Economic Community of West African States (ECOWAS), the Inter-Governmental Authority of Development (IGAD) and the Southern African Development Community (SADC).
94. Killander, *supra* n. 118, p. 95.
95. Tussie, D.: Latin America: Contrasting Motivations for Regional Projects. In: *Review of International Studies*, Vol. 36, 2009, p. 170.
96. Malamud, A., Gardini, G.L.: Has Regionalism Peaked? The Latin American Quagmire and Its Lessons. In: Fioramonti, L. (ed.): *Regionalism in a Changing World: Comparative Perspective in the New Global Order*. London and New York: Routledge, 2013, p. 123.
97. "There is a growing awareness that long-term sustainable economic growth is impossible without the legal security and certainty provided by the rule of law-in particular in times of international economic openness and cooperation". See: Schmitz, *supra* n. 120, p. 2.

6 Regional Judicial and Non-Judicial Bodies and Their Importance for Proper Functioning of Regional Systems

6.1. Regional Courts

The legal basis of regional organizations usually comprises three sources namely: constituent international treaty, other treaties adopted within the regional organizations and eventually the rules of their internal legal order. Similarly, as with respect to other regional legal acts, the position and condition of the application and/or interpretation of the rules of international law can be, from time to time, subject to different views between member states of organizations, between member states and bodies of organizations, between legal persons and individuals and the member states or bodies of organizations. Taking into account both the particularity and legal nature of these issues, there are mainly regional judicial bodies charged with corresponding competences to deal with them. Their legal regulations form either part of the constituent instruments of the regional organizations, and/or are included into special additional protocols. It should be noted that the establishment of these courts assumes the existence of legally binding regional norms creating rights and obligations for parties (including the subjects entitled to bring the cases before a regional court).This is the main difference from the so-called Asian approach (Asian Way) of regionalism, preferring the cooperation of member states without formal legalization and based on the idea of non-binding commitments and non-legalistic methods of dispute resolutions.

Referring to their competences, three kinds of regional bodies can be identified today. Firstly, they are regional courts vested with the competence to resolve different disputes, interpret international treaties and/or adopt non-binding advisory opinions and other sources of legal orders of regional organizations using specific procedures (preliminary rulings procedures, advisory opinion procedure). These competences have practical effects by improving compliance, with commitment to and implementation of regional agreements and stimulating regional economic activities. Secondly, there are courts with the above-mentioned regional competence supplemented by the protection of human rights (ECJ, some subregional African courts). Thirdly, there are special regional courts on human rights protection (ECHR, Inter-American Court of Human Rights) and in the near future their competences can be even expanded.[1]

Generally speaking, whereas these courts usually form part of the regional institutional structure, their jurisprudence helps mainly to maintain the legal stability and/or respect of rule of law within a regional dimension with positive effects on the good functioning of a concrete regional project. Legal writing generally characterized these courts (set up after the end of the Cold War) as "new style" courts because they have far-reaching compulsory jurisdiction and allow also non-state actors to initiate judicial procedures before them. With respect to compulsory jurisdiction, it is typical for regional courts mainly within regional trade systems, where all members of the organization are equally accountable to binding legal rules.[2]

Speaking broadly, the contribution of international judicial bodies to international law (regardless of their universal or regional nature) may consist in the "gap-filling" of international treaties (for example, through implied rights), in the adoption of a binding interpretation of the treaty (and eliminating unclarity or overly general content in the treaty) and stabilization of the recognized meaning of the treaty (contribution for stability and uniform interpretation and application of international treaties). Similarly, as with other segments of the current regionalism there is an evident uneven level of the occurrence of regional courts across the continents.

6.1.1. Preliminary Rulings Procedures of Regional Courts

It should be noted at the outset that the main purpose of the judicialization of international law in the last quarter of 20th century remains the settling of disputes between state parties through treaty-based judicial bodies as one segment of the system of peaceful settlement of disputes in international organizations. With respect to traditional means of the settlements of disputes, the setting up of international courts increasingly replaced the non-judicial diplomatic model of dispute settlement and of ad hoc arbitration by judicial proceedings before permanent courts.[3] Alongside their basic disputable jurisdiction the interpretation of treaties within and through specialized procedures before international judicial bodies represents a sui generis "collateral" consequence of the process of judicialization. The judicial practice confirms that any international court has been instituted only for advisory jurisdictions and this jurisdiction is still secondary to that of disputes settlement by binding decisions. Beyond their traditional role of the settlement of disputes, the regional courts have therefore also further jurisdictions regarding the specific importance for the proper functioning of the institutional and legal systems of regional organizations. The first of them is the jurisdiction to interpret international treaties relevant for regional organizations and/or rules of their internal legal orders through preliminary rulings procedures. As regards to a brief characteristic of preliminary rulings procedures it is to be noted that on the request of domestic court(s) of member states of regional organizations an international judicial body can render an authoritative interpretation of the regional treaty(ies) or other relevant legal acts defined usually in the constituent instrument of organization. Their original idea is based on the principle of cooperation and/or dialogue between international and national courts of member states in order to achieve the uniform interpretation of relevant treaty and/or specific rules of legal order of international organization needed for the "living" case before domestic court. The courts are, however, not entitled to interpret the provisions of national legal orders and examine the facts of the concrete case before domestic courts.

The current practice brought some models of such cooperation that vary from one to the other regional grouping. The main differences among them concern mainly the "rigorousness" of their jurisdiction and legal relevance of their interpretive findings. Nevertheless, its basic idea is common whereby: ". . . in systems where the function and application of the law of the regional organization is exercised in a "widespread" manner by domestic courts, there is a risk of a conflict of judgments and an uneven application of the said law within the Member States that could compromise attainment of the above-mentioned goal".[4] Within such systems the existence of the regional judicial body entitled to give uniforms interpretation of relevant legal norms is desirable.

Among the examples of practical illust of ration of the interpretive jurisdiction of regional judicial bodies, one can firstly mention the ECJ because (and according to Article 267 of the Lisbon Treaty) the ECJ shall have preliminary rulings concerning "The Interpretation of Treaties" on the request of any court or tribunal of a member state. Also a number of other regional organizations of economic nature outside Europe have set up judicial bodies vested *inter alia* with the preliminary rulings powers. Among them one can mention the COMESA Court, the Caribbean Court of Justice, the Court of Justice of Andean Community, Central American Court of Justice (CACJ).

Regardless of the specificities of the preliminary rulings proceedings of the above-mentioned courts, they, in principle, reflect the EU idea of direct cooperation between the regional court and domestic courts of member states of international organizations before which a question essential to rendering their judgments has been raised. As regards, concretely, the judgments of the ECJ concerning the interpretation, application or validity of the EU legal order, they should guarantee the uniform interpretation and correct application of EU law within the legal orders of its member states.

Despite the undisputable importance of these proceedings for the proper interpretation and application of treaties by their state parties, preliminary ruling procedures have their own limits. As has been mentioned above, according to the criterion *ratione materiae* the subject matters of these procedures are only constituent instruments of regional organizations, international treaties concluded within them and eventually the legal rules of their internal legal orders. It may be remarked that an authoritative interpretation is given only for the needs of a concrete "living" case before a domestic court. Constituent instruments of some international organizations, however, confirm the importance of an interpretive finding also within the larger context of the interpretation and application of regional international treaty by their other state parties (member states of international organizations). This larger context practically depends on the "surrounding" regional regulation of preliminary rulings procedure related both to the binding nature and eventual *erga omnes* effect of the preliminary rulings judgments interpreting an international treaty. In this context an important role can also be played by the practice of the member states of international organizations as well as the legal value given to the judgments adopted within preliminary rulings procedure in the case law of a judicial body.

A good example of an effective regional preliminary ruling procedure before an international judicial body is the European Union and European Court of Justice (ECJ). According to Article 267 of the Treaty on the Functioning of the European Union (hereinafter known as the TFEU), the ECJ carries out preliminary rulings at the request of courts or tribunals of the member states on the interpretation of the Treaties and the validity of the acts of various institutions of the EU. A judgment given by the ECJ under Article 267 TFEU is binding on the national court hearing the case in which decisions are given.[5] With respect to its larger legal relevance, it should be, however, added that within the legal space of the EU it binds all national courts and tribunals of EU member states. In this context the binding effect of the preliminary ruling judgment can be explained by the main purpose of the procedure according the Article 267 of TFEU, namely to ensure uniform interpretation and application of union law and the unity and consistency of all bodies of the EU legal order.

It should be pointed out that according to Article 267, paragraph 4, of the TFEU, an urgent preliminary ruling procedure is laid down if the question raised by court or a tribunal of member states concerns a person in custody. In such a case the ECJ shall act with the minimum of delay.[6]

It is worth noting a special contribution of the ECJ for the advancement of European regional integration through its case law establishing both the principle of direct effect in a preliminary ruling proceedings (Van den en Loos Case—1963) and the principle of the supremacy of EU law over national law (*Costa v. E.N.E.L.* Case—1964). On the basis of these judgments the ECJ was able to significantly advance the integration process and today is "clearly seen as a successful supranational court that has furthered regional integration through its many rulings".[7]

Another difference consists in the optional or compulsory nature of preliminary rulings procedures. The analysis of the basic documents of regional organizations and rules of their tribunals enables identifying three models of these procedures. Among the first one can mention the EFTA Court where the request of court or tribunal of EFTA state (concerning the interpretation of EEA Agreement) is only optional as well as the Court of Justice of ECOWAS and Central American Court of Justice (CAJC) with respect to the Central American Integration System (SICA). It seems doubtful if the main task of such kinds of procedures are really to guarantee the uniform interpretation of relevant treaties and/or other legal rules by all member states of international organizations.

Other treaties include the compulsory model of preliminary rulings procedure ordering domestic courts or tribunals to seek preliminary rulings from international courts. Among others are the Caribbean Court of Justice (CCJ), the Eastern Caribbean Supreme Court (ECSC), the Tribunal of the Southern African Development Community (SADCT)[8] and the Benelux Court of Justice (BCJ). In these cases the failure of the domestic court to seek the preliminary ruling is, however, not sanctioned by specific infringement proceedings.

Within Article 267 of the Lisbon Treaty, the "mixed" position between the optional and compulsory model represents the EU system whereby lower domestic courts or tribunals of member states may request the ECJ to give a preliminary ruling procedure (if they consider that a decision on the question is necessary to enable them to give judgment) and the other shall bring the matter before ECJ (provided that it is about the court or tribunal of member state against whose decisions there is no judicial remedy under national law.) Also Article 12 (2) of the WAEMU Court Protocol (West African Economic and Monetary Union) provides for a preliminary reference procedure similar to that of the European Union, both for the questions on the interpretation of community law and for questions on the legality of Community Measures. National courts in the last instance are obliged to refer and lower Courts have the possibility to refer the case before regional court. Finally, Article 17 of the CEMAC Court of Justice Convention (Central African Economic and Monetary Community) provided also for a European-style preliminary ruling procedure because a national court may refer questions raised on the interpretation of CEMAC law to the CEMAC Court and similarly, as in EU national courts, in the last instance are obliged to refer.[9]

Finally, within the third group, consisting of the ECJ, the EAC Court of Justice, the COMESA Court of Justice, the UEMOA Court of Justice, and the CEMAC Court of Justice, the compulsory preliminary rulings proceedings combined with the infringement proceedings is applicable in the case when a domestic court of a member state fails in its obligation to seek a preliminary ruling entailing a breach of the law of the relevant organization. These infringement proceedings ". . . in the regional systems can be directed specifically at a breach of the obligation to seek a preliminary ruling".[10] These proceedings should strictly guarantee the proper and uniform functioning of a regional treaty system and legal rules of the internal legal order of organizations.

What appears from the above analysis is an uneven "rigorousness" in the preliminary rulings procedures evinced at different levels in their contribution to the uniform interpretation and application of international treaties within regional organizations. There is, however, no doubt that the compulsory model of preliminary ruling procedure, as well as the compulsory model combined with eventual infringement procedures, represent a more efficient contribution to the uniform interpretation and application of regional treaties by their state parties in comparison with optional models. Such a contribution may be reinforced provided that the interpretive judgments have a binding nature with *erga omnes* effects. One can share the view according to which: ". . . models of judicial cooperation channelled into preliminary rulings procedures—especially those that envisage compulsory preliminary references allied to infringement proceedings for breach of that obligation—are more likely to achieve the objective and application of the integrated law".[11]

The above-outlined models of preliminary rulings proceedings reflect different approaches of regional organizations to the uniform interpretation and application of regional treaties and other legal rules as one of the specific legal tools required for the guarantee of their uniform interpretation and application and the effective functioning of a concrete regional organization. Within the organizations characterized by the compulsory model of the preliminary rulings procedure the needs to guarantee effectiveness and the main goals of the organization prevent the possibility of individual different and/or erroneous interpretations of regional treaties or legal rules of internal legal orders by the domestic courts of member states. On the other hand, international organizations having the optional procedure of preliminary ruling procedures do not insist on the crucial role of the obligatory uniform interpretation of regional rules for the effective functioning of a regional organization. This is, however, not detrimental to the eventual application of other proceedings dealing with the legal consequences of non-application of preliminary ruling procedures in the circumstances of a concrete case and a concrete international organization.

Finally, with respect to the evolving effects of the preliminary rulings procedures for domestic judicial bodies, it is worth emphasizing that: "Preliminary rulings gradually have been transformed from mere instruments that guarantee the uniform interpretation of regimes' laws by national jurisdiction to powerful instruments for the control of legality of national legal orders. Hence, preliminary rulings give national courts the possibility to transform themselves into custodians of the international or rather supranational regime".[12]

6.1.2. Advisory Jurisdiction of Regional Courts

One of the consequences of the judicialization of international law in the late 20th century is a growing number of advisory jurisdictions within judicial bodies of regional organizations from different geographic areas. Among the examples of practical illustration of the interpretive jurisdiction of regional judicial bodies one can mention Protocol No. 16 to the Convention at Protection of Human Rights and Fundamental Freedoms stating that the highest courts and tribunals of the "High Contracting" party may request from the European Court of Human Rights a non-binding advisory opinion ". . . on questions of principle relating to interpretation or application of the rights and freedoms defined in the Convention or the Protocols" (Article 1. para.1).[13]

According to Article 32 of the Agreement between EFTA States on the Establishment of a Surveillance Authority and a Court of Justice[14] the EFTA

Court shall have jurisdiction to give advisory opinions on the interpretation of the EEA Agreement. Where such a question is raised before any court or tribunal in an EFTA State: "that court of tribunal may, if it considers it necessary to enable it to, request the EFTA Court to give such an opinion".

Some regional African judicial bodies are also vested with the advisory powers. One can mention the ECOWAS Court of Justice, The Court of Justice of COMESA, African Court of Human and Peoples' Rights, the Caribbean Court of Justice.

As another example from the American continent one can mention the American Convention of Human Rights[15] confirming (Article 62 paras.1,1) the right of their State Parties to declare that they recognize as binding ipso facto the jurisdiction of the Inter-American Court of Human Rights on all matters relating to the interpretation or application of the American Convention. Such jurisdiction can be recognized not only by special declaration but by special agreement as well. Unlike the above-mentioned advisory competence (EFTA Court), the competence of the Inter-American Court of Human Rights is strictly optional, founded either on the special declaration or special agreements of state parties.

And finally some of the republics of the former USSR created Commonwealth of Independent States (CIS, 1991) and its Charter (1993) includes an Economic Court among the principal organs of this grouping. Its constituent instrument is the Agreement of the Statute of the Economic Court (1992). In addition to its contentious jurisdiction, the Economic Court also has advisory jurisdiction because (and according to Article 32 of the CIS Charter) it may interpret the: "agreements and other acts of the Commonwealth on economic issues". Article 5 of the Statute of the Economic Court confirms that decisions on interpretation may be given not only by rendering judgments in specific cases but also by the issuing of abstract opinions at the request of the highest legislative and executive organs of member states, their highest economic and commercial courts, or CIS institution. This list has been in practice extended to include NGOs. The 1992 CIS Statute does not make any distinction between opinions on a dispute and abstract opinions regarding such interpretation.[16] Judicial bodies are however not requested by the domestic courts and for the need of "living" domestic judicial proceedings whereby the subjects entitled to ask for them are the different bodies of the "maternal" international organization and their member states.

Unlike the above-mentioned preliminary rulings procedure, advisory jurisdictions produce legal opinions of a non-binding nature concerning either the legal problems and/or questions regardless of its arising within legal disputes or not. Generally they may be characterized as qualified legal advices needed for the proper interpretation and application of international law or legal rules of the internal legal orders of regional organizations. The comparison of preliminary rulings procedures and advisory jurisdiction at the same time confirms that some of regional judicial bodies (ECHR, COMESA Court of Justice, Caribbean Court of Justice) provided both kinds of these proceedings for the needs of different subjects.

With respect to their legal relevance, it is generally recognized that advisory opinions are authoritative, but non-binding statements on interpretation of international law by an international tribunal or arbitration body[17]—having the "soft law"[18] nature and "less controversial" character when compared with binding judgment.[19] It is, however, worth noting that their non-binding nature is without prejudice to their undoubted importance for clarifying the relevant provision(s) of international treaties through their authoritative interpretation. Due to this, they are able to: ". . . encourage but not compel states to behave in a certain manner".[20]

The procedural rules allowing the active involvement of other interested states or other subjects (differing from the requesting body) within the advisory procedure provides the judicial body with a broader information basis founded on the information and comments of all interested parties which: ". . . may be considered to be a means of legitimating the decision".[21] This procedural possibility of non-requesting subjects for its active involvement in the advisory proceeding can help the acceptance of qualified and well-reasoned advisory opinions within a larger circle of member states of an international organization.

This relevance of advisory opinions may have a specific role also within the framework of potential legislative activity of concrete international organizations whereby: ". . . their persuasive authority can and does induce states or others organs to act in accordance with advisory opinion thus a contribution to the creation to customary law"[22] provided that it shall be followed and conform to the relevant state practice.

Finally, advisory opinions have their own irreplaceable contribution in the process of the uniform interpretation and application, not only in the agreements of concrete international organization(s) but, depending on the nature of the interpreted international treaty, also within a larger community of states.

Within the general context of international law characterized by its increasing complexity, specialization and growing judicialization, a question concerning the role and importance of regional judicial bodies with respect to the interpretation of treaties may be legitimately raised. The rapid evolution and extension of international law complicate the possibilities to encompass every situation in traditional international agreements and to renegotiate them. Less detailed or complex agreements, combined with the interpretive jurisdiction of an international judicial body, offers the potential solution to interpretive problems for the near future. Within regional international organizations, interpretive powers of regional courts may depend, for example, on the degree of "rigidity" of their legal orders requiring general and uniform interpretation and application of their rules by all member states as a necessary condition for the guarantee of their proper functioning. The future practice of "cohabitation" of international treaties and international judicial bodies will reveal if, and to what extent, the state parties of international treaties will be (more or less) willing to exploit their jurisdiction related to the interpretation of treaties.

A last note relating to the regional judicial bodies, concerns the restriction of their interpretive jurisdictions *ratione materiae*. Taking into account the fact that these bodies usually form the segment of the institutional structure of regional organizations, their powers cover only treaties adopted within the scope of their functions and guaranteeing their speciality and effective functioning. It is, therefore, to be noted that: ". . . tribunals established within an international organization are primarily concerned with the law of treaty on which they are founded as well as with the secondary law derived from this treaty, so that international law plays only a supplementary role concerning, for example, questions of validity and construction of the treaty".[23]

6.1.3. Advisory Jurisdiction and/or Interpretive Findings of Regional Non-Judicial Bodies

The post-war practice of international organizations confirms that the interpretation of international treaties adopted within international organizations is not carried out exclusively by their judicial bodies. It should be pointed out that apart from treaty-based judicial bodies there are also international treaties (mainly in the form of constituent instruments of international organizations) establishing non-judicial bodies empowered also to interpret the treaties mainly on the request of member states.

A few examples may be useful to quote to illustrate this practice. According to Article 84 of the ICAO Convention, any disagreement between member states concerning the interpretation or application of the Convention shall be decided by the Council if the agreement cannot be reached by negotiations[24] within the Council of Europe Convention on Transfrontier Television 1989; its Standing Committee is entitled: "to examine at the request of one or more parties questions concerning the interpretation of the Convention".[25] Also, State Parties of the NAFTA Agreement established the Free Trade Commission (Art. 2001 (1)), entrusted with the competence to interpret the Agreement and: "An interpretation by the Commission of a provision of this Agreement shall be binding on the Tribunal established under this section" (Art. 1131 (2)).[26]

The WTO agreement contains the provision: "The Ministerial Conference and the General Council shall have the exclusive authority to adopt interpretation of this Agreement and of the Multilateral Trade Agreements . . . The decision to adopt an interpretation shall be taken by a three-quarter's majority of the members".[27]

Another example is the Executive Board of the International Monetary Fund (IMF) having the power: "to decide questions of interpretation of the IMF Articles that arise between the Fund and a member or members".[28]

International law, however, also confirms the existence of treaty mechanisms for an authoritative interpretation of treaties beyond the structures of international organizations. Taking into account both the universal nature of human rights treaties concluded under the auspices of UN, and the absence of a world human rights court, the specific institutional system of interpretation and monitoring of these treaties and their compliance by state parties has been set up in the form of Committees as specific human rights treaty bodies. Today, eight Committees work connected with the concrete human rights treaties and vested with the above-mentioned competences.[29] As regards to the manner and complexity of the interpretation of human rights treaties, they vary depending on the specific procedures of each Committee. Their practice, however, confirms the common final outcomes of their interpretation through General Comments. In this respect it should be pointed out that the Committees: "carry out this competence normally played by states (in lieu of states) and they are bound to the same extent as states by rules of interpretation by which states would be bound. Regular reference to the Vienna Convention by the treaty bodies indicate that they recognize the relevance of its principles within their work".[30] The talk regarding rules of customary international law laid down in Articles 31 and 32 of the VCLT and their application by the Committees is not only an option but an obligation. The findings provided in General Comments and related to the interpretation of human rights treaties are in principle respected by their state parties.[31]

In regards to the treaty-based non-judicial bodies empowered to adopt General Comments, a number of Committees are currently charged with this power (CERD, CESR, HRC, CRC, CEDAW, CAT, CMW). Although the content of their General Comments obviously differ as regards to their scope, they generally: ". . . sets out in some details basic premises, normative content, states' obligations, violations and implementation at the national level and international obligations".[32] They are usually adopted unanimously.

Legal scholars differ in opinions concerning their real weight and relevance although they recognize their non-binding nature whereby: "None of the human rights treaties explicitly confers on the relevant treaty bodies the power to adopt binding interpretations of the treaties, and the practice of at least some states suggest that this power has not been conferred implicitly, as part of the implied power that a body established by treaty is considered to possess in order to carry out the functions conferred on it by the state parties".[33] At the same time this does not mean that General Comments do not have any real significance because they "can contribute to community expectations of appropriate state behaviour under human rights treaty obligations"[34] and /or "can assist legislators who are trying to draft laws in compliance with a Covenant"[35] and "can effectively amount to something close to a codification of evolving practice".[36] As regards to the state parties, they are under obligation to engage with the Committee's interpretation and give it important weight although they "ultimately have the right to reject its finding".[37]

It should be pointed out that the interpretive power is not "automatically" excluded from the treaty-based bodies vested with different kinds of advisory jurisdiction. Among existing examples one can mention the Seabed Dispute Chamber exercising such jurisdiction according to Article 191 of the

UN Convention on the Law of Sea (1982)[38], the Advisory Committee on Legal Texts of International Criminal Court[39] and Interpreting Guidance of International Committee of the Red Cross on the notion of "Direct Participation in Hostilities under International Humanitarian Law"[40] prepared on an expert basis.

Regardless of the different nature of international bodies vested with the interpretive power and their various procedural specificities, the result of these activities represents an authoritative interpretation of the relevant international treaty. Within the larger context of international law, the legal effects of these activities may even exceed the scope of a concrete international organization when taking into account their relations to the general principle of rule of law at a regional level. Bearing in mind that the rule of law essentially requires: "predictability through the rules that are general, prospective and clear . . . the concept of interpretive powers empowering a designated non-judicial body to interpret a body of law is beneficial to the rule of law because it increases predictability of the norms . . .".[41] As regards to judicial bodies: "By offering their law interpretation, law application and dispute settlement services, international courts can promote legal certainty, maintain the credibility of the legal undertakings of states, raise the costs of non-compliance and defuse intra regime tensions".[42]

It should also be finally added that the idea of a common (agreed) interpretation of international treaty has already been practically applied also within the area of treaty interregionalism. This fact confirms the Joint Interpretative Instrument on the Economic and Trade Agreement (CETA) between Canada and the European Union and its member states (2016). According to its preamble: "This interpretative instrument provides in the sense of Article 31 of the Vienna Convention on the Law of Treaties, a clear and unambiguous statement of what Canada and the European Union and its Member States agreed in a number of CETA provisions that have been the object of public debate and provides an agreed interpretation thereof. This includes, in particular, the impact of CETA on the ability of governments to regulate in the public interests, as well as the provisions of investment protection and dispute resolution, sustainable development, labour law and environmental protection".[43]

6.2. Regional Systems of the Protection of Human Rights

Within the evolution of new regionalism since the 1990s, the growing trend of both the regional human rights systems and regional human rights institutional structures may be identified. Regional mechanisms of human rights today cover five parts of the world, namely: Africa, the Americas, Europe, Arab countries and Asia-Pacific. They naturally differ in the reasons for their origin, which result from different concepts of human rights and the need of interested states to establish a regional framework for human rights protection. As regards to their effectiveness as a whole, and the extent of their practical "everyday" efficiency for the protection of human rights, they may be briefly structured as follows:

Europe and the Americas—Advanced regional systems of human rights protection. These systems have a whole set of regional human rights treaties with the respective supervisory, expert and judicial systems. The Inter-American system is followed to a large extent by the European system, although some problems still prevent its future development because the system is not universal, and the lack of direct access of individuals to the Inter-American Court of Human Rights (obligatory through the Inter-American Commission on Human Rights).

Africa—An emerging regional system requiring further consolidation. Some of the greatest problems are: the absence of political will of some states to fully cooperate and participate in the regional system, the structural "overlapping" between pan-African and subregional courts, the lack of direct access of individuals to regional judicial bodies and objections against the supranational nature of regional judicial bodies.

Arab countries—An emerging regional system *in statu nascendi* with respect to the initial stage of standard setting and implementation machinery, lack of institutional practice and an operational human rights regional court and the inconsistency of regional human rights documents with international human rights standards.

Asia-Pacific—A region without an effective regional institutional structure of human rights protection. Taking into account the great cultural and political diversities among states, a lack of homogeneity currently prevents any foreseeable regional integration project. It therefore seems more realistic to expect subregional human rights mechanisms.[44]

As regards the characteristic of the states which established a regional structure for the protection of human rights, it should be pointed out that: "It is true that the most used and arguably most effective adjudicatory mechanisms tend to be in the more democratic Europe and the Americas, but African supranational courts are a puzzling contrast".[45]

If concrete human rights are not sufficiently protected at the domestic level the international system of human rights comes into play either at the level of the global or regional judicial and non-judicial structures. The treaties that obviously create regional human rights systems have in principle the same structure: the first contains the list of the individual rights and in some cases also the duties of the states that have joined into regional system. The second part of these treaties obviously creates either specific non-judicial mechanisms for the monitoring of the compliance of human rights, or judicial or quasi-judicial bodies for the cases of violations of the rights, and eventual combinations and "cohabitations" of these mechanisms within regional human rights systems.

Institutional structures charged with the protection of human rights can be divided into a panregional (or continental) grouping, comprising of: in the case of Africa, the African Union (AU); in the Americas, the Organization of American States (OAS); in Europe, the Council of Europe (CoE); among Arab states, the League of Arab States (LAS) and a number of subregional systems. Each of the above noted panregional systems has its own judicial body, namely: the European Court of Human Rights (ECHR, 1959), the Inter-American Court of Human Rights (IACHR, 1979),the African Court of Peoples and Human Rights (ACPHR, 2004) and the Arab Court of Human Rights (ACHR, 2014). The key feature of each of these systems (except the Arab states) consists in a complaint mechanism through which relevant subjects can seek justice and ask for reparation for human rights violations. Within these systems only states may be held responsible for human rights violations so the prosecution or individual responsibility for human rights violations are excluded. The practice confirms that judicial bodies within some of the originally economic regional organizations gradually acquired human rights jurisdiction as a consequence of the adaption and/or enlargement of their constituent instruments or adoption of special protocols (Court of Justice of the EU (2009), ECOWAS Court of Justice (2005)). These bodies are not generally considered to be human rights courts because their principal mandate is not human rights protection, but they may be authorized to consider individual complaints concerning human rights violations or directly apply human rights treaties. With respect to the SADC and EACJ Court of Justices they are able to review human rights issues through the interpretation of and within the good governance principle. The nature and duties of each judicial body for the protection of human rights are embodied both in the constituent instrument and each body's statutes or rules of procedure.[46]

Not all of the panregional organizations have established only judicial bodies with the mandate to promote and protect human rights. Special commissions and/or committees have also been charged with the powers in the area of human rights (African Commission on Human and Peoples' Rights, Inter-American Commission of Human Rights, Arab Human Rights Committee). These bodies in particular prepare reports on human rights practices, carry out country visits and monitor emerging human rights themes and the rights of vulnerable groups by appointed experts ("rapporteurs and/or special rapporteurs"). Comparing the commissions with human rights courts, only the latter receive complaints and render binding decisions and do not engage in monitoring or promotion activities.

It is, however, worth noting that human rights commissions do not strictly have an autonomous position within regional human rights systems because under certain circumstances they are authorized to initiate concrete proceedings before human rights courts with specific *locus standi.* It should also be pointed out that even: "In Asian sub-regions where there has been a strong sense of informal regionalism and where allusion to politically charged and sensitive matters such as human rights have been eschewed in the past, there is now an embryonic (albeit strong) inclination to embrace the institutionalization of human rights".[47]

These different kinds of regional institutionalization reflect the specificity and importance of human rights protection both on the national level of the member states and consequently within the concrete regional organization. Taking into account the absence of a world human rights court, the legal writing, however, confirms some advantages of regional systems (compared with a possible global human rights system) whereby: "Countries from a particular region often have a shared interest in the protection of human rights in that part of the world and the advantage of proximity in terms of influencing each other's behaviour and ensuring compliance with common standards. Regional systems also allow both the possibility of regional values to be taken into account when human rights are defined and a regional enforcement mechanism exists which can resonate better with local conditions than a global universal system".[48] The Vienna Declaration adopted by the World Conference on Human Rights (1993) also expressly emphasized the fundamental role of the regional arrangements in the promotion and protection of human rights.[49]

6.2.1. Regional Protection of Human Rights in Europe

As has been noted above, the European human rights system belongs to the most advanced, and its origins, rooted in the beginning of the 1950s, reflect the reaction to the great human rights violations committed during the Second World War, and the defence against all forms of totalitarianism. The founding states of this system believed that human rights needed to be respected so as to secure democracy and avoid and prevent conflict between East and West Europe.[50] The European Convention on Human Rights (ECHR) and Fundamental Freedoms (hereinafter known as the Convention 1950) is the central European human rights instrument, which was gradually complemented by the 16 Additional Protocols concerning both the new human rights gradually subjected to judicial control of the European Court of Human Rights (Protocols 1, 4, 6, 7, 12 and 13) and the improvement of the control mechanism of the European Court of Human Rights (mainly Protocols 11 and 14). The Convention is focused mainly on civil and political rights and its Article 15 stipulates the right of derogation under special circumstances.

The ECHR does not contain provisions relating to self-determination, rights of minority groups, children, refugees and aliens. Social economic and cultural rights are embodied in the European Social Charter (1961) and the control of these rights is in the hands of a non-judicial body of the European Committee of Social Rights (ECSR). This committee, composed of independent and impartial experts, monitors state compliances with the European Social Charter. The supervisory mechanism is based on a system of collective complaints and national reports indicating how European States implement the Charter in practice.

As regards to the structural and institutional mechanism of the human rights protection in Europe during the first 50 years of the ECtHR activity (until 1998), the system was comprised of two bodies, namely, the Commission of Human Rights, having a quasi-judicial and screened function, and the European Court of Human Rights of a non-permanent nature, having a judicial function in the affairs referred to by the Commission.[51]

The Protocol No. 11 of the ECHR (1998) substantially changed this procedural mechanism in three important areas: it established the ECtHR as a permanent judicial body, it abolished the Commission of Human rights, and it allowed all alleged victims of violations of human rights (regardless of their nationality) to lodge their complaints directly to the ECtHR after exhaustion of local remedies within the concerned state party.[52] As regards to the latter, it should be pointed out that: "This represents a crucial development since individual complaints have been the means by which the great majority of Convention violations have been identified throughout the ECtHR history".[53]

It is worth noting that ECtHR is the only international court to which any individual, NGOs or group of individuals have access for the purpose of enforcing their rights under the Convention and where: "The right of individual application is today both an essential part of the system and a basic feature of European legal culture in this field"[54] and its main importance for the European system of human rights confirmed the ECHR because: "The Convention right to individual application . . . has over the years become of the highest importance and is now a key component of the machinery for protection the rights and freedoms set out in the Convention".[55] The inter-states complaints are still possible but for different political and other reasons they are used only rarely. Judgments of the ECtHR are legally binding and may provide financial compensation for damages suffered to individuals due to the violation of their human rights or freedom caused by a state party of ECHR. The ECHR is, however, not entitled to proceed *ex officio* and only on its own initiative.

Within the European human rights system, Protocol No. 11 reinforced its judicial nature by making it compulsory and transformed the existing supervisory system, creating a single full-time court to which individuals have direct access. The ECtHR through its jurisprudence reviews the compliance of the state parties of the Convention with their obligations issuing from Convention, interprets the Convention using the evolutive interpretation of referring to its nature as a "living instrument" and renders advisory opinions on legal questions arising from the interpretation of the Convention and its Protocols.[56]

The right to request that the Court give an advisory opinion on a question of principle relating to the interpretation or application of the rights and freedoms defined in the Convention or the protocols thereto has been granted to the highest national courts and tribunals of a "High Contracting Party" (and for the pending cases before domestic court) by the Protocol No. 16 to the ECHR (2013).[57]

The main goal of advisory procedure (similar to the preliminary ruling procedure before the ECJ) is clarifying the provision of the Convention and the Court's case law and thus providing guidance in order to assist State Parties in avoiding future violation of the ECHR. The procedure is optional and advisory opinions are not binding.

The efficiency of the European system of human rights is guaranteed through its supervisory mechanism, although it has no specific means to force member states to comply with the judgments of the ECtHR. There is a Committee of

Ministers charged with the power to supervise the execution of the court decisions. Within this context, the execution of the ECtHR judgments is regarded as an integral part of the "trial" for the purposes of Article 6 of the Convention, and the Court infers the right of execution from "the principle of the rule of law".[58] Within the larger context, a full execution of judgments helps to enhance the Court's prestige and the effectiveness of its action, and has the effect of limiting the number of applications submitted to it.

Since its creation at the beginning of 1950s, the European system has permanently expanded and gradually become the most successful regional project of human rights protection: "It is no exaggeration to state that the Convention and its growing and diverse body of case law have transformed Europe's legal and political landscape, qualifying the ECtHR as the world's most effective human rights tribunal".[59]

Unlike the other regional courts, the ECtHR, has become a victim of its own success because since the early 1980s it has been permanently confronted with the exponential increase of individual complaints and the need to adopt the necessary procedural and structural reforms in order to reduce a chronic backlog and to make this judicial body more effective. Legal writing confirms that a combination of different factors caused this adverse situation including: "the Court's positive public reputation, its expansive interpretations of the Convention, and the distrust of domestic judiciaries in some countries and the entrenched human rights problems in others have attracted tens of thousands of new individual applications annually. The huge volume of cases shows no sign of abating and threatens to bury ECtHR judges and Registry lawyers in paper".[60]

In comparison with other regional human rights courts, one can share the view that: "There is a fundamental conflict between the size of the population who have access to the Court with the right to lodge an individual application and the Court's responsibility as the final arbiter in human rights matters for so many different states. No other international court is confronted with a workload of such magnitude while having at the same time such a demanding responsibility for setting the standards of conduct required to comply with the Convention".[61] Although Protocol No. 11 has simplified the proceedings before ECtHR, regarding reinforcing their judicial character in practice it proved inadequate to cope with the continuous rise in the number of individual applications as a result (among other things) of the enlargement of the Council of Europe. As a consequence, the urgent need has arisen to adjust the existing mechanism and particularly to guarantee the long-term effectiveness of the ECtHR so that it can continue to play its principal role in the protection of human rights in Europe.

The legislative result of the effort to adapt the mechanism of the ECtHR to the situation endangers the effectiveness of the judicial system of ECHR represents Protocol No.14 to the Convention for the Protection of Human Rights and Fundamental Freedoms amending the Control system of the Convention (hereinafter known as Protocol 2004).

The State Parties in its preamble took *inter alia* into account "the urgent need to amend certain provisions of the Convention in order to maintain and improve the efficiency of the control system for the long term, mainly in the light of the continuing increase in the workload of the European Court of Human Rights and the Committee of Ministers of the Council of Europe". Unlike Protocol No. 11.: "Protocol No. 14 makes no radical changes to the control system established by the Convention. The changes relate more to the functioning than to the structure of the system. Its main purpose is to improve it, giving the ECtHR the means and flexibility it needs to process all applications in a timely fashion, while allowing it to concentrate on the most important cases which require in-depth examination".[62]

To achieve this goal, the Protocol concentrated on three areas, namely: the reinforcement of the Court's filtering capacity in the respect of unmeritorious applications, a new admissibility criterion concerning cases in which the applicant has not suffered significant disadvantage and measures for dealing with repeating cases. The main goal of these measures is: "to reduce the time spent by the Court on clearly inadmissible applications and repeating applications so as to enable the Court to concentrate on those cases that raise important human rights issues".[63] The principal aim was to increase the Court's capacity by introducing smaller judicial formations with specific competences (single judge formation in respect of the admissibility of petitions and a three-judge Committee to give judgments in cases coming within well-established case law) and having more time to deal with cases of greater legal importance or urgency.

This goal is fully compatible with the Convention because if its purpose is to protect the rights and freedoms, it must not merely vindicate them but to do so relatively quickly and efficiently. It should be noted that the situation of the ECtHR has significantly improved thanks to the effectively implemented reforms of Protocol No. 14 and, above all, as a result of new working methods, particularly the effective filtering of new applications. Therefore, the President of the ECtHR could state with satisfaction at the beginning of 2003: "To adapt the phrase so often used in relation to this Court, it is no longer a victim of its own success".[64] And the last Annual Report of the European Court of Human Rights (2016) states that: "the single-judge cases have been virtually eliminated and this is a welcome development . . .".[65]

6.2.2. Regional Protection of Human Rights in the Americas

With the end of military dictatorships in a number of South/Central American countries, it became possible for an Inter-American human rights system to start working at the beginning of the 1980s. Its main goal was to provide a framework to make a coalition against communist-inspired threats and to defend effective political democracy. The American states adopted in April 1948 a Charter of the Organization of American States (hereinafter known as the Charter) and established the Organization of American States (OAS) referring to Article 52 of the UN Charter. The Charter *inter alia* contains some articles related to fundamental human rights. In the same year (and even before the approval of the UN Universal Declaration of Human Rights in December 1948) the American Declaration on the Rights and Duties of Man was adopted by American states as an impetus for the creation of the regional American system of human rights. A set of civil, political, economic, social and cultural rights are embodied in the declaration. Among other instruments of the American normative human rights system one can mention the American Convention on Human Rights (1969) complemented by two protocols, namely: the Additional Protocol to the American Convention on Human Rights in the Area of Economic Social and Cultural Rights (1988), and the Protocol to the American Convention on Human Rights to abolish the Death Penalty (1990). The American Convention contains mainly the civil and political rights, except in Article 2, and in one general provision on economic social and cultural rights.

A number of specialized international conventions related to torture, violence against women and on forced abductions of people were signed and ratified during the 1990s by the member states of OAS. By the adoption of these international instruments the American states have created the Inter-American system for the promotion and protection of human rights.

As regards to the Inter-American institutional structure, the Inter-American Commission on Human Rights (1959, hereinafter as the Commission) and the Inter-American Court of Human Rights (1979, hereinafter as the Court) are the main institutions in charge of the promotion and protection of human rights within the Americas. Both bodies can review individual complaints concerning alleged human rights violations and may issue emergency protective measures. As regards to the Commission it is one of the main organs of the OAS and its function is to promote the observance and protection of human rights. In order to fulfil this function it is entitled to make recommendations to member states, publish reports, and since 1966 has acquired the competence to examine individual petitions for alleged violations of human rights. All such petitions must, however, pass through the Commission before being submitted to the Court.

One of the specifics of the Inter-American system consists in the fact that the Commission deals with individual complaints through two legal procedures. The first of them is based on the OAS Charter and the American Declaration on the Rights and Duties of Man is binding on all member states of the OAS irrespective of their ratification of the American Convention on Human Rights. This individual complaint procedure based on the OAS Charter results in the conclusion and/or recommendation of the Commission that does not have the character of a legally binding decision. The second procedure relates to the states who ratified the American Convention on Human Rights. According to the relevant article of the Convention (Article 44), any person or group of persons or any NGO may lodge a complaint objecting to an alleged violation of the American Convention by its State Party. The complainant must exhaust all domestic remedies and its complaint must be lodged within six months after the final decision of the domestic proceeding. The Commission as a "filter body" decides on the admissibility of each complaint and prepares a report on the facts of the case and its conclusion. Only the State concerned and the Commission can decide to refer the case to the Court; an individual does not have this right.[66]

Direct participation, pleadings, motions and evidence in the Court Proceedings were granted to alleged victims and/or their representatives in 2001 by the amended Rule of Procedure of the Court although individuals still have no right to bring their case directly to the Court (Article 61 of the American Convention on Human Rights).[67] The court judgment can decide on the violation of the right or freedom protected by the Convention. Its judgment shall be final and the State Parties to the American Convention are obliged to comply with the judgments in any case to which they are parties. Apart from complaints procedures the Inter-American Court performs an evolutionary interpretation of the American Convention following the idea that human rights treaties are living instruments whose interpretation must take into account the changes over time and current conditions.[68]

6.2.3. Regional Judicial Protection of Human Rights in Africa

It is useful to note at the outset that some of the main goals of the African system of human rights were safeguarding independence, collective security, territorial integrity and the promotion of solidarity among African states. The comparison of its system with other regions confirms that Africa became the third region (continent) after Europe and the Americas to put into place a panregional intergovernmental system for human rights protection. It is, however, to be noted that there is a great difference between the scope of the normative acts dealing with human rights in Africa, on the one hand, and a real possibility to ask for their judicial protection before panregional or subregional judicial bodies on the other.

The main source of the normative nature is represented by the African Charter on Human and Peoples' Rights (1981, hereinafter as the African Charter or Banjul Charter)) which was gradually completed by other panregional regulations, including the Charter of the Rights and Welfare of the Child (1990), the Protocol to the African Charter on Human Rights on the Rights of Women in Africa (2003), etc. Apart from traditional individual human rights, the African Charter recognizes some collective rights and so-called third generation rights because within the legal traditions of the continent special responsibility is born by every person to his or her family, community and mankind. Also, there are a number of instances where the African regional and subregional treaties make specific reference to human rights referring mainly to the African Charter of Human Rights either as an objective or as a fundamental principle. In this context it can be concluded that: "there exists a clear conceptual linkage between regional economic trade rules in Africa and human rights rules in

Africa. In particular, specific reference to the provisions of the African Charter implies that all three generations of human rights are considered fundamental in the formulation and implementation of trade rules".[69]

As regards to the institutional structure for the protection of human rights, its foundation starts with the African Commission of Human and Peoples' Rights (hereinafter as the African Commission) established by the African Charter of Human Rights in order: ". . . to promote human and peoples' rights and ensure their protection in Africa" (Article 30 of the African Charter of Human Rights). Its mandate and function as well as procedures confirm that the intention of its parties has been concentrated on the different kinds of promotion of human rights in Africa mainly at the level of states and among states. Although the Commission may also decide complaints (communications) of individuals, organizations and states concerning alleged violations of the African Charter by the member states of the AU, it is not competent to render binding decisions.[70] Its recommendations are not binding and there is no effective mechanism for their enforcement. Since 1987, when the African Commission was created, "it has been severely criticized as a toothless bull-dog that only barks but cannot bite because the decisions of the Commission are not binding on State Parties. Secondly, African states are still tied to the apron string of the much-vaunted principles of state sovereignty and reserve domain".[71]

The first pan-African judicial body was established by Constitutive Act of the African Union (Art.18, 2000)[72] and its "functional" legal basis represents the Protocol to the Court of Justice of the African Union (2003).[73] Without going into details, suffice it to say that this Court has no relevance for the effective protection of human rights in Africa because its competences are formulated too generally and are concentrated mainly on the disputes related to the interpretation and application of different legal regulations (Constitutive Act of the AU, AU treaties, all subsidiary legal instruments adopted within the Union, any questions of international law, all acts, decisions regulations and directive of the organs of the Union, etc., according to Article 19 of the Protocol).

The first judicial body vested with the charge to protect human rights in Africa was created by the Protocol to the African Charter on Human and Peoples' Rights on the Establishment of the African Court on Human Rights and People's Rights (1998) (hereinafter as the Court). The Protocol came into force in 2004 and the first case was decided in 2009.[74]

To reach its main mandate the Court jurisdiction is extended to all cases and disputes submitted to it concerning the interpretation and application of the African Charter; this Protocol and other Human Rights instruments are ratified by the states (Article 3). The Court is entrusted with the power to provide advisory opinions on any legal matter relating to the Charter or any relevant human rights instruments (Article 4). With respect to the access to the Court, it is available to the Commission, the State Party against which the Commission lodges a complaint and African intergovernmental organizations

(Article 5). The complaint concerning an alleged violation of the Human Rights Charter can bring before Court either the state whose citizen was a victim of such violation or directly persons who have suffered provided that the State Party at the time of ratification of the Protocol makes a declaration accepting the jurisdiction of the Court to receive cases from individuals (Article 5 para. 3 of the Protocol). To exercise these competences properly, the Court should complement and reinforce the protective mandate and functions of the African Commission to enhance its efficiency. In the practice the entire responsibility of human rights protection is really imposed on the African Commission. As a result of this development two distinct pan-African courts were established in a relatively short period (2000–2005). Against this promising background there has therefore been a surprising further development in the fate of these courts. Despite this fact, or perhaps because of this fact, the heads of states and governments, at the initiative of the president of AU Conference (Nigerian President of the Conference, Mr. Obasanjo) decided in July 2004 to merge the African Court of Human Rights and Peoples' Rights with the African Court of Justice. The formal Protocol on the statute of a merged African Court of Justice and Human Rights was adopted in July 2008. The reason for this decision was of an economic nature because the African Union could not afford two distinct judicial institutions. In January 2005 the Chiefs of States subsequently decided to activate the African Court of Human Rights and Peoples' Rights regardless of the previous decisions to merge. Until the Protocol on the African Court on Human Rights and Justice comes into force (15 state parties ratification is required) the African Court on Human and People Rights will continue to exist in its full and complete form. Article 2 of the Statute of the African Court of Justice and Human Rights[75] confirms that the court shall be the main judicial organ of the African Union. According to one of its goals, it should: "complement and strengthen the mission of African Commission on Human and Peoples' Rights as well as the African Committee of Experts on the Rights and Welfare of the Child".

As regards to its institutional structure, the merged Court has two sections, namely: the General Affairs Section and Human Rights Section. The first of them includes all cases and legal disputes relating to the interpretation and application of different legal regulations (Constitutive Act of the AU, AU treaties, all subsidiary legal instruments adopted within Union, the interpretation and application of the African Charter of Human Rights, the Charter on the Rights and Welfare of the Child, any questions of international law, all acts and decisions, regulations and directives of the organs of the Union, etc., according to Article 28 of the Protocol.)

The entities entitled to bring the cases to the Court relating to the interpretation and application of legal instruments are: the State Parties of the Protocol, the Assembly, the Parliament and other organs of the Union, as well as staff members of the African Union (Article 29). Within the Human Rights section, the Court deals with the cases of any alleged violation of the rights guaranteed by the African Charter, the Charter on the Rights and Welfare of the Child, The Protocol to the African Charter on Human Rights on the Rights of Women in Africa. The cases may refer to the Court State Parties of the Protocol, the African Commission on Human and People Rights, African intergovernmental organizations, the African National Human Rights Institution and the African Committee of Experts on the Rights and Welfare of the Child. As regards to individuals and relevant NGOs (accredited to the AU), they have access to the Court only when the relevant state at the time of signature, ratification, accession or at any time thereafter make the declaration accepting the jurisdiction of the court to receive cases submitted by the individuals or relevant NGOs (Articles 8 and 30 of the Protocol).

From the brief analysis of the pan-African judicial bodies carried out above, the following conclusion can be made. First of all, the denial of the individual's direct access to the Courts confirms the lack of effective legal protection of human rights in Africa available to victims of the alleged violations of human rights. In this context, it is pertinent to share a current opinion: "Only a few African states are willing to make Special Declarations allowing individuals to have direct access to the Court. The implication of this is that individuals and NGOs of states ratified the Protocol, but are yet to make a declaration that would allow access to the Court (and later the merged Court) through the African Commission and the State itself. A true denial of direct access to the individual is a 'step' back in access to justice for all in Africa".[76] If the states are hesitant in making special declarations, the African system will be similar to that of Inter-American system[77] because the Court will receive most of cases from the Commission. This situation is not desirable because it deprives the Court of its purpose, which was to grant individuals and NGOs an effective judicial remedy for the protection of their human rights.

Provided conditions for the proceedings of the Human Rights Court related to the African Human Rights Charter have been met, some legal problems can arise. First and foremost, problems result from the unique characteristics of the Charter because it protects not only civil and political rights (following the example of other regional human rights conventions) but also social, economic and cultural rights. In addition to these individual rights, the Charter also recognizes collective or group rights or peoples' rights. The African Charter guarantees socio-economic rights and gives them the same status as civil and political rights. The state parties in the Preamble of the Charter state that: "civil and political rights cannot be disassociated from economic, social and cultural rights in their conception as well as universality and that the satisfaction of economic, social and cultural rights is a guarantee for the enjoyment of civil and political rights".[78]

The main difficulty results from the fact that social and economic rights are normally not justiciable neither before national nor international courts due to their specific "programmatic" nature and the dependence of the material and financial level of the national economy of each state.[79] International practice also confirms that only the reporting (and not complaints) procedure is considered as most pertinent for the area of social and economic rights. It is therefore possible to agree with the opinion in which: "The yardstick of the African Human Rights Court will adopt to determine whether or not a state has violated socio-economic rights will be more problematic because African states, like other countries, have different economic policies. It will be difficult for the court to decide that such violations have occurred where resources are not available".[80]

Another problem lies with the judicial enforcement of socio-economic rights before the domestic courts of Africa.[81] Additionally, critical opinion with respect to the African Charter concerns rather broad "claw back clauses" related to civil and political rights (Articles 6, 8, 9) because it is sufficient that restrictions of these rights will be in accordance with the national legal orders (without the necessity to identify some of the reasons of public interest, e.g. national security, public safety, public health, public order, etc.). Such limitations have been criticized because they subject rights guaranteed by the Charter to domestic laws, thus weakening their content, scope and effectiveness. This approach permits the national laws of African states to take precedence over generally recognized human rights standards embodied in the sources of general international law. This is one of the reasons emphasizing the need to review the text of the Charter in order to reflect more adequately on the current international human rights standards.

The above-mentioned facts, confirming a certain weakness of the African Union's Human Rights system, contributed to the granting of human rights jurisdiction to the subregional ECOWAS Court to the EACJ, and the SADC Court's willingness to entertain human rights cases, invoking the vague "good governance" provisions. This situation, however, generates another problem of a procedural nature whereby: "a brief examination of these Treaties and of the African Court of Human Rights Court Protocol clearly indicate the existence of a rich zone of overlap, potential competition and possible complementarity. It also presents rich possibilities of forum shopping in the enforcement of regional human rights".[82]

With respect to the ECOWAS, its primary function still remains the examination of disputes arising out of the interpretation and application of the ECOWAS treaty. Its revised version, however, pointed out that the respect, promotion and protection of human rights of the African Charter remains one of the fundamental principles of the Treaty. The Supplementary Protocol to the Protocol of the Community (ECOWAS) Court of Justice (2005)[83] greatly expands its jurisdiction because "the court has jurisdiction to determine a case of violation of human rights that occurs in any Member States" (Art. 5, para.4), allowing the individual an application for relief for violation of their human rights (Article 9, para. 4) provided that such application is not anonymous and not made while some matter is pending before another international court. Unlike Europe and the Americas systems of human rights, there is no obligation for individuals to first exhaust local remedies before bringing the cases before the ECOWAS Court.

The positive aspects of this regulation consist in the fact that ECOWAS Court of Justice acquired compulsory jurisdiction and that the individuals have been granted (for the first time) the right to direct access to the judicial body charged with the protection of human rights on the subregional basis. The SADC Treaty, although making no direct reference to the African Charter, also commits members to the fundamental principles of human rights, democracy and rule of law. Similarly, the COMESA treaty also established the recognition, promotion and protection of human rights as a fundamental principle of the system in addition to liberty, fundamental freedoms and rule of law and similar provisions that may be identified also within the EAC Treaty.

6.2.4. The Emerging Regional Human Rights System of Arab States

The Charter of the League of Arab States (hereinafter as LAS, Charter) was adopted in 1945 by seven states and LAS today represents one of the oldest regional organizations founded before the UN and before the end of the Second World War. Taking into consideration the specificity of the international and regional situation in the middle of 1940s there is no mention of human rights in the Charter and it established neither non-judicial institution for the protection of human rights nor a judicial body. The first regional instrument that related to human rights was represented by the Arab Charter of Human Rights (1994) but had a number of problematic provisions because it does not meet international norms and standards (the application of the death penalty for children, non-acceptable treatment of women and non-Arab citizens).[84]

One of the main weaknesses of the Charter consists in the lack of any procedural human rights mechanism. Under the increasing pressure from the criticism of this fact and common efforts of the representatives of different NGOs—as well as the gradually changing approaches of the member states of LAS—a new version of the Arab Charter of Human Rights was adopted in 2004 in Tunisia.[85] A new "modern" version of the Arab Charter contains four main categories of human rights, namely: traditional individual rights (right to life, right to be free from slavery, interdiction of inhuman and degrading treatment, etc.—first category), rights related to judicial proceeding (the equality of all persons before law, the rights to due process and fair trial—second category), civil and political rights (freedom of movement, respect for private and family life, the right of private property, the right to information, freedom of opinion, etc.—third category) and economic, social and cultural rights (right to work, right to form trade unions, right to social protection and education, etc.—fourth category).[86]

The new and progressive articles of the Arab Charter confirm equality between men and women in the Arab world (Article 3, para. 3), protection of children's rights (Article 34, para. 3) and the rights of handicapped people (Article 40).[87] But unlike its equivalent in Africa, Europe and the Americas, the Arab Charter has no judicial body to interpret and enforce it, and remains without any real value within human rights protection. Another international instrument "completing" the Arab normative system was the Arab Declaration on the Rights of Child (1983).

As regards the regional institutional structure of human rights protection it is exiguous and does not provide effective remedies for the victims of the alleged violation of human rights in Arab states as well as not contributing effectively to the improving the standards of human rights protection. There are some factors which led to this not very optimistic conclusion. Among the first can be mentioned the nature and competences of the bodies entrusted with the power to deal with human rights issues. Although the Arab Charter established an Arab Human Rights Committee (Article 45), its system is concentrated on the monitoring of the compliance of states with their obligations issuing from the Charter. The Committee receives a periodic report (every third year) from each State Party but parties can make neither individual nor state petitions to the Committee if there is reasonable suspicion of an alleged violation of any right guaranteed by the Charter. After analysing the concrete report, the Committee prepares a non-binding recommendation as deemed appropriate. The Committee lacks the mandate and competencies to receive and adjudicate individual complaints, to receive and consider alternative reports and to address urgent human rights situations in the LAS member states. The practice confirms that as well, as in other fields a lot more could be done to enhance the protection mandate of the Committee, namely in terms of developing expertise, the interpretation of the provisions of the Arab Charter and developing a proper jurisprudence that could be used by judicial bodies at the national level of member states.

The member states of the LAS have therefore attempted to improve the human rights situation through the first Arab regional judicial body. In September 2014 a ministerial meeting of the LAS approved the statute of an Arab Court for Human Rights (hereinafter as the Court).[88] According to its Statute, the Arab Court of Human Rights is an independent Arab judicial organ to reinforce the desire of State Parties to implement their obligations regarding human rights and freedoms and help to achieve the purposes and objectives of the Arab Charter on Human Rights. It is worth noting that since the moment of the approval of the Statute the Court has been subjected to permanent criticism from various sources and levels. The prominent Arab lawyer and war crimes expert Cherif Bassiouni dismissed the court as little more than a "Potemkin Tribunal" and according to another opinion its author is not sure "whether the court is likely to be a part of the human rights solution in the Arab world or part of the problem".[89] The jurisdiction of the court is formulated generally referring to: "all suits and conflicts resulting from the implementation and interpretation of the Arab Charter of Human Rights or any other Arab Convention in the field of human rights involving the member state"[90] As regards to the admissibility of a case, the requirements demand: the exhaustion of the local remedies, only one jurisdiction of regional human rights court resulting from a ban to bring the same case also before other regional human rights court and a six-month period for bringing the case after a final decision of the domestic court (Article 18).

With respect to the access of the Court, the State Parties have chosen the model which is most unfavourable for the real judicial protection of human rights. According to Article 19 of the Statute, it restricts the access to the State Party whereby citizens who claim to be victims of human rights violation have the rights to access court provided that both claimant state and the defendant state are parties to this Statute and to NGOs that are accredited and working in the field of human rights in the state whose subject claims to be a victim of human rights violations. It is to be noted that decades of experience of existing human rights courts and UN human rights bodies, typically, for diplomatic and political reasons, almost never make use of interstate complaints procedures regarding human rights issues. By denying individual victims the right to have direct recourse to the Court, the Statute of Arab Court of Human Rights defeats the very purpose and raison d'etre of a regional human rights court.[91]

6.2.5. The Asia-Pacific Human Rights System

Unlike Europe, Africa and the Americas, the Asia-Pacific remains the only region without a specific panregional human rights treaty and judicial and/or non-judicial mechanism for the promotion and protection of human rights. During the last quarter of the 20th century progress was achieved on the sub-regional level, where some regional entities were established with a more or less emphasis on human rights. One can mention the South Asian Association for Regional Cooperation (SAARC, 1985) which adopted the Social Charter, including the protection of children and vulnerable groups, and the Pacific Island Forum (PIF, 1971) supporting the ideas of promotion of human rights. The most active in the field of human rights was undoubtedly ASEAN, which adopted in the first after the millenium decade various non-legally binding declarations related to human rights, including: the Declaration on the Elimination of Violence Against Women in the ASEAN Region (DEVAW, 2004), the Declaration Against Trafficking in Persons Particularly Women and Children (2004) and the ASEAN Declaration on the Protection and Promotion of the Rights of Migrant Workers (2007). The first attempt at a precise "codification" of human rights was represented by the ASEAN Human Rights Declaration adopted in November 2012 containing *sui generis* "a road map for regional human rights development".[92]

It is fair to note that the adoption of these declarations has had mainly a symbolic value and reflected the intention of Asian states to improve the human rights situation in the region rather than accept any binding obligations in this area. The protection of human rights is, though, embodied among one of the purposes of the ASEAN Charter in order: "to promote and protect human rights and fundamental freedoms with due regards to the rights and responsibilities of the member states of ASEAN" along with democracy, rule of law and good governance (Article 1, para. 7 of the Charter).

As regards to the institutionalization in the area of human rights protection, for this moment it is possible to identify mainly the ASEAN Intergovernmental Commission on Human Rights (hereinafter as the AICHR, Commission) established in 2009 on the basis of Article 14 of the ASEAN Charter.[93] The ASEAN foreign ministers endorsed its Terms of Reference in July 2009 and October 2010, and latter is recognized as the official "date of birth" of the AICHR. The Terms of Reference limit the Commission's role (as an intergovernmental body forming an integral part of the ASEAN organizational structure) to promotion and protection of human rights as a consultative body of the ASEAN (Article 3 of the Terms of Reference) without binding powers.

In order to comply with its main task, the AICHR is empowered *inter alia* to develop strategies for the promotion and protection of human rights and fundamental freedoms, develop the ASEAN Human Rights Declaration, provide the ASEAN with advisory and technical assistance on human rights, develop common approaches and positions on human rights matters, etc. Its decision-making is by consensus. The mandate of AICHR, however, does not contain an explicit provision for receiving individual complaints of human rights violations.[94] The scope and specificities of its mandate confirm its position as an overreaching body mainly for the promotion of human rights in the ASEAN.

The institutional structure of the ASEAN relating to human rights has been gradually completed by two sectoral bodies, namely: the ASEAN Commission on the Rights of Women and Children (ACWI 2010) and ASEAN Committee on Migrant Workers (ACMW, 2007). Like the AICHR, neither the ACWI nor the ACMW have a specific mandate to receive and investigate complaints of human rights violations from women, children or migrant workers.

Finally, a growing informal ASEAN network of human rights currently includes various civil society groupings, NGOs and national coalitions on human rights in some of the member states, etc.[95]

This brief institutional and normative overview confirms that the ASEAN approach to human rights is clearly different from the above-highlighted regional systems in Europe, the Americas and Africa. These systems are based on the key instruments (including the treaties with shorter or longer lists of guaranteed human rights) and institutional structures set up by the commissions and/or courts which can pressurize states to respect human rights. These systems clearly provide access and redress for individuals to a regional judicial or non-judicial body where there are no effective remedies at the national level and the regional courts render binding judgments which can lead to compensation for injured persons. The existing ASEAN structure does not contain these crucial elements and prefers the "modest" gradualist process building of the ASEAN regional human rights system through a systematic step-by-step approach.

It should be, however, taking in account that a number of obstacles of different natures prevent the ASEAN and its bodies from building a strong and effective mechanism for the protection of human rights. Some of them result from the so-called Asian way of regionalism which emphasizes the principles of independence, sovereignty and non-interference into the internal affairs of ASEAN member states;[96] the principle of full consensus for adopting also the non-legal documents; different attitudes of ASEAN member states to human rights (Indonesia, the Philippines and Thailand are their supporters, while Singapore and Malaysia belong to the "wait-and see" category); the democratic deficit in some of the ASEAN member states and the purely intergovernmental nature of ASEAN. As regards to other problems at the Asian level, a variety of languages, religions, political systems, ethnic compositions and differences in economic performance as well as an absence of similar cultural heritage prevents further attempts to build a pan-Asian system of human rights.[97]

To sum up, the above allows one to conclude that there is a low probability for Asia to have single, unified human rights system that enjoys a comprehensive membership of the states across the Asian region. However, it is not impossible to induce and encourage states to accept the regional human rights system by increasing the benefit of membership. The first step might be developing a human rights mechanism under the existing regional cooperative mechanism. It might be desirable to recognize human rights concerns as a crucial component of the overall cooperative mechanism by imposing an obligation such as accepting human rights standards and the undertaking of legal reforms for any states who wish to remain respected members.

The above analysis clearly confirms the uneven level and complexity of regional human rights systems in different parts of world. Their particularities result from a set of various factors having historical, religious, ethnic and other natures. A specific factor represents the strict concept of sovereignty, preventing external control of human rights respect before a regional judicial body on the basis of an individual complaint of a concerned person. This is one of the main reasons for different approaches to the regional human rights structures excluding the direct access of the individuals to the regional judicial body. Among them one can mention the optional (non-compulsory jurisdiction) of the regional judicial body, the preventive "filtering" systems before non-judicial bodies (commissions) combined with their right the bring the case before the judicial body, the systems in which different entities are entitled to bring the case before judicial body but the individual has no such right, etc.

Notes

1. "In the future we may well see regional courts increasingly involved in criminal law matters. Already the European Court of Justice adjudicates disputes involving police and judicial cooperation, the European Court of Human Rights reviews questions regarding the administration of justice in the criminal law systems and the Inter-American Court of Human Rights exercises quasi criminal jurisdiction. And as dissatisfaction with the International Criminal Court grows we may also see a rise of regional criminal bodies outside the western world, probably firstly in Africa". See: Alter, K.J., Hooghe, L.: Regional Dispute Settlement. In: Börzel, T.A., Risse, T. (eds.): *The Oxford Handbook of Comparative Regionalism*. Oxford: Oxford University Press, 2016, p. 547.

2. Alter, *supra* n. 92, p. 16.
3. Baudenbacher, C.: Judicialization: Can the European Model Be Exported to Other Parts of the World? In: *Texas International Law Journal*, Vol. 39, 2003 p. 382.
4. VIRZO, R.: The Preliminary Ruling Procedures at International Regional Courts and Tribunals. In: *The Law & Practice of International Courts and Tribunals*, Vol. 10, No. 2, 2011, p. 309.
5. Case C-446/98 *Fazenda Publica* (2000), ECR.I-11435, para. 49.
6. Chevalier, B.: Les nouveaux développements de la procédure préjudicielle dans le domaine de l'espace judiciare européen: la procédure préjudicielle d'urgence et les réformes principales prévues par le Traité de Lisbonne. In: *ERA Forum*, Vol. 9, No. 4, 2009, p. 591.
7. Alter, K.J.: The Global Spread of European Style International Courts. In: *West European Politics*, Vol. 35, No. 1, 2012, p. 145.
8. Legal writings often analyse the SADCT case *Campbell v. Republic of Zimbabwe* (2008) concerning the expropriation of the farmer M. Campbell's land by the Zimbabwean government. The SADCT ruled in favour of the complainant and ordered Zimbabwe to end expropriation and pay compensation to those whose lands has already been seized. The Zimbabwean government failed to accept the court's ruling and the Tribunal was later (2000) suspended by the member states of the SADC. Later development resulted in the reduction of the availability of the Tribunal with respect to individual person(s) because since 2012 its jurisdiction was confined to member states and in practice has been "effectively transformed into a dormant institution void of its original purpose". Fanenbruck, Meisner, *supra* n. 19, p. 15.
9. Eliantonio, M., Roer-Eide, H.: Regional Courts and *locus standi* for Private Parties: Can the CJEU Learn Something From the Others? In: *The Law & Practice of International Courts and Tribunals*, Vol. 13, No. 1, 2014, pp. 46–47.
10. Virzo, *supra* n. 149, p. 306.
11. *Ibidem*, p. 309.
12. Romano, C.P.R.: The Proliferation of International Judicial Bodies: The Pieces of the Puzzle. In: *New York University Journal of International Law & Politics*, Vol. 31, No. 4, Summer 1999, p. 748.
13. Protocol No. 16 to the Convention on the Protection of Human Rights and Fundamental Freedoms, Strasbourg 2013, Council of Europe Treaty Series, No. 124. Available at: https://rm.coe.int/1680084821
14. Agreement Between the EFTA States on the Establishment of a Surveillance Authority and a Court of Justice. Available at: www.efta.int/sites/default/files/documents/legal-texts/the-surveillance-and-court-agreement/Surveillance-and-Court-Agreement-consolidated.pdf
15. American Convention on Human Rights "Pact of San José, Costarica" on November 22, 1969. Available at: www.refworld.org/docid/3ae6b36510.html
16. Danilenko, G.M.: The Economic Court of the Commonwealth of Independent States. In: *International Law and Politics*, Vol. 31, 1999, p. 903.
17. Interpretation of Peace Treaties With Bulgaria, Hungary and Romania, Advisory Opinion of the ICJ, I.C.J. Reports 1950, 65, 71.
18. "Judicial decisions in contentious cases are said to be 'hard' because states have given the court jurisdiction to issue a binding opinion. Advisory opinions are said to be 'soft' because in most instances states have not given the court jurisdiction to issue a binding opinions". See: Alvarez, J.E.: The New Dispute Settlers: (Half) Trust and Consequences. In: *Texas International Law Journal*, Vol. 38, 2003, p. 405, 427.
19. Pasqualucci, J.M.: Advisory Practice of the Inter-American Court of Human Rights: Contributing to the Evolution of International Human Rights Law. In: *Stanford Journal of International Law*, Vol. 38, No. 2, 2002, p. 241, 246.

20. Pasqualucci, *supra* n. 177.
21. Oellers-Frahm, K.: Lawmaking Through Advisory Opinions? In: *German Law Journal*, Vol. 12, No. 5, 2011, p. 1050.
22. Oellers-Frahm, *supra* n. 179, p. 1052.
23. Tomuschat, C., *supra* n. 23, pp. 401–402.
24. Convention on ICAO, December 7, 1944, 15 UNTS, p. 296. Available at: www.icao.int/publications/Pages/doc7300.aspx
25. European Convention of Transfrontier Television (1989), Article 21, Letter c). Available at: https://rm.coe.int/168007b03
26. Dolzer, R., Schreuer, C.H.: *Principles of International Investment Law*, 2nd Edition. Oxford: Oxford University Press, 2012, p. 32.
27. Marrakesh Agreement Establishing the World Trade Organization, April 15, 1994, 1867. U.N.T.S., 154, 159, Art. IX. Available at: www.wto.org/english/docs_e/legal_e/04-wto.pdf
28. Article XXIX of the IMF Agreement states that: "a) Any question of interpretation of the provisions of this Agreement arising between any member and the Fund or between any members of the Fund shall be submitted to the Executive Board for its decision". Available at: www.imf.org/external/pubs/ft/aa/pdf/aa.pdf
29. Committee on the Elimination of All Forms of Racial Discrimination (CERD), Human Rights Committee (HRC), Committee on Economic, Social and Cultural Rights (CESCR), Committee on the Elimination of Discrimination against Women (CEDAW), Committee against Torture (CAT), Committee on the Rights of the Child (CRC), Committee on Migrant Workers (CMW) and Committee on the Rights of Persons with Disabilities (CRPD). United Nations Office of the High Commissioner for Human Rights, Human Rights Bodies. There is also a Sub-Committee on Prevention established under the Optional Protocol to the Convention against Torture and other Cruel, Inhuman or Degrading Treatment or Punishment. A Committee on Enforced Disappearances (CED) will be established once the Convention on the Protection of All Persons from Enforced Disappearance enters into force. See: International Convention for the Protection of All Persons from Enforced Disappearance [hereinafter Convention Against Enforced Disappearance], art. 26(1), 2006, 14 IHRR 582. Available at: www.ohchr.org/EN/HRBodies/CED/Pages/ConventionCED.aspx
30. Mechlem, K.: Treaty Bodies and the Interpretation of Human Rights. In: *Vanderbilt Journal of Transnational Law*, Vol. 42, 2009, p. 919.
31. "In practice states rarely put forward their own interpretations of specific rights. They typically base their reports on the interpretations offered by treaty bodies in General Comments, the reporting guidelines and the questions provided to them. See: International Law Association: Committee on International Human Rights and Practice, Final Report on the Impact of Findings of the Human Rights Treaty Bodies, London 2004, paras. 631–657. Available at: file:///C:/Users/J%C3%A1n%20Klu%C4%8Dka/Downloads/Conference%20Report%20Johannesburg%202016.pdf
32. Mechlem, *supra* n. 189, p. 927, 931.
33. International Law Association, *supra* n. 190, para.18.
34. Rodley, N.: The Role and Impact of Treaty Bodies. In: Shelton, D. (ed.): *Oxford Handbook of International Human Rights.* Oxford: Oxford University Press, 2013, p. 639.
35. Keller, H., Grover, L.: General Comments of the Human Rights Committee and their Legitimacy. In: Keller, H., Ulfstein, G. (eds.): *UN Human Rights Treaty Bodies: Law and Legitimacy.* Cambridge: Cambridge University Press, 2012, p. 129.

36. Rodley, *supra* n. 193, p. 611.
37. Ulfstein, G.: Individual Compliants. In: Keller, H., Ulfstein, G. (eds.): *UN Human Rights Treaty Bodies: Law and Legitimacy.* Cambridge: Cambridge University Press, 2012, p. 115.
38. The Seabed Dispute Chamber shall give advisory opinion on the request of the Assembly or the Council on the legal questions arising within the scope of their activities.
39. Setting Up in Line With Article 52 of the Rome Statute of International Criminal Court Together With Article 4 of the Regulations of the Court (2004). Available at: www.icc-cpi.int/nr/rdonlyres/ea9aeff7-5752-4f84-be94-0a655eb30e16/0/rome_statute_english.pdf
40. The main purpose of Interpretive Guidance is "to provide recommendation (totally 10) concerning the interpretation of international humanitarian law (IHL) as far it relates to the notion of direct participation in hostilities". See: Interpreting Guidance of International Committee of the Red Cross on the notion of "Direct Participation in Hostilities Under International Humanitarian Law", ICRC, Geneva, 2009, p. 9.
41. Kaufmann-Kohler, G.: Interpretive Powers of the Free Trade Commission and the Rule of Law. In: *Fifteen Years of NAFTA Chapter 11 Arbitration*, Juris Net, LLC 2011, pp. 186–187. Available at: www.arbitration-icca.org/media/1/13571335953400/interpretive_powers_of_the_free_trade_commission_and_the_rule_of_law_kaufmann-kohler.pdf
42. Shany, *supra* n. 93, p. 82.
43. Doc.12865/1/16/REV1 WTO 275 SERVICES 24 FDI 20 CDN 19, Brussels, October 27, 2016, p. 3.
44. The Role of Regional Human Rights Mechanisms, European Parliament, Directorate General for External Policies-Policy Department, Doc.EXPO/B/DROI/2009, 25, pp. 11, 19–20.
45. Alter, Hooghe, *supra* n. 144, p. 549.
46. In order to ensure the legitimacy and effectiveness of the international judicial process and to enhance public confidence in the international judiciary some regional and other courts newly adopted their own ethical codes (Code of the Judicial Conduct of the Court of Caribbean Community, Resolution on Judicial Ethic—ECHR (2008), Code of Judicial Ethics—International Criminal Court (2005), Code of Conduct of the ECJ (2016)).
47. Kingah, S.: Regional Courts and Human Rights in the Developing World. In: *UNU-CRIS Working Paper*, W-2013/11, p. 4.
48. Heyns, C.H., Padilla, D., Zwaak, L.: A Schematic Comparison of Regional Human Rights Systems: An Update. In: *African Human Rights Law Journal*, Vol. 5, No. 2, 2005, p. 308.
49. Article 37 of the Vienna Declaration states: "Regional Arrangements play a fundamental role in the promoting and protection of human rights. They should reinforce universal human rights standards as contained in international human rights instruments and their protection. The World Conference on Human Rights reiterates the need to consider the possibility of establishing regional and subregional arrangements for the promotion and protection of human rights where they do not already exist". Available at: www.ohchr.org/EN/ProfessionalInterest/Pages/Vienna.aspx
50. Robertson, A.H.: *Human Rights in the World: An Introduction to the Study of the International Protection of Human Rights.* Manchester: Manchester University Press (MUP), 1982, p. 81.
51. The text below confirms that this kind of human system is still operational in the Americas and Africa, having, however, their own specificities.

52. The Preamble of the Protocol No. 11 emphasized *inter alia* that: "Considering the urgent need to restructure the control machinery established by the Convention in order to maintain and improve the efficiency of its protection of human rights and fundamental freedoms, mainly in view of the increase in the number of applications and the growing membership of the Council of Europe"; and "Considering that it is therefore desirable to amend certain provisions of the Convention with a view, in particular, to replacing the existing European Commission and Court of Human Rights with a new permanent Court";. Available at: www.echr.coe.int/Documents/Library_Collection_P11_ETS155E_ENG.pdf
53. Sadlier, G.: The ECHR- A Victim of Its Own Success. In: *Cork Online Law Review*, No. 7, 2007, p. 68. Available at: http://corkonlinelawreview.com/editions/2007/COLR%202007%207%20Sadlier.pdf
54. Report of the Group of Wise Persons to the Committee of Ministers, Doc. CM (2006) 203, p. 3. Available at: https://search.coe.int/cm/Pages/result_details.aspx?ObjectID=09000016805d7893
55. Case *Mamatkulov and Askarov v. Turkey*, ECHR, App.No. 46827/99 and 46951/99, 122, Febr. 4, 2005.
56. According to Article 1 para. 1 of the Protocol No. 2 to the Convention on Human Rights and Fundamental Freedoms. Available at: www.echr.coe.int/Documents/Library_Collection_P2_ETS044E_ENG.pdf
57. Protocol No. 16 to the Convention on the Protection of Human Rights and Fundamental Freedoms, Strasbourg 2013, Council of Europe Treaty Series, No. 124.
58. ECtHR, *Hornby v. Greece*, Judgment on 19 March 1997, § 40.
59. Helfer, L.R.: Redesigning the European Court of Human Rights: Embeddedness as a Deep Structural Principle of the European Human Rights Regime. In: *The European Journal of International Law*, Vol. 19, No. 1, 2008, p. 126.
60. Caflisch, L.: The Reform of the European Court of Human Rights: Protocol No. 14 and Beyond. In: *Human Rights Law Review*, Vol. 6, No. 2, 2006, p. 404.

    The ECtHR with 47 judges and 250 registry lawyers has an annual working capacity of around 28,000 cases. The practice confirms that the numbers of individual complaints permanently and considerably exceeds this capacity because over 50,000 new complaints are lodged every year. In 2016, 53,500 applications were adopted to a judicial formation, which was an overall increase of 32 percent compared with 2015 (40,550).
61. Report of the Group of Wise Persons to the Committee of Ministers, *supra* n. 213, p. 4.
62. Explanatory Report to Protocol No. 14 to the Convention for the Protection of Human Rights and Fundamental Freedoms Amending the Control System of the Convention, p. 7 para. 35. Available at: https://rm.coe.int/CoERMPublicCommonSearchServices/DisplayDCTMContent?documentId=09000016800d380f
63. Explanatory Report to Protocol No. 14 to the Convention for the Protection of Human Rights and Fundamental Freedoms Amending the Control System of the Convention, *supra* n. 221, p. 8, para. 37.
64. Speech given by Mr. Dean Spielmann, President of the ECtHR, on the Occasion of the Opening of the Judicial Year, 25 January 2013. In: *Annual Report of the ECJ, 2013*, Council of Europe, ECHR, 2013, p. 26. Available at: http://curia.europa.eu/jcms/upload/docs/application/pdf/2014-06/qdag14001enc.pdf
65. Annual Report of the ECJ, 2017, Council of Europe, European Court of Human Rights, 2017, p. 7. Available at: www.echr.coe.int/Documents/Annual_report_2016_ENG.pdf

66. A similar model existed in the European System until 1998 until the moment of the entry into force of Protocol No. 11 to the European Convention on Human Rights and Fundamental Freedoms. Protocol No. 11 established European Court on Human Rights as a full-time, permanent body overtaking the task of the former Commission, which was abolished. A right to direct access of the individuals to the ECHR has been granted as compulsory.
67. For more details relating the Inter-American System of Human Rights see: The Role of Regional Human Rights Mechanisms. European Parliament, Directorate General for External Policies-Policy Department, Doc.EXPO/B/DROI/2009, 25, pp. 75–81.
68. IACHR—Advisory Opinion OC16/99, October 1, 1999:

    Para 114. This guidance is particularly relevant in the case of international human rights law, which has made great headway thanks to an evolutive interpretation of international instruments of protection. That evolutive interpretation is consistent with the general rules of treaty interpretation established in the 1969 Vienna Convention. Both this Court, in the Advisory Opinion on the Interpretation of the American Declaration of the Rights and Duties of Man (1989)79, and the European Court of Human Rights, in *Tyrer v. United Kingdom* (1978), 80 *Marckx v. Belgium* (1979), 81 *Loizidou v. Turkey* (1995), have held that human rights treaties are living instruments whose interpretation must consider the changes over time and present-day conditions.

    Para 115. The corpus juris of international human rights law comprises a set of international instruments of varied content and juridical effects (treaties, conventions, resolutions and declarations). Its dynamic evolution has had a positive impact on international law in affirming and building up the latter's faculty for regulating relations between States and the human beings within their respective jurisdictions. This Court, therefore, must adopt the proper approach to consider this question in the context of the evolution of the fundamental rights of the human person in contemporary international law.

69. Musungu, S.F.: Economic Integration and Human Rights in Africa: A Comment on Conceptual Linkage. In: *African Human Rights Law Journal*, Vol. 3, No. 1, 2003, p. 92.
70. According to its Preamble the Parties of the African Charter of Human Rights take into consideration: "The virtues of their historical tradition and the values of African civilisation which should inspire and characterize their reflection on the concept of human and peoples rights". Available at: www.achpr.org/files/instruments/achpr/banjul_charter.pdf
71. Yerima, T.F.: Comparative Evaluation of the Challenges of African Regional Human Rights Courts. In: *Journal of Politics and Law*, Vol. 4, No. 2, 2011, p. 120.
72. Constitutive Act of the African Union. Available at: www.achpr.org/files/instruments/au-constitutive-act/au_act_2000_eng.pdf
73. Protocol to the Court of Justice of the African Union. Available at: www.peaceau.org/uploads/protocol-court-of-justice-of-the-au-en.pdf
74. Protocol to the African Charter on Human and Peoples' Rights on the Establishment of the African Court on Human Rights and People's Rights. Available at: www.achpr.org/files/instruments/courtestablishment/achpr_instr_proto_court_eng.pdf
75. Protocol on the Statute of the African Court of Justice and Human Rights. Available at: www.peaceau.org/uploads/protocol-statute-african-court-justice-and-human-rights-en.pdf

76. Yerima, *supra* n. 230, p. 123.
77. Within the Inter-American system all communications to the Inter-American Court of Human Rights must pass through Inter-American Commission before being submitted to the Court. The Commission decides on the admissibility of the communication and prepares report on the facts of the case and its own conclusion.
78. African Charter of Human Rights. Available at: www.achpr.org/files/instruments/achpr/banjul_charter.pdf
79. A traditional example of the programmatic nature of the economic and social rights provides International Covenant of Economic, Social and Cultural Rights (1966) because each State party: "merely to undertake steps . . . to the maximum of its available resource with a view to achieving progressively the full realisation of the rights recognized".
80. Mbazira, C.H.: Enforcing the Economic, Social and Cultural Rights in the African Charter on Human and Peoples' Rights: Twenty Years of Redundancy, Progression and Significant Strides. In: *African Human Rights Law Journal*, Vol. 6, No. 2, 2006, p.361.
81. Yerima, *supra* n. 230, p. 121.
82. Odinkalu, C.A.: Contemporarity, Competition or Contradiction: The Relationship Between the African Court of Human and Peoples' Rights and Regional Economic Courts in East and South Africa. In: *Paper Presented at a Conference of East and Southern States*, Botswana, 2003, p. 21.
83. ECOWAS Court of Justice was established in 1995 being operational since 2001. See: Supplementary Protocol- Doc.A/SP.1/01/05 on January 2005.
84. Al-Midani, M.A.: The League of Arab States and the Arab Charter on Human Rights. Available at: www.acihl.org/articles.htm?article_id=6
85. Arab Charter of Human Rights has entry into force in 2008.
86. Arab Charter on Human Rights. Available at: http://www.humanrights.se/wp-content/uploads/2012/01/Arab-Charter-on-Human-Rights.pdf
87. Al-Midani, *supra* n. 242.
88. English Version of the Statute of the Arab Court of Human Rights. Available at: www.acihl.org/texts.htm?article_id=44&lang=en-GB
89. Stork, J.: New Arab Human Rights Court Is Doomed From the Start. In: *International Business Time*, Human Rights Watch, November 2014, pp. 1–5. Available at: www.hrw.org/news/2014/11/26/new-arab-human-rights-court-doomed-start
90. Statute on the Arab Court of Human Rights (English Version). Available at: https://www.acihl.org/texts.htm?article_id=44&lang=ar-SA
91. The Arab Court of Human Rights: A Flawed Statute for an Ineffective Court. Publication of the International Commission of Jurists, 2015, pp. 5–6. Available at: http://icj.wpengine.netdna-cdn.com/wp-content/uploads/2015/04/MENA-Arab-Court-of-Human-Rights-Publications-Report-2015-ENG.pdf
92. ASEAN Human Rights Declaration and the Phnom Penh Statement on the Adoption of the ASEAN Human Rights Declaration (AHRD). Available at: www.asean.org/storage/images/ASEAN_RTK_2014/6_AHRD_Booklet.pdf
93. Article 14 of the ASEAN Charter states that: "1) In conformity with the purposes and principles of ASEAN Charter relating to promotion and protection of human rights and fundamental freedoms the ASEAN shall establish an ASEAN human rights body. This ASEAN human rights body shall operate in accordance with the Terms of Reference to be determined by the ASEAN Foreign Ministers Meeting". Available at: www.asean.org/wp-content/uploads/2012/05/11.-October-2015-The-ASEAN-Charter-18th-Reprint-Amended-updated-on-05_-April-2016-IJP.pdf

94. In March 2012 human rights advocates attempted to bring some complaints of human rights violations to the AICHR but they were refused because the Commission had neither competence nor any other mechanism to receive individual complaints. Complaints are now submitted to the AICHR *via* the ASEAN Secretariat and the Secretariat pass them on to the AICHR Chair. The Chair is consequently responsible for circulation the complaints among the AICHR members and the discussion of complaints takes place during a closed meeting. So far the AICHR has not taken any public action in regards to any alleged violation of human rights undertaken by an individual complainant.
95. "These measures symbolize the commitment of ASEAN leaders to recognizing human rights as an integral part of ASEAN's path toward a cohesive regional community". See: Wahyuningrum, Y.: The ASEAN Intergovernmental Commission on Human Rights: Origins, Evolution and the Way Forward. In: *International Institute for Democracy and Electoral Assistance (IDEA)*, Stockholm, 2014, p. 6. Available at: www.idea.int/sites/default/files/publications/the-asean-intergovernmental-commission-on-human-rights-origins-evolution-and-the-way-forward.pdf
96. These principles are expressly confirmed in the AICH Terms of Reference (Article 2.1. paras. a) and c). The ASEAN Intergovernmental Commission on Human Rights (Terms of Reference), ASEAN Secretariat, Djakarta, 2009, p. 4.
97. Kim, J.: Development of Regional Human Rights Regime: Prospects for and Implications to Asia. Available at: www.tokyofoundation.org/sylff/wp-content/uploads/2009/03/sylff_p57-1022.pdf

7 Interregionalism

7.1. Old and New Interregionalism

As we already mentioned, regional organizations are not being established in a vacuum, and despite not having stronger relations towards the international universal organizations (except for the UN Security Council under the UN Charter), this fact has never limited relations and cooperation between them.

There are also relationships being established among the subjects in various regions that can differ from regional organizations, and their intensity and form vary in different periods of development of regionalism.(within the concept of interregionalism). This is not a completely new phenomenon, since it emerged already with the first regional organizations in the second half of the 20th century as their associate element, and it has been growing into a general phenomenon within global international relations. There is no generally accepted definition of interregionalism in literature, and different writers have different definitions. The simplest definition says that interregionalism includes "regions mutually affecting each other",[1] while another says: "interregionalism relates to agreements made between two regionalisms . . .".[2]

The relations of interregionalism are carried out and developed within specific international forums (APEC, ASEM) which represent a certain novelty within international relations, since they are called for the purposes of interregional cooperation, and in the case of some of them we can already identify the features of a nascent institutionalism (e.g. in the form of permanent secretariats).

Both old interregionalism and new interregionalism have clearly differing features. Old interregionalism was typical for having a dominant position in the European Community (EC), which entered into relations of dialogue and cooperation both with the regional organizations and with the groups of states, or with individual states while maintaining its leading position of the most developed regional organization (*the hub and spokes model*). There were many characteristic features regarding the EC within the interregional relations at that time. The EC in its external relations took advantage of mainly interregional cooperation mechanisms as a means to make the integration relations stronger and advanced within other regional groups, to strengthen its own international position and, finally, to ensure international regional security, stability and prosperity outside their own borders. As an example, the relations between the EC and ASEAN began in 1978, resulting, after two years of meetings, with the signing by ministers of foreign affairs of the Cooperation Agreement in 1980—and, similarly, with the SAARC in 1985—though such cooperation was focused on trade and technical matters and without a political focus.

During the old regionalism period, interregional relations had seen developments between the regional groups mainly of a trade and economic nature without a relevant institutional basis. The development of interregional relations between political and security regional groupings was slowed down by being oriented internally as well as by the Cold War atmosphere.

After the Cold War ended and new regionalism started, the new interregionalism had more favourable conditions for its development, i.e. the removal of obstacles that had been created by the hegemonic policy of superpowers and enclosed blocks, a strict division of spheres of their influence, the closed character of regional organizations, etc.

The new interregionalism is typical for extending the geographical scope of its application, since new regional organizations start entering an interregional relationship in other parts of the world. Even though the EU[3] still plays an important role, the development of interregional relations with other regional organizations is enhanced also by the ASEAN in South-East Asia, MERCOSUR in Latin America, the Andean Community in Central America, GCC in the Persian Gulf and CER in Oceania. However, their contact and cooperation are sometimes of an *ad hoc* nature, with no serious efforts to make them regular and institutional and they have often a rather general agenda.

As it has been noted above, the current experience confirms that new regionalism produces new types and forms of relationships, not only within the regional organizations but among the other regional subjects, whose number and types grow, and that these relationships (though not on the same level) are becoming gradually institutionalized—a new phenomenon within international relations and international law.[4]

Because regional organizations from different parts of the world enter into interregional relationships, there is a trend to reflect the basic rules and principles that are typical for them. For this reason, the regional organizations in the developing world promote the rather flexible and informal character of their interregional relationships, with no detailed institutional structure and preferring informal consultations and exchanges of opinions. Such a trend can be identified in the South-East Asian countries which applied them to the interregional relations within APEC and ASEM. The EU approach is, however, typified by its attempts to formalize and institutionalize the interregional relations in reflecting their growing intensity and complexity. Regardless of the more or less flexible, or institutional form of interregional relations, the influential participants (especially the EU) use them to promote their own basic principles and values that they were built on in other regions (such as the rule of law, human rights, democracy and market economy). Such attempts can be observed in the treaty's interregionalism as well.

There are basically two reasons for new interregionalism starting so rapidly namely the development of a new regionalism after the Cold War and the globalization of international relations and economy. Since the beginning of the 1990s, literature has studied the new interregionalism both as a new phenomenon of international relations and as a new feature of the new regionalism. One of the basic issues of the research is the qualification of relations falling within the concept new interregionalism, its purpose and peculiarities. In summary, these relations can be divided into those that twin regional organizations in different regions, relations of regional organizations towards third states or a group of states in other regions as well as regional organizations participating directly or indirectly in other interregional structures.

As for a more detailed qualification of relations falling within the new interregionalism, the most quoted one is by H. Hänggi,[5] who divides it typologically into five groups according to participating subjects. The first group considers relations between a regional organization and a state from a different region (the quasi-interregional relations, or regionalism in a wider sense). The second group includes relations between regional organizations from different regions (interregionalism in a narrow sense). The third group deals with relations between a regional organization from one region with a regional group of states from the other (interregionalism in a narrow sense).[6] The fourth group includes relations between a regional group of states from one region and a regional group of states from the other region (interregionalism in a wider sense)[7] and finally group five concerns relations between groups of states from two or more regions (the megaregional relations, or interregionalism in a larger sense).[8] A common feature of these groups is that they reflect an uneven level of development of institutional regionalism in individual geographical areas, either in the form of a regional organization, regional group of states or a state from a different region, resulting in various possibilities or a combination of interregional relations.

In this respect we can talk also of multi-faceted regionalism, since the interregional relations are not restricted only to regional organizations and mutual relations between them (typical of the old interregionalism); yet there are more opportunities for the interregional relations to be established and developed also with a number of other subjects and with different agendas. Such an interregional approach might in practice represent an effective alternative to a bilateral system of relations among the states from different regions while not excluding its existence outside the scope of the agreed interregional agenda.

Regarding the first group, it reflects a situation in which a regional organization or a regional group of states exists in one region and is willing to enter into interregional relations with the interested state in the other region. Relations between such subjects cross the territorial scope of one region and are oriented to another region in the form of the quasi-interregional relation.[9] Their importance increases provided that the individual interested party is the state which has a dominant position in its region (e.g. the USA in South

America, India in South Asia).[10] Throughout the 1990s the relations among regional organizations and the third states in different regions increased significantly, becoming a significant part of new regionalism, with the EU and ASEAN, with long experience in this area, at the head of international organizations within this group.

New interregionalism, in a narrow sense, consists of relations among governmental regional organizations.[11] This second group of relations, typical for the old regionalism, also represents an important part of new interregionalism. It is worth noting that the EU and ASEAN also play an important role in this type of interregional relations, especially with respect to the relations of Western and Central Europe and East Asia.[12] Such relations are generally carried out through meetings held more or less regularly at the level of ministers, where common programmes and projects are drawn up and discussions are aimed at an exchange of information and cooperation within the agreed areas (mainly in economic areas including trade and investments). The EU is an exception in this respect, since it regularly requires a wider political agenda in the area of human rights and democracy. When regional organizations become involved in an interregional dialogue, there is a need for prior regional consultations and coordination of attitudes in order to work out common opinions so that the interregional dialogue is more transparent and there is closer cooperation.

The third group of the new interregionalism includes the interregional relations represented by various subjects. While it is the regional organization in one region, the other region is usually represented by a more or less coordinated group of states which want to enter into relations with a regional organization from another region. The establishment of such relations dates back to the beginning of the 1990s and is predominantly influenced by the EU in this group.

As an example of this group one can mention the EU-ASEM[13] relationship, which, however, offers no substitution for traditional bilateral relations between the European and Asian countries. Regular European-Asian summits in the form of multilateral conferences have been held every two years since 1996 by the heads of states, with discussions at the level of ministers, working groups of experts, etc. The basic principles that the meetings follow include: equal partnership, a multidimensional process of meeting, non-formality and promotion of mutual understanding. Experience proves that this type of interregionalism creates conditions suitable for fruitful dialogues between regions concerning current global issues and regardless of the fact that interregional partners are not identical. The ASEM provides the Asian side with real "regional" space in which the Asian states discuss and show interest in formulating common attitudes. They are based on informal discussions about specific issues (the *informal dialogue–based process*),[14] usually without having any formal or otherwise structured agenda.

Practice confirms that participating states regularly use such summits to promote their bilateral relations, where the intensity and content might differ from the official programme of the summit (e.g. states might give preference to current political and economic issues in their bilateral relations over the issues that are important globally). As a practical result, an interregional mechanism of this type might contribute informally to the development of bilateral relations among its members.[15] It should be added that two groups of non-governmental entities today form important parts of the EU-ASEM structure: the first group is the Asia-Europe Business Forum (AEBF),[16] a meeting of business leaders who met for the first time in 1996 and have acquired a strong position in the process of the ASEM interregional relations. The second group consists of non-governmental organizations from both regions which initiate and develop a mutual exchange of opinions among students, academics, journalists and young politicians. However, they have no official position in the ASEM process.

As a consequence, the first Common Asia-Europe meeting of non-governmental organizations[17] took place in 1996 along with the first ASEM summit. The ASEM shows that the interregional mechanism of this group is directly confronting the new global challenges and changing the international context. It is able to effectively connect the local, regional and international political and economic agendas and at the same time absorb the groups of subjects of a non-governmental nature concerned in both regions.[18] With respect to interregional relations between the EU and ASEAN, the ASEM represents a wider forum, enabling further development of their dialogue and creating space for a differential approach towards the European and Asian regions, as well as to third states. Most of the original agenda with respect to EU-ASEAN relations has been currently absorbed by the interregional process of the ASEM.

The fourth group of new interregionalism relates to regional groups of states from different regions. Unlike regional organizations, they are specific for being established for the purposes of participating actively within the interregional relations only.[19]

For example, the Europe–Latin America Rio Summit (1999), composed of 33 Latin American and Caribbean states on the one side and on the other the EU member states; then the Africa-Europe Cairo summit (2000), composed of 52 African states on the one side and the EU member states on the other; the East Asia–Latin America forum, composed of 13 East Asian states, Australia and New Zealand, as well as 12 Latin American countries. Their participation in interregional relations strengthens their regional identity based on common interest with no need to make formal institutionalization through regional organizations.

Finally, group five, consisting of relations between the states, group of states and regional organizations from two or more regions is also a reflection of a new interregionalism (megaregionalism).

Similarly to the new regionalism, the new interregionalism is not located evenly from the geographical point of view and it is concentrated in the Triad composed of North America, Western Europe and East Asia.[20] Each type of interregional relations we have mentioned is applied within this area (although not evenly regarding the scope and intensity), from quasi-interregionalism to megaregionalism. In addition, there are interregional relations outside the Triad which have been developed (especially through the EU and ASEAN), mainly in Latin America and Africa.

From the above we can imply that the new interregionalism as the *sui generis* phenomenon currently includes not only traditional relations between the regional organizations, but also other subjects of governmental and non-governmental character that are interested in interregional cooperation. It is at the same time a dynamic process depending on the changes occurring to the interregional relations (a group of states is replaced by the regional organization, or vice versa), and it currently forms a permanent part of international relations with prospects for future development.[21]

There is neither a uniform definition of interregionalism, nor uniform opinions regarding its functions. Sometimes interregionalism is referred to as an instrument to maintain balance among participants. Practice shows that the most powerful participants of the Triad use the interregional forums to maintain both mutual balance and balance with the states outside the Triad, provided that these states are able to compete with the dynamics of its development in the field of economy. It concerns mainly institutional and economic (not power) balance, the need of which depends on activities carried out by other interregional participants.

Examples suggest that NAFTA was established as a reaction to the establishment of the European common market. The relation developed between the EU and MERCOSUR represented a European reaction to the Free Trade Area of the Americas (FTAA). Reinforcing the relations between the MERCOSUR member states and Europe represented efforts to restrict the influence that America had within the southern hemisphere, etc. The system FEALAC (Forum for East Asia–Latin America Cooperation) represents efforts that Asian and Latin American members made to diversify their economic and political relations for purposes of catching up with the strong American and, partially, European influence. Australia joined the IOR-ARC because it failed to be accepted by the ASEM and India because it was excluded from the ASEM and APEC; the AEC (2015) represents a counterbalance in respect of the economic and commercial markets of China and India, etc.

Another segment of interregionalism includes a specific institutional element of interregional relations, since their existence requires more intensive cooperation among participants which is not possible (at a certain level) to provide *ad hoc*. However, current results within this area are not very distinctive. As was already mentioned, the idea of a stronger institutional structure of interregional relations is not generally accepted since the approach of the EU and regional groups in developing countries in this respect clearly differ. In a wider context we can, however, infer that if such organs or institutions become established, they contribute to the gradual institutional diversification of international law.

Another function of interregionalism is to build and reinforce the regional identity of its participants (ASEM, APEC). Practice confirms that such identity is formed mainly through different kinds of interregional dialogues at different levels which give grounds to common concepts of how the regional groups should work and develop relations among themselves, as well as form common attitudes towards global problems.

In this context interregionalism can be regarded as a useful process through which the regions represented by different subjects acknowledge and define or determine themselves as regional entities with respect to another region or regions.

Possibly the final function of interregionalism is the rational function. It is based on the fact that in the current multipolar world the interests of states within the global institutions (forums) currently differ, while the number of issues of technical character in their agenda is increasing. Such circumstances slow down the decision-making process, make it difficult for institutions to carry out their activities and, moreover, possibly decrease their legitimacy.

Interregional dialogue can enhance members' common attitudes with respect to global issues and thus negotiations at a global forum might be more efficient and easier.

In connection with the development of interregional relations, there is quite naturally a question arising about the role of international law with respect to the potential regulation of such relations. Further analysis of interregional relations will show that these relations are today regulated by international treaties (bilateral and multilateral) which the states and regional organizations conclude with respect to these issues. There have been no doubts[22] as to the treaty-making powers of the states. However, the treaty-making power of international organizations is neither automatic, nor general and they are expressly regulated in their constituent instruments. For a rather long period of time there had been no rules of general international law that would govern the different aspects of the process of international treaties concluded by international organizations. It was not until the latter half of the 1980s that the International Law Commission prepared the draft of the Convention on the Law of Treaties between States and International Organizations or between International Organizations of 1986[23] codifying the rules of existing practice of international organizations in this area.

Considering the qualification of interregional relations, the international treaty's regulation can be observed in the first "quasi-interregional group" in the form of treaties concluded between the international organization on the one side and the third state from another region on the other. International treaties are also found within the second and the third group, which means within the interregional relations between two regional organizations and between the regional organization and the states (group of states) from a different region. Because of the significant position of the EEC-EC-EU, which has been for a long time a leading player and initiator of interregional relations governed by international law, due attention shall be paid to the analysis and the benefits it brings for international law.

7.2. The EC-EU Interregional Treaties

The Treaty on the Functioning of the European Union, as amended by the Treaty of Lisbon (hereinafter as the TFEU) Article 216, stipulates that the

EU may conclude an agreement with one or more third countries or international organizations where the Treaties so provide or where the conclusion of an agreement is necessary in order to achieve, within the framework of the Union's policies, one of the objectives referred to in the Treaties, or is provided for in a legally binding Union act or is likely to affect common rules or alter the areas of their competences. The competence of the EU to conclude treaties is not unlimited, though, and the Union has competence when respecting the division of powers and its member states under the Article 3 et seq. TFEU. The TFEU Article 317 thereof also states that the EU may conclude with one or more countries' or international organizations' association agreements establishing an association involving reciprocal rights and obligations, common actions and special procedures. Their common aim is to create a legal and economic regime for cooperation between the third (non-member) states or the international organization and the EU.

The EU interprets the term third states in two ways. The first interpretation relates to the states "with a chance" to become EU members which have already applied for membership, but still fail to comply with conditions as required. The association agreements in such a sense anticipate their future membership.[24] In accordance with Article 49 TFEU, such association agreements may be concluded with only a limited number of states because only European states may apply for membership in the Union.

The second group includes the association agreements with third states whose objective is not membership in the EU, but which serve other purposes. They create a legal framework for cooperation of the EU with third countries within a specific area of mutual relations[25] or they serve to promote political and economic cooperation with the aim of creating a free trade zone, as well as ensuring conditions necessary for free trade with industrial goods, in the agricultural area and services, to enhance cooperation with respect to political, social, economic and cultural matters, and in the justice area.[26]

It should be pointed out that the EU's efforts to conclude these association agreements reflect, in virtue of Article 21 Section 1 TFEU, general principles that the EU complies with when carrying out its external policies and which it seeks to advance in the wider world. This concerns democracy, the rule of law, the universality and indivisibility of human rights and fundamental freedoms, respect for human dignity, the principles of equality and solidarity and respect for the principles of the UN Charter and international law. Under this Article, the Union seeks to have these values respected in the process of developing relations and building partnerships with third countries and international organizations, as a necessary condition in order to strengthen regionalism and regional cooperation and as one of the guarantees of international peace and security.

Another group of international treaties is envisaged by Article 198 of the TFEU, which determines the association of the overseas countries and territories having special relations with Denmark, France, the Netherlands and the United Kingdom. The purpose of their association with the EU is to promote their economic and social development and to establish close economic relations between them and the EU as a whole. Article 212 TFEU envisages the treaties related to economic, financial and technical cooperation with third countries other than the developing countries (the partnership agreements).[27] Additionally, Article 214 of the TFEU entitles the EU to conclude other treaties with third countries and international organizations in order to regulate humanitarian needs, technical assistance, etc.

The EU treaty practice also confirms the existence of various "combination" agreements, including the stabilization and association agreements with former Yugoslavian Republic of Macedonia (of 2004), with Albania (2007, 2009), Bosnia and Herzegovina (2008, 2010), as well as more concrete specialized treaties, i.e. on free trade with Norway, Ireland, Switzerland (all in 1973), on customs union with Andorra (in 1991), Turkey (in 1995) and San Marino (1992), etc.[28]

A brief excursion through EU treaty practice shows its diversification and orientation by means of which it establishes relations with third countries, taking into account their specificities but without prejudice to the fundamental principles that the EU and its external policy is governed by. Their application usually goes beyond the scope of trade or economic cooperation because the indivisible treaty condition determines respect for the rule of law, human rights and market economy, whereby the democracy of the legal environment is enhanced within third countries and which is the condition necessary not only to develop and stabilize economy, but also to strengthen the rule of law in a wider context of current international law. Summing up the practice of EU confirms its permanent efforts to cooperate with the integration process of developing countries through comprehensive agreements with third states and regional groupings which cover not just trade but also trade-related issues, development and political aspects.

Variation can also be observed in the case of the interregional treaties of the EU that belong to the second and the third groups, which are the treaties concluded with another regional organization or its member states or a group of states. They differ in terminology and the content of objectives in which they pursue. The name of the state parties suggests what entities (or to what extent) their constituent instruments are entitled to conclude such treaties. We can infer that the interregional treaties, where at least one of the parties is the regional organization, are essential for the purposes of developing external relations and confirm its capability to be a representative of its own rights within the international relations.

Cooperation Agreement Between Member Countries of ASEAN and the European Community—Kuala Lumpur of 1980[29]

The ASEAN was for the EC the first treaty partner in the area of interregional cooperation and their initial contact took place in the 1970s, with the Treaty on

Cooperation concluded in 1980. In wording and content the treaty reflects the beginning of cooperation and in its four brief articles specifies the cooperation between the contracting parties in the area of trade, economy and development together with the granting of the most favoured nation clause. According to its Preamble, the purpose of the Treaty is to develop international cooperation between the parties on the basis of freedom, equality and justice. Unlike further treaties, however, it includes neither the obligation to respect democracy and human rights nor political dialogue between parties. Similarly to other treaties, the Treaty does, however, contain an institutional segment represented by the Joint-Cooperation Committee (Article 8). Its main aim is to supervise compliance with the Treaty and make its fulfilment easier by state parties.

Cooperation Agreement Between the European Economic Community on the One Part and the Cartagena Agreement and the Member Countries Thereof—Bolivia, Colombia, Ecuador, Peru and Venezuela on the Other Part of 1983[30]

Even though the European Community in this treaty recognizes the Andean group of states as a developing region, the Cartagena Agreement (the Andean Pact) involves both the less developed and more developed countries (Article 2). This is, however, without prejudice to the development of mutual cooperation in the field of economy and trade and in the developing field in granting the most favoured nation clause and respecting the principles of equality, justice and advancement. According to Parties such cooperation strengthens regional organizations and increases economic growth, social and cultural development and represents a balancing factor in international relations. Specific cooperation is exercised by various means: mutual exchange of information, technical and financial aid, cooperation of developing programmes and projects, promotion of operators in individual areas by establishing the expert organs, etc. This Treaty also contains the institutional element represented by the Joint Cooperation Committee (Article 5) composed of the representatives of the European Economic Community[31] and the Cartagena Agreement. The Joint Cooperation Committee takes measures to ensure the efficiency of various forms of cooperation within agreed areas, and thus its fulfilment is easier. It can make recommendations (including settlements of disputes) and, when needed, establish specific sub-committees.

Framework Agreement Between the European Economic Community and the Cartagena Agreement and Its Member Countries, Namely Bolivia, Colombia, Ecuador, Peru and Venezuela on April 23, 1992[32]

Because the cooperation between the EEC and other contracting parties to the Cartagena Agreement was successful during the 1980s, its participants decided to prepare the next treaty on cooperation which would reflect the level achieved and provide conditions suitable for further development—the 1992 Framework Agreement between the EEC and the Cartagena Agreement and its member countries.

According to the Preamble, its principal purpose is to consolidate, deepen and diversify relations between the parties in various areas, in particular economy, trade and development. Unlike the Treaty of 1983, the scope of cooperation between the parties is now more comprehensive and structural as it covers industrial cooperation, investment cooperation, financial cooperation, science and technology cooperation, cooperation in the area of copyright and industrial property, the mining area, transport and telecommunication, tourism, environment (and others), while mutually granting the most favoured nation clause. The democratic basis of cooperation between the parties is extended (Article 1), based on respect for democratic principles and human rights which guide the domestic and international policies of both the EEC and the Andean Pact. Within the Framework Treaty, these principles constitute its essential component. In addition to more general areas and forms of cooperation, the Treaty also concerns practical measures, such as establishment of joint ventures, conclusion of licence agreements, technological and technical know-how transfer, technical and investment aid and others. This Treaty additionally contains an institutional element represented by the Joint Cooperation Committee set up in accordance with a previous agreement of 1983 with its specialized three sub-committees (Sub-committee on science and technology, Sub-committee on industrial cooperation and Sub-committee on trade cooperation).

Political Dialogue and Cooperation Agreement Between the European Community and Its Member States of the One Part and the Andean Community and Its Member Countries (Bolivia, Colombia, Ecuador, Peru and Venezuela) of the Other Part of 2003[33]

This agreement goes beyond the traditional orientation of interregional cooperation agreements as it is concentrated mainly on political cooperation between parties. The Treaty expressly confirms (Article 2) that its purpose is to govern the political dialogue and cooperation between the parties and it contains the necessary institutional arrangement for its application. Upon developing political dialogue and strengthening the cooperation, the parties seek to achieve a common objective of strengthening and deepening their relations in all fields constituting the subject matter, as well as other issues relating to their common interest (international security, regional development, human rights, corruption, illegal migration, combating terrorism and drug trade, money laundering and others). The parties mutually believe that the aim of the political dialogue is also a broad exchange of information and to provide the basis for common initiatives at an international level. Such political dialogue will be carried out at various levels, from the top level, to the head of states or prime ministers, ministerial level and to the cooperation at a level of working groups through diplomatic channels. This political dialogue between the parties shall be based on respect for democratic principles and fundamental human rights, as laid down in the Universal Declaration of Human Rights, which governs both domestic and international policy of the parties and within the Treaty constitute its essential component. The Political Dialogue and Cooperation agreement also contains an institutional element, referring to previous agreements of 1983 and 1993 which established (and later approved) the existence of the Joint Committee. The subject matter shall be agreed by the parties and in accordance with the agreement (Article 52) it shall be responsible for its proper application. A Joint Consultative Committee shall assist to promote dialogue with economic and social organizations of civil society of state parties. The parties encourage the European Parliament and the Andean Parliament to establish an Inter-Parliamentary Committee.

Interregional Framework Cooperation Agreement Between the European Community and Its Member States of the One Part and the Southern Common Market and Its Party States of the Other Part[34]

The next agreement is the 1995 Interregional Framework Cooperation Agreement between the European Community and its Member States on the one side, and the Southern Common Market and its Party States, on the other. Whereas the European party is identified easily, the Latin American party comprises of states which signed the Agreement on common market, known generally as the MERCOSUR,[35] in Asunción in 1991. A specific article of the Framework Agreement (Article 2—Definition of the Parties) defines that the Parties shall mean the Community or its Member States or the Community and its Member States (subject to competences referred to in the treaty on establishment of the European Community) on one side and the MERCOSUR, or its state parties in accordance with the Treaty on establishment of the MERCOSUR on the other. Unlike the above-mentioned agreements on cooperation, the Framework Agreement is more ambitious as the objectives defined therein are not only to strengthen relations and cooperation between the parties, but also to prepare conditions enabling the creation of an interregional association between the Parties (Article 2 Section 1). The Preamble of the Framework Agreement and Article 2 further define that it should cover political and economic interregional association based on political cooperation and diversification of common trade in order to prepare its gradual and reciprocal liberalization, taking account of the sensitivity of certain goods. The cooperation between the Parties in the fields of trade and economy, integration matters and other common areas of interest shall ensure the achievement of this objective.

A specific element of the Framework Agreement is the system of political dialogue between the parties that would progress towards the conditions necessary for an interregional association. In accordance with Article 3 of the Framework agreement, the dialogue should be regular and its particulars are defined in the Joint Declaration on Political Dialogue between the EU and MERCOSUR, constituting the Annex thereto.[36] It specifies that the political dialogue shall concern both regional and multilateral matters, where the latter might result in the coordination of the Parties' approaches within the multilateral international organizations. The political dialogue shall also include mutual contacts between the representatives of the parties (at various levels), exchange of information, etc. Regular meetings shall be held either between the heads of states, MERCOSUR parties and EU high representatives. Annual meetings of the ministers for foreign affairs or of other ministers shall be held as deemed necessary by the Parties. A significant part of the Framework Agreement consists of provisions governing cooperation in the fields of trade and economy, e.g. agriculture and industry, customs matters, intellectual property, entrepreneurship, investment, transport, energy, science and technology, telecommunication, information technology, environmental protection and others.

Article 1 of the Framework Agreement provides for the respect for the democratic principles and fundamental human rights laid down in the Universal Declaration of Human Rights, which inspires the domestic and external policies of the Parties and within the agreement constitutes its essential element.

Similarly to previous agreements, the Framework Agreement between the EC and MERCOSUR also contains an institutional element represented by the Cooperation Council creating a forum for political dialogue and responsible for its proper application. The agenda of its meeting might be any issue relating to the Agreement or bilateral or multilateral issues that the Parties are interested in. The Cooperation Council is composed of members of the European Union and of members of the European Commission, on the one hand, and members of the MERCOSUR Council and members of the MERCOSUR Market Group, on the other. In addition, the Framework Agreement sets up the Joint Cooperation Committee that assists the Cooperation Council in the execution of its tasks and deals with the agenda agreed in advance either in Brussels or in any other MERCOSUR party. Its activities are aimed at consultations and preparation of measures to liberalize trade, including future programmes for cooperation, exchange of views on such matters and preparation of proposals and recommendations. The Parties shall also set up a Joint Subcommittee on Trade to ensure implementation of measures related to trade.[37]

In addition, the EC signed the Cooperation Agreement with the states of the Gulf,[38] the Free Trade Agreement (FTA) with the Overseas Countries and Territories,[39] etc.

Partnership Agreement Between the Members of the African, Caribbean and Pacific Group of States on the One Part and the European Community and Its Member States on the Other (The Cotonou Agreement)[40]

This Partnership Agreement geographically covers the widest scope, with over 100 contracting parties and a total population of around 1.5 billion people. It regulates partnership relations between the European Community and its member states and the group of states from three different geographical areas. According to the Preamble, its purpose is to strengthen partnerships between the parties based on political dialogue, development of cooperation and economic and trade relations. Article 1 stipulates that it aims at making economic, cultural and social development within African, Caribbean and Pacific groups of states (ACP countries) deeper and faster, with a view to contributing to peace and security and a stable and democratic environment. In accordance with the Agreement, the partnership assumes the creation and exercising of agreed cooperation programmes not only through official representatives of parties, but also through parliaments in ACP countries, regional organizations, the African Union, local and decentralized organs at a national and regional level, representatives from the private sector, economic and social partners, non-governmental organizations or other representatives from civil society. Such cooperation shall be exercised on the principles of equality between the partners, availability to parliaments and local authorities of ACP countries, while the agreed cooperation programmes shall adapt to a level of development achieved in a particular area, with special reference to regional integration (Article 2).

The objective of political dialogue between the parties (Article 8) is to foster mutual understanding and cooperation through exchange of information and consultations. Political dialogue is aimed not only at treaty priorities and programmes, but also at any other matters of general or regional interest, including the issues of regional integration. Through dialogue, the parties shall contribute to peace, security and stability and promote a democratic political environment. In addition to general matters, the Agreement assumes that objectives of political dialogue shall include also specific issues of international policy such as traffic in arms, organized crime, combating drugs, children's rights, discrimination of any nature, etc. As regards to its institutional structure, the process of dialogue assumes the participation not only of official representatives of the parties, but also regional organizations, civil society representatives and the ACP countries' parliaments. The cooperation between the parties in the fields covered by political dialogue and development, trade and economic cooperation shall be based on the respect for human rights, democratic principles and the rule of law which promote partnership between the parties and are a part of their internal and foreign policies, while constituting an essential element of the Partnership Agreement.

The institutional structure of the Partnership Agreement (part two of the Agreement) comprises the Council of Ministers, Committee of Ambassadors and Joint Parliamentary Assembly. In addition to these bodies having more or less general competences, the Joint Ministerial Trade Committee of a specialized nature has been established, too. When necessary, the parties can meet at the level of the heads of states. The Council of Ministers arranges political dialogues and meets regularly once a year, while the representatives of economic and social partners and other civil society representatives may attend it too. For such a purpose, their negotiations shall take place parallel to the official political dialogue of state parties. The Council of Ministers shall notify the Joint Parliamentary Assembly of any decisions, recommendations and views they have adopted in its report.

The Committee of Ambassadors comprises permanent representatives of the EU states and the heads of missions of ACP states to the EU. Its main aim is to assist the Council of Ministers in the fulfilment of its tasks, including monitoring implementation of the Agreement and progress achieved in the process of exercising the Agreement.

The Joint Parliamentary Assembly is a consultative body, composed of equal number of members of the European Parliament, on the one hand, and members of parliaments designated by the ACP states on the other. Its main objective is to promote democratic processes through dialogue and consultation, facilitate understanding between the peoples of the EU and those of the ACP states, discuss annual reports of the Committee of Ministers on implementation of the Agreement and adopt resolutions and make recommendations to the Committee of Ministers with a view to achieving the objectives of the Agreement. The Joint Parliamentary Assembly shall meet twice a year in plenary sessions, alternating between the EU and an ACP state. Because in February 2020 the Cotonou Agreement will expire, the European Union already elaborated working material dealing with the perspective of the new partnership relations of the EU with ACP countries after 2020. Assuming that a new partnership will be confirmed within a legally binding agreement, a partnership consisting of three distinct regional partnerships with Africa, the Caribbean and Asia Pacific under a common umbrella is proposed with an opening for closer involvement of other countries. This umbrella would define the common values, principles and essential elements that underpin the cooperation between state parties, building on the significant *acquis* of the ACP. The new partnership should remain flexible and able to adapt to its own progress and the ever-changing environment. The following fundamental principles have been identified for the proposed new partnership project: dialogue, mutual accountability, broad participation of state and non-state actors and ownership.[41]

Agreement Establishing an Association Between Central America on the One Hand and the EU and Its Member States on the Other[42]

So far the highest level of interregional legislation is represented, undoubtedly, by the Agreement establishing an association between Central America, on the one hand, and the EU and its member states on the other, which laid down the strongest institutional and substantial tie between the EU and Central American partners. A number of other agreements, however, preceded the conclusion of the Association agreement in order to prepare suitable political and administrative conditions necessary for the conclusion thereof.[43]

Similarly to previous agreements, a specific provision (Article 352) defines the parties, with in the case of Central America: Costa Rica, El Salvador, Guatemala, Honduras, Nicaragua and Panama, on the one hand; and on the other, the EU or its member states, within their respective areas of competence determined by EU primary law. The objectives of the Agreement are to strengthen and consolidate the relations between the parties through a bi-regional association based on mutual and common principles, namely political dialogue, development and trade, mutual respect, reciprocity and common interests.

The objective of political dialogue is to create a privileged political partnership based on the respect for democracy, peace, human rights, rule of law and sustainability of development under current protection of common values and objectives embodied in the UN Charter.

The means of political dialogue are based on an exchange of views and information leading to joint initiatives of the parties at international level, with the subject matter of dialogue including any issues of common interest either at the regional or international level. In particular: disarmament, ban on weapons of mass destruction, fight against terrorism and other crimes breaching international law. The priority of political dialogue is to strengthen international peace and security, promote and stabilize democratic institutions, respect human rights and fundamental freedoms and the rule of law, promote sustainable economic development, deepen the process of regional integration in Central America and its economic and social development.

Regarding trade relations, the parties establish a free trade area in accordance with the GATT Rules of 1994. Other objectives in the field of trade include the expansion and diversification of trade in goods through the reduction or the elimination of tariff or non-tariff barriers to trade, liberalization of trade in services, facilitation of trade in goods through the agreed customs rules and tariffs, technical standards and measures, as well as sanitary and phytosanitary provisions, effective protection of intellectual property, establishment of an effective and predictable dispute settlement mechanism, etc. According to state parties, these general provisions shall be further specified in the Agreement and in XXI technical annexes.

Pursuant to Article 1 of the Agreement, the cooperation within the agreed areas shall be based on the respect for democratic principles and fundamental human rights as laid down in the Universal Declaration of Human Rights, guiding the internal and international policies of the parties and constituting an essential element of the Agreement.

The structure of the institutional segment corresponds to the level and complexity of the Agreement. It comprises the Association Council, charged with the control of the fulfilment of the Agreement objectives and supervising their practical implementation. This body meets at ministerial level at regular intervals, not exceeding a period of two years, and extraordinarily whenever circumstances so require (Article 4). Upon agreement by the parties, the Association Council may take decisions and recommendations. The Association Committee shall assist the Association Council and shall be responsible for the general implementation of the Agreement, where for this purpose it can set up special sub-committees.

The Association Parliamentary Committee is an organ composed of members of the European Parliament on the one side and of the Central America Parliament (PARLACEN) on the other. Its main task is to be a common forum for exchanging views regarding the implementation of the Agreement or any other current issues. The outcome of its negotiations are recommendations, submitted to the Association Council. There is also a Joint Consultative Committee which is a consultative body of the Association Council. Its main role is to submit opinions and positions of civil society representatives to the Association Council regarding the implementation of the Agreement and to promote dialogue and cooperation between the organizations of civil society in the EU and those in Central America.

7.3. Treaty Interregionalism and International Law

Despite limited analysis of interregional EC-EU agreements with other regional groupings, as well as their member states and/or other state parties, some partial conclusions concerning their relevance for international law can be drawn. First of all, the different scope and level of these agreements, the institutional variety and uneven complexity of the subject matter of regulation should be pointed out, as they differ in areas with respect to relations with individual regional groups and reflect the acquired level of mutual relationships and willingness of the parties to regulate such relationships by means of international treaties. In this respect one can speak about a certain individualization forming an inherent feature of the current interregionalism treaties. Depending on development, the interregional agreements reflect various stages of cooperation reached between their parties (e.g. EC-Cartagena Agreements).

Another common feature these agreements have is the institutional aspect, where those having a more complex character (association agreements, partnership agreements) have obviously a more complex institutional structure comprising a combination of bodies with general competence (various Joint Committees) along with the specialized bodies of expert nature. More or less developed and specialized interregional institutional structures of general and specialized natures allow one to describe the current interregionalism as the institutional one.

Although the international agreements the EC-EU concluded within the framework of its interregional relations regulate especially various types and forms of trade, economic and development cooperation, their contribution to general international law is apparent and undoubted. It is based especially on the fact that the essential element of such treaties represents the obligation of their parties to respect the democratic principles of general international law and fundamental human rights and freedoms (obviously with reference to the Universal Declaration of Human Rights), as well as the rule of law, and that the internal and external policies of the parties should be based on the latter.[44] Taking into account the significant and sometimes dominant position of the EU within such relations, it seeks to ensure that the general values and principles of international law will be observed also within its interregional relations with third countries, their groups, as well as with international regional organizations in various parts of the world. In the context of treaty interregionalism, the respect for these principles and values of international law forms the basis and essential assumption for purposes of successful cooperation between the parties in their interregional relations.[45] Monitoring and ensuring that the interregional agreements are complied with in the process of their practical application is enhanced by the institutional structure of treaties, political dialogue between the parties and the agreed consultations regime. Unlike the sanction systems of regional organizations, they are, however, lacking within the structure of interregional agreements.

Another contribution of interregional agreements to general international law is represented by the system of the political dialogue of their state parties where its scope regularly exceeds the interregional trade and economic framework of cooperation between the parties. Treaty provisions dealing with its various aspects today form an inherent part of the external treaties of the EU. Its importance is underlined by specific agreements concerning only political dialogue (i.e. agreements with the Andean Community and Central America).[46] Successful political dialogue might result in the coordination of positions eventually formulating joint proposals of the state parties of interregional agreements at global summits or important international conferences, within the UN, the World Trade Organization or any other international organization.

As a result, treaty interregionalism, through its political dialogue system, is able to make proposals or recommendation in order to deal with global issues of the contemporary world within international conferences or the universal international organizations.

With regards to the contribution of interregionalism to the democratization of general international law, it should be pointed out that the entities aimed at exercising different interregional relations are not restricted to representative bodies of regional organizations or to the official organs of states. They tend to involve other structures and entities, such as associations of civil society representatives, business and entrepreneurs associations, social and trade union partners and non-governmental organizations in the interregional and politic dialogue where their own views, positions or recommendations can be formulated. The aforesaid is relevant not only with respect to the development of interregional relations itself, but that the developing countries apply those provisions to strengthen the legitimacy and importance of these entities within their civil society and in a wider context, their democratic (multidimensional) environment, too.

Summing up, the existing agreements mapping various levels of interregional relations and establishing various forms of cooperation between their parties play two roles. The first is their real regulative function with respect to the agreed subject matters of their cooperation. The second of these agreements represents a certain "pattern" for those regional groups or other regional subjects wishing to build their interregional relations on the basis of international law.

Finally within the wider context of international law of treaties, current treaty interregionalism comprises a set of international treaties with regularly mixed nature of their parties (states and international organizations) when the rules of international law may by applied within the process of their preparation and legal existence.[47]

Notes

1. Gilson, J.: New Interregionalism? The EU and East Asia. In: *Journal of European Integration*, Vol. 27, No. 3, 2005, p. 309.
2. Reiterer, M.: Interregionalism as a New Diplomatic Tool: The EU and East Asia. In: *European Foreign Affairs Review*, Vol. 11, 2006, p. 223.
3. See at least Teló, M.: *European Union and New Regionalism: Regional Actors and Global Governance in a Post-Hegemonic Era*. Aldershot: Ashgate Publishing, 2007, 406 p.

   Warleigh-Lack, A.W., Robinson, N., Rosamond, B. (eds.): *New Regionalism and the European Union: Dialogues, Comparisons and New Research Directions*. London: Routledge, 2011, p. 297.
4. The more or less institutional relations arising within the new interregionalism are sometimes called as transregionalism. Valle, V.M.: Interregionalism: A Case Study of the European Union and Mercosur. In: *GARNET Working Paper*, No. 51, 2008, p. 6.
5. Hänggi, H.: Interregionalism as a Multifaceted Phenomenon (In Search of a Typology). In: Hänggi, H., Roloff, R., Rüland, J. (eds.): *Interregionalism and International Relations*. London and New York: Routledge, 2006, pp. 31–61.
6. For instance with respect to ASEM, there is the EU on the one side, while the "Asian side" includes a group consisting of the ASEAN and also the ASEAN+3, which means the other states (China, Japan and South Korea), as well as other three members of the SAARC (India, Pakistan, Mongolia). As a consequence, the ASEM includes in total two regional organizations (EU, ASEAN), plus the Asian regional group (the ASEAN+3+3).
7. For instance the FEALAC (Forum for East Asia-Latin America Cooperation).
8. An example of such megaregion is the "transpacific" APEC consisting of almost all the member states of the NAFTA, state parties with Australia–New Zealand Closer Economic Relations Trade Agreement (CER), ASEAN and "ASIA-10" group and two South American states (Chile and Peru). In practice, there is interregional connection being established between South America, East Asia and Pacific space. Unlike other interregional mechanisms, the APEC has a small secretariat based in Singapore.
9. As an example of this type of interregionalism we can give the relations between the EU and Mexico, Chile, China, Japan, India, USA and Canada.

The ASEAN has such relations with China, Japan, South Korea, USA, Canada, Australia and New Zealand.

10. Since 2013 the official negotiations between the EU and the USA have started in order to prepare the Transatlantic Trade and Investment Parthership (TTIP).
11. For example, the EU-MERCOSUR, EU-ASEAN, EU-Andean Community, EU-SADC, ASEAN-SARC, ASEAN-MERCOSUR, ASEAN-CER, ASEAN-Rio Group, CER-MERCOSUR.
12. The first summit of the EU-ASEAN was held in 1978.
13. Literature concerns: " . . . Asia-Europe Meeting . . . as one of the most advanced and original examples of inter-regionalism". See: Mols, M.: Cooperation With ASEAN: A Success Story. In: Edwards, G., Regelsberger, E. (eds.): *Europe's Global Links: The European Community and Inter-Regional Cooperation*. London: Pinter Publishers, 1990, pp. 143–160.
14. The object of discussion held up to now was, for example, the UN reform, ban on weapons of mass destruction, international terrorism, illegal migration, problems related to the World Trade Organization, etc.
15. ASEM has neither its own secretariat nor seat, and summits alternate between Asia and Europe. Ministers of foreign affairs are in charge of summits, assisted by informal coordination group composed of two Asian and two European representatives.
16. Asia-Europe Business Forum.
17. Joint Asia-Europe NGO Conference 1996.
18. As stated by H.W. Maull and N. Okfen: "ASEM has developed into a complex process of cooperation involving governments (at the level of leaders, ministers and senior officials) business and societies in the broad variety of activities, from summit meeting to seminars and workshops". See: Maull, H.W., Okfen, N.: Comparing Interregionalism: The Asia-Pacific Economic Cooperation (APEC) and the Asia-Europe Meeting (ASEM). In: Hänggi, H., Roloff, R., Rüland, J. (eds.): *Interregionalism and International Relations*. London and New York: Routledge, 2006, p. 221.
19. For example, the group of African states consists of member states of the former Organization of African plus Morocco and Cairo summit; the Asia group of states consists of the ASEAN member states plus three partner states of North-East Asia dialogue; the member states of the Rio group and Caribbean community in the case of Latin America states, etc.
20. Three-quarters of trade are produced in areas within these regions and around 90 percent of direct foreign investments are concentrated there.
21. As stated by H. Hänggi: ". . . interregionalism appears to have become a lasting feature of the international system. It may be expected that a wide array of forms and types of interrregionalism will continue to coexist thereby further enriching (and complicating) the emerging multi-layered system of global governance". In Hänggi, H.: Interregionalism: Empirical and Theoretical Perspectives. Paper Prepared for the Workshop: *Dollars, Democracy and Trade: External Influence on Economic Integration in Americas*. Los Angeles, May 18, 2000, p. 13. Available at: www.cap.lmu.de/transatlantic/download/Haenggi.PDF
22. Article l Sec. 1 of the Vienna Convention on the Law of Treaties of 1969 states that: "Each state is capable to conclude treaties". Available at: https://treaties.un.org/doc/publication/unts/volume%201155/volume-1155-i-18232-english.pdf
23. Article 6 of the Convention of 1986 states that the capacity of international organizations to conclude treaties is governed by the rules of that organization.

Available at: http://legal.un.org/ilc/texts/instruments/english/conventions/1_2_1986.pdf

24. For instance, the Association agreement with Greece in 1961, the Association agreement with Turkey in 1963, or the European agreements on association concluded with 10 countries in the 1990s. The Preamble of the Association agreement with Slovakia of 1993 states that: ". . . a final aim of the Slovak Republic is its accession to the Community" and this accession ". . . shall help the Slovak Republic achieve this objective".
25. For instance the Sector Agreement on Cooperation with Switzerland.
26. For example the Association Agreements with Tunisia (1998), Algeria (2005), Morocco (2000), Egypt (2004), Israel (2000), Syria (1977), Jordan (2002), Chile (2002, 2005), Lebanon (2003).
27. Agreements of such character that have recently been concluded include the ones with the CARIFORUM countries (Antigua, Granada, Haiti, Jamaica, Dominican Republic, Barbados, Bahamas (2009); Ivory Coast (2009); Cameroon (2009)).
28. To make the picture complete it should be pointed out that the formalized interregional relations between the EC-EU existed not only in the form of international treaties. The exception which proves the rule is the Joint Declaration on the establishment of official relations between the European Economic Community and the Council for the Mutual Economic Assistance on June 25, 1988.
29. Cooperation Agreement Between Member Countries of ASEAN and European Community, Kuala Lumpur, March 7, 1980. Available at: http://ec.europa.eu/world/agreements/SummartOfTreatyAction.do?step=0&treatyId=373
30. Cooperation Agreement Between the European Economic Community of the One Part and the Cartagena Agreement and the Member Countries Thereof—Bolivia, Colombia, Ecuador, Peru and Venezuela of the Other Part on December 17, 1983. In: *Official Journal of EC*, L 157, June 24, 1988.
31. The Community is within the common committee represented by the European Commission with representatives from the member states—Article 3 Council Regulation (EEC) No 1591/84 of June 4, 1984 concerning the conclusion Cooperation Agreement between the European Economic Community of the one part and the Cartagena Agreement and the member countries thereof—Bolivia, Colombia, Ecuador, Peru and Venezuela, of the other part on December 17, 1983.
32. Framework Agreement on Cooperation Between the European Economic Community and the Cartagena Agreement and Its Member Countries, Namely the Republic of Bolivia, the Republic of Colombia, the Republic of Ecuador, the Republic of Peru and the Republic of Venezuela on April 23, 1992. Available at: http://ec.europa.eu/world/agreements/downloadFile.do?fullText=yes&treatyTransId=864
33. Political Dialogue and Cooperation Agreement Between the European Community and Its Member States of the One Part, and the Andean Community and Its Member Countries (Bolivia, Colombia, Ecuador, Peru and Venezuela) of the Other Part on December 15, 2003. Available at: http://eur-lex.europa.eu/legal-content/EN/TXT/?uri=CELEX:52003PC0695(01)
34. Interregional Framework Cooperation Agreement Between the European Community and Its Member States, of the One Part and the Southern Common Market and Its Party States of the Other Part on December 15, 1995. Available at: www.sice.oas.org/TPD/MER_EU/negotiations/Framework1995_e.pdf
35. It Includes Argentina, Brazil, Paraguay, Uruguay.
36. Joint Declaration on Political Dialogue Between the European Union and Mercosur. Available at: www.sice.oas.org/TPD/MER_EU/negotiations/ministerial_october2004_e.pdf

37. The heretofore negotiations, however, confirm that the preparation of interregional association is not an easy process. Even though the Cooperation Council started negotiations in 1999, the negotiations were suspended in 2004 without any preliminary agreement and although "revitalized" in 2010, so far have not reached any significant results.
38. Cooperation Agreement Between the European Community and Its Members States and the States of the Gulf 1988. Available at: http://trade.ec.europa.eu/doclib/docs/2008/september/tradoc_140300.pdf
39. Free Trade Agreement Between the European Community and the Overseas Countries and Territories.
40. Partnership Agreement Between the Members of the African, Caribbean and Pacific Group of States of the One Part and the European Community and Its Member States on the Other Part on June 23, 2000 (Cotonou Agreement), Revised in Luxembourg on June 25, 1995 and Ouagadougou on June 22, 2010. Available at: https://ec.europa.eu/europeaid/sites/devco/files/cotonou-agreement-2000_en.pdf
41. For more details see: EC-Joint Communication to the European Parliament and the Council (a renewed partnership with the Countries of Africa, the Caribbean and the Pacific), Doc.JOIN (216), Final, pp. 25–26.
42. Agreement Establishing an Association Between Central America on the One Part and the EU and Its Member States on the Other Part on June 29, 2012. Available at: http://eur-lex.europa.eu/legal-content/en/TXT/PDF/?uri=CELEX:22012A1215(01)&rid=1
43. In particular it includes the Cooperation Agreement of 1985, the Framework Cooperation Agreement of 1993, the Political Dialogue and Cooperation Agreement of 2003. The last one was, however, replaced by the Association Agreement of 2012.
44. The specification in this area is the Association Agreement between the EU and Central America, which, for purposes of the regulation of interregional relations, brings (Article 1 Section 3) its own definition of the "rule of law": "entailing in particular the primacy of law, the separation of powers, the independence of judiciary, clear decision making procedure at the level of public authorities, transparent and accountable institutions, the good and transparent management of public affairs at local, regional and national levels and the implementation of measures aiming, preventing and combating corruption". Available at: http://eur-lex.europa.eu/legal-content/en/TXT/PDF/?uri=CELEX:22012A1215(01)&rid=1
45. Another specific impact of treaty interregionalism concerns the institutional structure of regional organizations. It should be pointed out that the regional organizations in the developing world more or less complete their institutional structure and adapt it to a certain extent to the EU structure, also for the purposes of their active participation in the process of exercising of the interregional agreements. For example, the MERCOSUR set up a Commission of permanent representatives and the MERCOSUR Parliament, Andean Community (elected directly), the Andean Parliament, Andean Council of Ministers, Court of Justice of the Andean Community, ASEAN Council, Permanent Representatives Committee, Secretariat, Secretary General, etc.
46. Political dialogue is dominant also within relations of the EU with other subregional organizations, such as the Caribbean Community (CARICOM), and the Rio Group (since 1990).
47. Vienna Convention on the Law of Treaties Between States and International Organizations or Between International Organizations of March 1986 (A/Conf.129/15). Available at: http://untreaty.un.org/cod/avl/pdf/ha/vcltsio/vcltsio-e.pdf

8 Relation of Regionalism and Regional Organizations With Respect to General International Law

8.1. Regional Rules as Confirmation and Development of International Law

Historically, regional organizations were not established inside an international legal vacuum, but in the background of general international law which in the course of the 20th century was expanding and specializing as a consequence of the changing needs of the international community. During such development, the regional organizations came across certain relations and contacts with general international law, despite having a different scope and intensity in individual areas and periods. The aforementioned applies mainly to regional treaty-making because their legal rules might have had a larger or smaller impact on general international law, too; this was because general international law has no rule restricting the scope and content of regional law-making to matters related only to the regional organization and the subject of its activities. Similarly, the process and the law-making of general rules of international law does not exclude that the originally regional rule might be at the beginning of the process of the rise of rule of general international law provided that the wider international community of states regards it useful. As a result, the regional international treaties adopted might not only confirm or develop the rules of general international law[1] but they might act as initiators to start the process of general international law rules. If the originally regional norms and institutes of regional law overlap into general international law, they lose their regional character and can be regarded as a regional contribution for the purposes of development of general international law.

It is, therefore, possible that regional rules might gain the character of general rules in the future, provided that their content reflects not only the particularity and specification of regional relations but also that the scope and application within the international group is wider.[2] Non-regional members can "become familiar" with them through a customary or treaty way.

The treaty-making activities of the regional organization might therefore result in making international treaties available also to third states and these treaties might become (with regard to its purpose and content) the ground for a multilateral treaty instrument.[3]

To sum up, through their law-making regional organizations are able to contribute to the confirmation of general international rules, to the development among the parties of the regional treaty or serve as a trigger to create a new rule of international law. They, however, do not substitute the system of general international law and each regional treaty system has to be interpreted fully in accordance with the principles of general international law.[4]

The aforesaid is not to the detriment of the "*soft law*" rules, which are accepted and applied more and more frequently within the regional organizations (recommendations, resolutions, opinions, codes of conduct, etc.) and which, despite having a legally unbinding character, may have a real impact on the conduct of the member states of the regional organization. This impact is apparent when these rules have been adopted in a transparent and democratic way and when their content is useful, practical and needed for the proper functioning of the organization. Such soft rules are currently recognized not only as useful for the organization itself, but they can play a role in the process of formation of regional treaties and customary rules. It is appropriate to add that international organizations are to a limited extent also subject to internal legal orders of their "host" states to such a scope and manner as compatible with their privileges and immunities.

Finally, the international organizations may have an impact on the formation and development of customary international law. One can note in this respect that membership of states either in a regional or universal organization does not limit their right to participate in the process of the formation of regional or universal customary law. The legal writing also confirms that: "These measures of international organizations can help to reduce the time consuming process of the formation of customary rules"[5] because: "In the contemporary age of highly developed techniques of communication and information, the formation of a custom through the medium of international organizations is greatly facilitated and accelerated . . ".[6] The ICJ in its advisory opinion on the Legality of the Threat or use of Nuclear Weapons f.e. clarified the contribution of the UN principal organ for the formation of customary rule stating that: "General Assembly resolutions . . . can in certain circumstances provide evidence important for establishing the existence of rule or the emergence of an opinion iuris. Or a series of resolutions may show the gradual evolution of the opinion iuris required for the establishment of new rule".[7] The aforesaid proves that today there are no strict dividing lines between the regional legal systems and general international law.

8.2. The Rules of General International Law Governing Activities of International Organizations

The dynamic growth of international organizations, followed by the extension and specialization of their competences in the post-war period, made their rules cease to be sufficient enough to regulate all aspects of their activities. As a result, they started to be completed within the rules of general international law in the second half of the last century. Therefore, the complex legal basis of regional organizations currently consists of not only their constituent acts, their own legal orders, but also of the rules of general international law.[8]

The International Law Commission (the "Commission") was charged with the task of elaborating the drafts of the codification conventions in the 1970s and 1980s regulating the specific activities of the international organizations and their relations with states.[9] These did not concern specific issues of individual international organizations, but activities common to international organizations regardless of their different orientation and number of member states (universal, regional). Including the codification matters related to international organizations in the working programme of the Commission did not represent a problem since the aim, according to its Statute, is to promote the progressive development of international law and its codification, and the Commission is entitled to carry out this function both in the field of public international law and private international law (Article 1 Sections 1 and 2 of the Statute of the International Law Commission).[10] In this context it should be therefore noted that the development of international organizations gradually resulted in the number and scope of legal problems arising out of their relations between organizations and states and between international organizations, and these problems had only partially been solved by the "traditional" interstate codification treaties. This was a point of departure for involving the international organizations in codification procedures.

Because the codification and the progressive development of international law is not confined to specific entities of international law (e.g. only states versus states), the subject matter of the Commission's activities might also include the specific rules applied among states and international organizations for purposes of their codification and/or progressive development. Analysing various codification outputs of the Commission implies that various types of international organizations' activities were not carried out to the same extent, because in some of them they constitute only a smaller part of legal regulation (with the states still playing the significant role) while in others it concerns the outputs that deal mainly with international organizations.

As with the codification topics related to the states, the international organizations also comprise the element of international law codification and its progressive development to a different degree. Although some codification drafts could have been based on the long and more or less stable practice of international organizations, emphasizing their codification aspect (representation of states in international organizations, conclusion of international treaties between the international organizations and the states or the international organizations themselves), the regulation of a further topic was based on relatively weak practice (the responsibility of international organizations for international unlawful acts). The codification outputs carried out by the Commission up to now include four international conventions, one draft of articles and one Guide to Practice on Reservations to Treaties. These are: the Vienna Convention on the Law of Treaties of 1969, the Vienna Convention on the Representation of States in their Relations with International Organizations of a Universal Character of 1975, the Vienna Convention on Succession of States in respect of Treaties of 1978, the Vienna Convention on the Law of Treaties between States and International Organizations or between International Organizations of 1986, the Draft Articles on the Responsibility of International Organizations of 2011 and the Guide to Practice on Reservations to Treaties of 2011.

The fact that the codification of these topics related to international organizations took place after similar topics had been completed in relations between states was relevant for the orientation of the Commission's work relating to international organizations. The results of the Commission's work prove that preparation of some codification drafts was more or less inspired by its previous works in the interstate topic e.g. within the preparation of the Vienna Convention on the Law of Treaties between States and International Organizations or between International Organizations of 1986[11] or the Draft Articles on the Responsibility of International Organizations of 2011.

The outcome of the Commission's work was the unified rules of international law, despite the diversity and different nature of international organizations. As a result, the organizations' rules apply only to a limited extent, and in cases expressly set forth in the codification convention and, unless provided otherwise, all other issues are regulated by the codified rules. To be more concrete, the privileged position of the organization's own rules has been recognized in the Vienna Convention on the Law of Treaties of 1969 (Article 5), the Vienna Convention on Succession of States in respect of Treaties of 1978 (Article 4), the Vienna Convention on the Law of Treaties between States and International Organizations or between International Organizations of 1986 (Article 6), as well as in the Draft Articles on the Responsibility of International Organizations of 2011 (Article 64).

In preparation of the Convention on the Representation of States in their Relations with International Organizations of a Universal Character of 1975, the Commission's draft concentrated on multilateral diplomacy and organizations of universal character. The member states of regional organizations remain free to choose the most suitable form of their representation following also their model from organizations of universal character.

1. The first international convention that concerned international organizations partially was the Vienna Convention on the Law of Treaties of 1969,[12] which governs traditional interstate treaties but does not exclude those having the nature of the constituent instrument of the international organization (either regional or universal).

   Regarding its terminology, the Vienna Convention in Article 2 (Use of Terms) states that "international organization" means intergovernmental organization. The scope within which the rules of the Vienna Convention apply to the constituent instrument of an international organization, as well as to other treaties adopted within the organization, is governed by Article 5 of the Convention (Treaties constituting international organizations and treaties adopted within an international organization) which affirms that the Convention applies to any treaty which is the constituent instrument of an organization and to treaties adopted within an international organization, without prejudice to any relevant rules of the organization.

In such cases the provisions of the Convention fall under a possible derogation in favour of the international organization's own rules.[13] Taking into account the diversity and importance of issues that can be regulated by legal order of an international organization, the Convention did not attempt to define them. Subject to different legal regulations in the legal order of an international organization, other treaty rules under the Vienna Convention apply within the international organization without restrictions. The Vienna Convention, however, excludes from the scope of its application international organizations founded by instruments other than treaties,[14] and those whose legislative outcomes have a *soft law* nature.

2. The next codification topic concerning international organizations represents the Draft of the Convention on the Representation of States in their Relations with International Organizations of a Universal Character. Even though the Commission's members during the preparation work recognized that the representation of states within international organizations of universal character in principle should not differ from the representation within the organizations of regional character, they took into account that the regional organizations are so diverse that it would be difficult to formulate unified rules, since their peculiarities require specific rules.[15] These were the main reasons why the Vienna Convention on Representation of States in their Relations with International Organizations of a Universal Character of 1975[16] concentrated on multilateral diplomacy between the states and the UN and its specialized agencies, as well as among other international organizations of universal character.[17] The Vienna Convention offers the only example when its regime applies to the representation of states within the international organizations subject to the number of member states.

In addition to types of representations of member states in international organization (permanent missions) and of non-member states (permanent missions of observers), the Convention brings also guarantees for the proper performance of their competences through the system of immunities and privileges in respect to their premises and accommodation (Articles 19–27), and specific immunities and privileges guaranteed to heads of missions and of their members (Articles 28–41). In accordance with the Preamble to the Convention, their existence is a functional necessity because "the purpose of privileges and immunities contained in the Convention is not to benefit individuals but to ensure the efficient performance of their functions". Analysis of the Convention, and the Explanatory Report thereto, proves that the Commission has been inspired by and inclined towards the Vienna Convention on Diplomatic Relations of 1961 and the Convention on Special Missions of 1969. Article 2 Section 2 of the Convention states that the fact that it applies only to universal organizations is without prejudice to the application of their provisions to the representation of states in their relations with other organizations, if they are applicable under international law independently of the Convention.[18] Consequently, the member states, or the non-member states, may use the Vienna Convention of 1975 as a model in setting up their representations within the regional organizations. The Convention, however, does not govern privileges and immunities of international organizations that fall under special legal regulations.

3. The legal position of the constituent instruments of international organizations as well as treaties adopted within their framework within the succession to treaties is laid down in the Vienna Convention on Succession of States in respect of Treaties of 1978.[19] Article 1 defines the scope of its application to the effects of succession of states into treaties concluded between states. Such determination excludes treaties where the parties are entities other than states (international organizations). Regarding, however, the treaties between states, the Convention relates also to those which are the constituent instruments of international organizations regardless of their universal or regional nature and also to treaties concluded within the international organizations.

An essential question the Convention had been seeking an answer to in relation to the categories of treaties was whether the notification of succession[20] should be applied in relation to a multilateral treaty constituting international organizations and treaties adopted within such organizations in the same way that it is in the case of other multilateral treaties. The Convention deals with this issue specifically in relation to both categories of treaties. With respect to the effects of a succession of states in respect to the treaty which is the constituent instrument of an international organization, its application has to be without prejudice to the rules concerning acquisition of membership in an organization and without prejudice to any other relevant rules of the organization (Article 4(a) of the Convention). This provision excludes "automatic" succession of third (non-member) states of organization in respect to the treaties constituting international organizations since according to them their succession might be subjected to the membership in an organization.

The application of this rule has a practical meaning because it enables the member states to evaluate whether the third state complies with the membership requirements in an organization. In this situation the third state, therefore, cannot take advantage of the notification of succession to a treaty constituting an international organization without, firstly, applying for membership. The other approach is weaker because some international organizations (for instance, the unions) do not expressly require membership as a precondition for the notification of succession in their constituent instruments. As a result, the third states may notify the succession in the constituent instruments of such international organization without previously acquiring their membership.

The second category includes treaties adopted within an international organization that can be succeeded under the Convention "without prejudice to any relevant rules of the organization" (Article 4(b) Convention). In relation to such treaties, the membership within an organization might play a significant role if the succession is subject to the membership.[21] Regarding both categories of treaties, the same rule applies and notification of succession to such treaties has to be without prejudice to any "relevant rules of the organization" which relate either to membership in an organization or to others conditions laid down by the rules of the organization. Provided that the third state is interested in becoming a member of an international organization, the application of succession to their treaties is limited to the scope and manner as determined by the legal order of the organization.[22]

4. Another topic related to the treaties of international organizations is regulated in the Vienna Convention on the Law of Treaties between States and International Organizations or between International Organizations of 1986.[23] Without going into too much detail, the treaty-making capacity of international organizations represents one of the most significant attributes of their international legal personality, and the Convention applies only to international organizations (Article 2) capable of concluding treaties with other subjects of international law. For the criterion of legislative activity of an international organization, it is not important whether it is a universal or regional organization, nor is the real scope of their legislative competence important.[24] The Commentary of the Commission to the Draft underlines that the provisions of the Convention should be applied in relation to treaties to which international organizations are parties, regardless of their universal or regional character eventually their openness or closedness. It concerns all international organizations.[25] With regard to the particularities of international organizations, their law-making capacity is usually restricted to treaties necessary for the proper performance of their competences, where the capacity to

conclude treaties is "governed by the rules of that organization" (Article 6 Convention). The aforesaid is, however, without prejudice to regional treaties of an "open nature" regulating the issues exceeding the regional framework (see above) and accessible for non-member states of international organizations.

5. The topic of treaties concluded between states and between international organizations and states or between international organizations was addressed by the Commission again in 2011. concentrating on the reservations and interpretative declarations of these treaties. Unlike the previous approach on this matter, when the Commission dealt with the treaties between states and with the treaties of international organizations separately, the reservations and interpretative declarations of states and of international organizations with respect to treaties are governed jointly in one document. This is seen in the Guide to Practice on Reservations to Treaties of 2011.[26] Under the reservation, the Guide understands a unilateral statement anyhow phrased or named, made by a state or an international organization, when signing, ratifying, accepting, approving or acceding to a treaty, whereby the state or the international organization purports to exclude or to vary the legal effect of certain provisions of the treaty in their application to that state or international organization.[27] The interpretative declaration means a unilateral statement, anyhow phrased or named, made by a state or an international organization, whereby these entities purport to explain or interpret the purpose or scope of the treaty or provisions thereof.[28]

    The Guide specifically and comprehensibly deals with all aspects of the reservations and interpretative declarations, including: the terms of their application (in relation to the treaty text), opportunities to apply them in respect of bilateral treaties, forms and methods of their notification to the parties, the period of time when it is possible to make such declarations, the entities entitled to make a declaration, the appeal and alternation of reservations and interpretative declarations, the reservations towards them and their legal effects, the interpretation of reservations and interpretative declarations, etc. One of the Guide's basic conclusions is that no matter what difference there is between the state and international organizations, many procedural aspects related to reservations and interpretative declarations are applied in the same, or a similar way—although some particularities of both the entities are sometimes reflected.

    Without going into details, one can mention that the reservations related to the territorial scope of treaties can be made only by the states, while the reservations and interpretative declarations on behalf of the organization are made by the head of the international organization and not the representative of a member state, etc. In the Annex to the Guide, the Commission formulated its conclusions on the reservations dialogue, stating that the purpose of reservations is to achieve a satisfactory balance between the purpose and objectives of an international treaty and guarantees protecting the integrity of multilateral treaties on the one hand, and to ensure the participation of their state parties as much as possible on the other hand.

6. Another codification outcome of the Commission's work is the Draft Articles on the Responsibility of International Organizations of 2011.[29] A principal argument for including this topic in the Commission's working programme was that if the international organizations have their own personality, and they are independent from the member states in exercising their own competences, they must be internationally responsible for breaching the rules of international law binding them. However, the "timing" for including this topic in the Commission's programme raised several doubts, mainly due to lack of proper fulfilment of elements required for the entry of a suitable topic into the codification process. Critics (including some members of the Commission too) refer mainly to the absence of practical examples of international organizations in regards to their responsibility for wrongful acts.

Consequently, the Commission had to rely on more or less detailed academic and doctrinal analyses of that matter or to copy the relevant provisions of the Draft Articles on the Responsibility of States for Wrongful Acts.[30] In fact, the Commission, in its General Commentary to the Draft Articles, expressly recognized that one of the principal problems concerning the responsibility of international organizations was caused due to their limited practice, which started to emerge not long ago.[31]

Despite criticism, the Commission continued in its work and prepared Draft Articles on the Responsibility of International Organizations. With respect to the criterion *ratione personae*, the Draft (Article 2(a)) relates to any international organization, which is "an organization established by a treaty or other instrument governed by international law and possessing its own international legal personality". In addition to the states, also the international organisations and other entities might become members.[32]

With respect to the regulation of the rules of responsibility, the Commission was mainly inspired by the responsibility of states,[33] which is the concept viewed critically by a number of international organizations which gave their views on the draft during preparatory works[34] as well as by the authors of international law.[35] The international organizations pointed to their peculiarities and differences of the states[36] and to the fact that the Commission failed to consider their diversity as a factor to be reflected in the formulation of special rules of responsibility.[37] The unified concept of responsibility was viewed critically by the International Monetary Fund, the World Health Organization, the International Labour Organization, NATO, the Organisation for Economic Co-operation and Development, while the Council of Europe and the International Maritime Organizations were in favour of such a concept.

It should be pointed out, however, that the Commission in its Draft did not neglect to consider peculiarities of international organizations completely. The special Article 64 (*Lex specialis*) of the Draft specifies that their articles do not apply where, and to an extent when, the conditions of an internationally wrongful act or the content of the international responsibility of an international organization are governed by special rules of international law. Such special rules may be included in the legal order of an international organization if it applies to the relations between an organization and its member states. Special rules may either supplement general rules of international responsibility or may replace them, and they concern a certain category of an international organization or one specific organization in its (their) relations with some or all member states.

7. The next outcome of the Commission was the Draft Articles on the Effects of Armed Conflicts on Treaties of 2011.[38] The Draft does not necessarily relate to states or to international organizations. It regulates the effects of armed conflicts on international treaties. Since the current international treaty law comprises not only treaties between states, but also between the states and international organizations, or between the international organizations themselves, the Commission has to determine the subject matter of this topic more precisely. Article 1 of the Draft therefore states that the effects of armed conflict relate to relations between states under an international treaty, while the Commentary specifies that the Draft does not apply to treaties between states and international organizations, or to treaties between international organizations. The reasoning is both "in the complexity of this matter and the improbability that the international organizations would engage in an armed conflict to the extent that their treaty relations are affected negatively".[39]

The Draft, however, covers the treaties between states to which international organizations are parties. Article 2 (Definitions) confirms that articles apply to treaties between states to which international organizations are also parties. A general rule contained in Article 3 applies to them stating that an armed conflict does not *per se* terminate or suspend the operation of treaties between state parties in a conflict, or between a state party in a conflict with a state that is not.

8.3. Problems Arising as a Consequence of Treaty-Making Competences of International Organizations and the General International Law

A growing number of international organizations in the second half of the last century called the international community to attend not only to the rules of general international law related to their specific activities (see above), but to the problems that their treaty-making power may eventually cause to general international law. Therefore, in 2002 the Commission included in its working programme analyses of this problem within the context of expansion and diversification of international law relating to the fragmentation of international law. The Commission's outcome is the Report of its Study Group relating to the development and diversification of international law as causes of its fragmentation.[40]

According to the Study Group, the fragmentation of international law is the consequence of its growing development and diversification associated with various sets of specialized and relatively autonomous groups of legal rules (commercial law, human rights law, environmental law) with their own institutional structures and principles. These rules, principles and structures are autonomous to each other and they are autonomous to general international law as well.[41] These sets of rules (including regional character): "do not necessarily comply with the general rules of international law, and in the case that the deviations from them became more significant and their occurrence more frequent, it would affect the unity of general international law".[42]

When analysing this aspect of fragmentation, the Study Group of the Commission concluded that the Vienna Convention on the Law of Treaties of 1969 is suitable in dealing with such issues upon application of the principles *lex specialis derogat legi generali*, the systemic interpretation of international treaties in accordance with Article 31 Section 3(c) of the Vienna Convention, the *lex posterior derogat legi priori* principle and according to Article 103 of the UN Charter.[43]

Another aspect of fragmentation is represented in a situation when international organizations apply rules of general international law resulting in different interpretations, without access to international judicial bodies. Under such a circumstance it is not possible to exclude the view that such an "loose" interpretation by regional or universal international organizations might after a certain time have a negative impact on the stability and unity of interpretation and later the application of rules of general international law.[44]

In this respect, doctrinal opinions have arisen enhancing the position of the International Court of Justice, which would be able to play a more significant role in ensuring the unified interpretation and stability of general international law principles through and within its advisory competence. This option would, however, assume the extension of a group of subjects entitled to request the advisory opinions. It has been suggested, that other subjects are to have access to the advisory competence of the ICJ. In particular the Secretary General and other entities different to the states[45] or the international or national courts who apply the rules of general international law. An international law doctrine dealing with this matter, however, does not support the creation of a new international judicial body vested with the competence to give a binding interpretation of the general rules of international law.

The Study Group at the same time also pointed to the institutional scope of fragmentation based on the parallel existence of two or more international judicial bodies having competing jurisdiction and the problems related to this procedural aspect of fragmentation.

It was, however, decided to put this issue aside as the international courts themselves are best equipped to deal with these problems using their own procedural codes.[46]

Note

1. The Resolution adopted by the Institute of International Law in Lisbon in 1995 (Problems Arising from a Succession of Codification Conventions on a Particular Subject) Section I (c) states that: "Regional codification convention means a codification convention concluded at the regional level which may reserve participation to the states belonging to the regional group concerned. Such a regional codification convention may, however, contain provisions which may codify or progressively develop rules of general public international law or rules of public international law applicable only as between states within the region".
2. For example, the originally Spanish-American rule *uti possidetis iuris*, is currently regarded as the "general principle of the international law". See: I.C.J. Reports 1986, paras. 20–21.
3. One can mention some conventions of the Council of Europe, e.g. the Framework Convention for the Protection of National Minorities of 1995, the European Convention on Nationality of 1997, or the Convention on Cybercrime of 2001 (with amending protocol of 2003), the Convention on the Protection of Children against Sexual Exploitation and Sexual Abuse of 2007 and others.
4. As stated by Jennings, R.: "Universality does not mean uniformity. It does mean, however, that such regional international law, however variant is part of the system as a whole and not a separate system and ultimately derives its validity from the system as a whole". In Jennings, R.Y.: *Collected Writings of Sir Robert Jennings*. Hague: Kluwer Law International, 1998, p. 341.
5. Wouters, De Man, *supra* n. 85, p. 26.
6. Dissenting Opinion of Judge Tanaka, ICJ Reports, 1966, 248 at 291.
7. ICJ Advisory Opinion-Legality of the Threat or Use Nuclear Weapons, I.C.J. Reports 1996, 226 para. 70.
8. The analysis of legal orders of international organizations confirms that these are usually composed of two parts, the internal order consisting the procedural, administrative, budgetary or other rules of similar character, ensuring due functioning of the organization's organs, and the substantial (regulative) rules regulating the competences and activities of organization's bodies and its member states in the area constituting the main subject matter of its activities. The second group of rules can be found either in international treaties or in the (specific) rules issued by the organization, or in both of these forms (e.g. the European Union).
9. With respect to the latter GA the UN invited the Commission of International Law already in 1958: "to give further consideration to the question of

relations between states and intergovernmental international organizations at the appropriate time . . .". See: GA Resolution Relations between states and Intergovernmental Organizations, No. 1289 (XIII) of December 5, 1958.

At its 20th session in 1968, the Commission of International Law decided the title of the topic without altering its meaning by changing the word "intergovernmental" to "international".

10. The Statute of the International Law Commission was adopted: UN GA Res. 174 (II) (21 November 1947): Establishment of an International Law Commission. Available at www.worldlii.org/int/other/UNGARsn/1947/75.pdf
11. "The Vienna Convention of 1969 provided the general framework for the Commission's draft Articles on treaties concluded by international organizations and consequently, the Commission noted its draft Articles relating to treated concluded by international organizations would have as their subject-matter". See: Watts, *supra* n. 53, p. 614.
12. Vienna Convention on the Law of Treaties of 1969.
13. The UN Charter in Articles 108–109 shall determine its own (specific) methods of amendments.
14. For instance, the Organization for Security and Co-operation in Europe (OSCE) has been established upon the Helsinki Final Act of 1975, which is not a treaty.
15. Draft Articles on the Representation of States in their Relations With International Organizations (With Commentaries) Yearbook of ILC, 1971, p. 284. Available at: http://untreaty.un.org/ilc/texts/instruments/english/commentaries/5_1_1971.pdf
16. For more details: Vienna Convention on the Representation of States in their Relations With International Organizations of a Universal Character of 14 March 1975- A/Conf.67/16. Available at: http://treaties.un.org/pages/ViewDetails.aspx?src=TREATY&mtdsg_no=III-11&chapter=3&lang=en
17. As regards the nature of international organization, the Commission regarding the Article 1 of a final Draft of articles suggests that: "The question whether an international organization is of universal character depends not only on the actual character of membership but also on the potential scope of its membership and responsibilities".
18. For the Vienna Convention see: Official Records of the UN Conference on the Representation of States in their Relations With International Organizations, Vol. II, UN Publication. Available at: http://untreaty.un.org/cod/diplomaticconferences/repofstates_intlorgs- 1975/docs/english/vol2/a_conf_67_index.pdf
19. Published in: Watts, *supra* n. 53, pp. 1186–1208.
20. The notification of succession in relation to a multilateral treaty shall under the Convention mean: "any notification, however phrased or named, made by a successor state expressing its consent to be considered as bound by the treaty". (Article 2 Section 1(g) of the Convention). Available at: http://legal.un.org/ilc/texts/instruments/english/conventions/3_2_1978.pdf
21. It should be noted that the International Law Commission has attempted twice (in 1963 and 1993) to include in its working programme the topic concerning the succession into membership of an international organizations, without success.
22. Consequences of a growing number of international organizations is, *inter alia*, that organizations with the same or similar subject matter of their activities are established in different periods. Even though this fact itself does not impede their activities and eventual cooperation, there is a question related to succession arising in some cases (the League of Nations succeeded by the

UN in 1946, the International Institute of Agriculture (IIA) succeeded by the UN Food and Agriculture Organization (FAO) in 1946, the Organisation of African Unity succeeded by the African Union in 2002). A basic difference between the traditional succession of states in respect of treaties and succession of states in respect of international organizations is that while the former relates to the state territory, the latter has a functional character. The reason for succession of international organizations is the common interest of member states to ensure functional continuity of a new organization either to a full, or limited extent.

23. Vienna Convention on the Law of Treaties between States and International Organizations or between International Organizations of March 1986.
24. As stated by the International Law Commission in its commentaries to the Final Draft (in particular Article 6): "Either an international organization has the capacity to conclude at least one treaty in which case the rules in the draft articles will be applicable to it . . .". See: Yearbook of ILC, 1981, Vol. II (Part Two), p. 124.
25. See: Watts, *supra* n. 53, p. 835.
26. Guide to Practice on Reservations to Treaties, Report of the ILC, GA, Official Records, Doc.A/66/10, Supplement No. 10.
27. Guide to Practice, Article 1 Section 1 (Definitions of reservations).
28. See reservation no.160—Article.1.2. (Definitions of Interpretative Declarations).
29. Responsibility of international organizations (Doc.A/66/10). Available at http://untreaty.un.org/ilc/reports/2011/2011report.htm
30. Annex of the UN GA Resolution No. 56/83 in January 2002.
31. Draft Articles on the Responsibility of International Organizations with Commentaries, (DARIO), doc. A/66/10, 2011, General Commentary, p. 3, para. 4.
32. *Ibidem*, para. 87.
33. "The topic of responsibility of international organizations was viewed as being 'necessary counterpart' and it would logically flow on from its work on state responsibility". See: Report of the International Law Commission on the Work of Its Fifty-Second Session (A/55/10), p. 135. Available at: http://legal.un.org/docs/?path=../ilc/publications/yearbooks/english/ilc_2000_v2_p2.pdf&lang=EFSRAC (Despite the General commentaries on the draft articles made by the Commission, stating that "they represent and autonomous text").
34. The European Commission on behalf of the EU expressed doubts: ". . . as to feasibility of subsuming all international organizations under the terms of this one draft in the light of the highly diverse nature of international organization of which the European Community is itself an example". See: ILC, 60 Session (2007), Responsibility of International Organizations and Observations Received From International Organizations, p. 4. Available at: http://daccess-ny.un.org/doc/UNDOC/GEN/N04/406/10/PDF/N0440610.pdf?OpenElement
35. Wouters, J., Odermatt, J.: Are All International Organizations Created Equal? Reflections on the ILC's Draft Articles of Responsibility of International Organizations. *Global Governance Opinions*, 2012. Available at: http://ghum.kuleuven.be/ggs/publications/opinions/opinions13-wouters-odermatt.pdf

The Czech doctrine of international law pointed out that: "the simple transposition of rules on state responsibility for the responsibility of international organizations should have certain limits. This concerns in particular the nature of rules of the organization which are different from the internal law of states or the issue of conduct *ultra vires* of the organization". See: Šturma,

P.: Drawing a Line Between the Responsibility of an International Organization and Its Member States Under International Law. In: *Czech Yearbook of Public & Private International Law*, Vol. 2, 2011, p. 4.

36. The European Commission on behalf of the EU also pointed out that: "EC . . . is differing from the classical model of an international organizations in a number of ways. The EC is not only the forum for its member states to settle or organize their mutual relations but also an actor in its own right on the international scene". Because of its specifications, the European Commission pointed out that ". . . regional economic integration organization reflected in modern treaty practice may require special consideration . . ." (doc.A/CN.4/545). Available at: http://daccess-dds-ny.un.org/doc/UNDOC/GEN/N04/406/10/PDF/N0440610.pdf?OpenElement
37. During the preparatory works there were many opinions supporting this trend: ". . . with regard to responsibility it may be unreasonable to look for general rules applying for all intergovernmental organizations . . . It may be necessary to devise specific rules for different categories of international organizations". Report of ILC, 54th session (2002), par. 470. Available at: http://untreaty.un.org/ilc/reports/2002/2002report.htm
38. Yearbook of the International Law Commission 2011, Vol. II, Part Two. Available at: http://untreaty.un.org/ilc/reports/2011/2011report.htm
39. A comment made by the Commission regarding Article 1 Section 4 states that: "the Commission decided not to include within the scope of the draft articles relations arising under treaties between international organizations or between states and international organizations owing to the complexity of giving such an additional dimension to the draft articles. And since international organizations rarely if ever engage in armed conflict to the extent that their treaty relations may be affected".

    Draft Articles on the Effect of Armed Conflicts on Treaties With Commentaries, UN 2011, p. 2, Section 4. Available at: http://untreaty.un.org/ilc/texts/instruments/english/commentaries/1_10_2011.pdf
40. ILC: Fragmentation of International Law: Difficulties Arising From the Diversification and Expansion of International Law: Report of the Study Group of the ILC (M. Koskenniemi), Geneva, 2006 (Doc. A/CN.4/L.702), pp. 1–25. Available at: http://daccess-dds-ny.un.org/doc/UNDOC/LTD/G06/628/63/PDF/G0662863.pdf?OpenElement
41. A report of the Commission group refers to such sets of rules as the "boxes" comprising "self-contained regimes", where the latter can be "geographically or functionally limited treaty systems . . .". An international law writer in this respect states that: "Faced with the contemporary explosion of legal norms, increasing normative specificity, the proliferation of international organizations and the multiplication of international tribunals, some have highlighted the risk of 'fragmentation' of International law into a more or less coherent set of "normative islands constituted by partial, autonomous and perhaps even 'self- contained legal sub-systems'". Prost, M., Clark, P.K.: Unity, Diversity and the Fragmentation of International Law: How Much Does the Multiplication of International Organizations Really Matter? In: *Chinese Journal of International Law*, Vol. 5, No. 2, 2006, p. 342.
42. A Report by the Study Group of the Commission in this respect states that: "Very often new rules or regimes develop precisely in order to deviate from what was earlier provided by the general law. When such deviation become general and frequent the unity of law suffers". In: Fragmentation of International Law: Difficulties Arising From the Diversification and Expansion of International Law, Geneva, 2006 (Doc. A/CN.4/L.702), p. 6.

43. ". . . although fragmentation is inevitable it is desirable to have a framework through which it may be assessed and managed in a legal and professional way. That framework is provided by the Vienna Convention on the Law of treaties . . . that already provides a unifying frame for these developments". ILC Report, 1996, p. 249.
44. One of the conclusions resulting from the Report on the fragmentation of international law states that: "the emergence of conflicting rules and overlapping legal regimes will undoubtedly create problems of coordination at the international level. But . . . no homogeneous, hierarchical meta-system is realistically available to do away with such problems". In Pronto, A., Wood, M.: *The International Law Commission 1999–2009 (Volume IV: Treaties, Final Draft Articles, and Other Materials)*. Oxford: Oxford University Press, 2010, p. 809.
45. Authors Vicuña and Pinto suggest: "broadening access to the Court by international organizations, eventually including NGOs, corporations and individuals" in order "to strengthen the Court's functions in respect of its role as the central judicial body of the international community". In: Vicuna, F.O., Pinto, C.: The Peaceful Settlement of Disputes: Prospect for the Twenty-First Century. *Preliminary Report Prepared for the 1999 Centennial of the First International Peace Conference.* Council of Europe, Doc. CAHDI, 1998, paras. 136–137.

    In his speech at the UN GA in 1994, M. Bedjaoui, a former Chairman of the International Court of Justice, pointed out that: "Access to the Court's advisory jurisdiction may henceforth appear unduly restricted if one thinks of the enormous potential of the advisory function and of the demand that exists. One might envisage the possibility that not only other organs of the Organization . . . might be able to request the advisory opinions of the Court but also that that option might be extended to third organizations not belonging to UN system but which make an eminent contribution to the maintenance of peace at regional level, for instance". See: ICJ-Statement of the President of Court: Address By Judge Mohammed Bedjaoui, President of the ICJ Delivered to Plenary Meeting of the General Assembly at Its 49 Session, on 13 October 1994.
46. "The issue of institutional competencies is best dealt with by institutions themselves". See: Fragmentation of International Law: Difficulties Arising From the Diversification and Expansion of International Law, Geneva, 2006 (Doc. A/CN.4/L.702), p. 58.

Summary

The phenomenon of regionalism is especially characteristic of the second half of the 20th century. A summary analysis of its various aspects and conclusions regarding its relations to current international law can be divided into several areas.

When assessing the phenomenon of regionalism from a historical aspect, prevailing opinion was that there are two main types: the post-war old regionalism, replaced by the wave of a new regionalism after the Cold War ended. A concept of old regionalism contained features of a bipolar world reflecting the position of the two leading superpowers, as well as basic characteristics of their Cold War foreign policy. It is, therefore, referred to as the hegemony regionalism, where the initiators, or external (supraregional) hegemonic leaders of regional groups were the USA and USSR (NATO, CENTO, SEATO, Warsaw Treaty Organization), whose aim was to ensure regional security against external attacks (the security regionalism) through systems of collective defence. Old regionalism was not of an open nature; it was internally oriented, designed for its members only, and its orientation was restricted to military, and, partially, economic areas. As a result, the regional groups of this era were understood as territorial, military and economic areas representing the sphere of influence of the superpowers and fully subjected to the needs of their foreign and international policies. As a consequence of the Cold War, the spread of regionalism was restricted as it focused on the political, military and security needs of the superpowers. Therefore, in this context it cannot be regarded as an autonomous, independent and even prosperous phenomenon of international relations of that time. This implies that along with the ending of the old superpower relationship and bipolarity of the Cold War, the regional grouping of old regionalism came to an end as well, although with some exceptions.

After the Cold War ended, regionalism moved to a new development stage called new regionalism, its structures being established without any significant influence on the part of former superpowers and built from below, i.e. at the state level and with non-governmental entities becoming participants as well.

From this viewpoint new regionalism may be regarded as a multilateral and multidimensional process of regional integration, including economic, political, social and cultural aspects not only among the states themselves, but also among states and other non-governmental entities. Unlike old regionalism, new regionalism is open to the global needs, trends and challenges of the international community with the aim of strengthening mutual cooperation among their subjects and removing any problems in economic and other areas. In the processes of economic globalization, which introduce new challenges and problems, states respond by establishing various regional groups, as global problems require solutions beyond the framework of one state and one national economy. Lasting differences in development and intensity of globalizing trends are, however, reflected in the uneven development of regionalism in economic, political and social areas across different parts of the world.

New regionalism in its overall context might be, therefore, understood as a continual process of changes that started after the Cold War and occurring at various levels, mainly at the level of states (the macro regions) but also at the interregional level (in relations between regional structures established by the states as well as between these structures and group of states or individual third states) at the subregional level and at the micro-regional level of non-governmental entities.

The reasons for establishing such regional groups represent not only military, territorial or security interests connected traditionally with the states and their foreign policies (even though they continue to exist also in new regionalism), but also areas in which the non-governmental entities, such as supranational corporations, non-governmental organizations, professional groups and social groups involved and local communities play an increasingly more important role. Areas of their interest include mainly international trade and finance, environmental, humanitarian and social issues.

Even though its beginnings are traced back to Europe, new regionalism currently has a worldwide character as it covers both developing and developed countries across almost all the continents and many non-governmental entities on a worldwide scale. Regarding its scope and dynamics of development, new regionalism today represents a significant factor of influence in international relations and international law, and, in specific areas, a prevailing form of cooperation between their subjects (EU on the European continent).

A significant feature is its democratizing nature, since the regional organizations of new regionalism often require their member states, prior to joining, to carry out necessary democratic reforms respecting the rule of law, political plurality of the domestic political system, protection of human rights and minorities contributing to the democratic legal area of the integration group. Similarly, relations between the regional groups within a system of interregionalism are required to respect the fundamental principles of international law. In this respect, the regionalism and its regional groups make an irreplaceable contribution to the process of democratization of international law and with respect to the *rule of law* principle.

Although the development of new regionalism demonstrates a growing trend and stronger cooperation between various entities, at different levels, it also proves that there is no worldwide single model of regionalism. There are currently various models of new regionalism applied differently in different regions depending on such factors as: historical development, democracy of individual states and other political specifications of future members, their attitude toward state sovereignty, the level of economic development, etc. It should be pointed out that new regionalism is not a uniform process but is performed at different speeds, through jumps and waves, and is affected by the various external or internal factors of future members of integration groups and the specificities of prevailing international relations.

Regionalism and regional organization in the second half of the 20th century thus became geographically more spread, their number rose, and despite some drawbacks they represented a significant and irreplaceable segment within international relations having a specific impact on general international law and international relations.

With regards to the dramatic entry of regionalism into the international community in the second half of the 20th century, there were debates over the impact it had on the Westphalian system of the international community, a system which counted on the exclusive position of states. According to the Westphalian principle of absolute sovereignty of states, dominant at the beginning of the 20th century, the international community fully respected the primacy of the territorial states as exclusive political players at a global level and their autonomy in managing their internal matters.

This system of the exclusive position of states started to emerge during the 20th century *inter alia* as a result of universal and regional intergovernmental organizations having their own international legal subjectivity which was different to the subjectivity of the member states, and creating their own system of legal rules. This reflected not just the exclusive will of the states but their own interests and purposes of the international organizations. Similar to sovereign states, many international organizations kept close relations with the states and other international organizations (including those that governed the rules of international law), had their own constitutions in the form of constituent instruments and their own systems for peaceful settlement of disputes, including judicial bodies.

As a result, the current international order may not be regarded as a continuation of the traditional Westphalian system of the international community because it consists of different subjects and various legal branches: environmental protection, trade law, humanitarian law, etc. These recognize the rights and obligations of non-governmental entities on the international scene and within which the legal acts and decisions of international organizations do not require the consent of the states.

The irreplaceable role of international law was common for both old and new regionalism as the states have established regional organizations on the basis of international law and complied with its rules when carrying out their activities. This traditional international legal framework is, however, within the legislative competences of regional organizations completed by their own legal orders of different levels and rigidity.

From the viewpoint of international law, one can speak about treaty (non-institutional) regionalism. This is a typical characteristic of certain regions, although the reasons for the conclusion of treaties might differ from region to region. A traditional reason is the existence of a geographical element crossing the border and relating to a specific group of states. A treaty will agree to the use of such geography in a commonly agreed manner and/or to protect it through regulating certain aspects of it by international law. Examples of this type include the treaties on regional rivers and lakes, or on geographically restricted parts of environment, e.g. Convention on the Navigation Regime on the Danube; the protection of environment in the Baltic Sea, the Black Sea, the Arctic or different regional environment biotopes.

Another aspect typical of treaty regionalism includes the geographical closeness (neighbourhood) of the states situated within a particular region. Treaty-making is in this case enhanced by their common historical roots, cultural, religious or other associations or the level and homogeneity of their economic systems. As an example one can mention the regional treaties for free trade zones, customs unions, the free movement of goods and persons within a region, regional agreements on human rights protection and on common defence. Practice confirms that this geographical aspect is not limited only to treaty regionalism alone; it can also represent a significant impulse for the establishment of regional groups within the framework of institutional regionalism.

In addition to the above-noted geographical elements, the strong interests of the states involved may also constitute a significant impulse for the conclusion of regional treaties in the period of new regionalism. Such regional legislation tends to be called functional because it is based on the intensive common interests particular to a groups of states, e.g. transboundary production systems, drilling and transportation of oil and gas and elements in the area of environment: acid rain, the Amazon rainforest, the ozone layer.

Institutional regionalism is traditionally expressed in the form of intergovernmental regional organization established obviously under the treaty in order to fulfil the agreed purpose. It is usually defined as a group of a limited number of states that are connected to each other through geographical relations and a certain level of mutual, economic or other interdependence. A prevailing trend in the second half of the 20th century shows that regionalism was promoted through institutional regionalism itself, and is reflected in a still growing number of international organizations of regional character and in the extension and specialization of the scope of their activities. As a result, they have played a yet more important role while entering into relations of cooperation with other regional organizations, non-member states or non-governmental entities.

A traditional model of institutional regionalism, in which the regional objectives and needs are being satisfied through a specifically defined legal basis, within an agreed institutional structure and within clearly defined competences of the regional organization's bodies, began to be subject to certain changes in the second half of the 20th century. The more sophisticated demands of a global nature meant that the regional organizations required a more comprehensive reaction through means of various non-formal, flexible and open systems of cooperation (*open, or networked regionalism*) within and between the regional organizations and non-governmental entities such as supranational economic groups and corporations, non-governmental organizations, representatives of civil communities, interest and professional groups. Such "soft" regional structures are currently typical of regional groups in Asia, Africa and Latin America and it might also have *pro futuro* impact on the stricter European integration model.

Such a trend is today reflected in membership diversification within regional organizations, resulting in the existence of hybrid institutional regionalism which the ASEAN is currently heading towards. Its existence is also a consequence of a strong belief that this hybrid membership of regional organizations might help them react in a better way to the problems of a specific region as well as to the problems of a global nature by enabling various non-governmental entities to participate more effectively in their activities. Further development of regionalism will show to what extent the global challenges and various regional models affect, or modify the traditional regional structures, as well as what role international law will play with respect to their establishment and functioning.

It should be noted that both intergovernmental and supranational (integration) models can be currently observed within institutional regionalism. For the intergovernmental approach, it is typical that the member states continue with full sovereignty, while established regional organs serve only to prepare and carry out their common projects as member states.

The supranational model means, however, that the member states have decided to transfer some parts of their sovereignty through, and within, the regional bodies, who have an autonomous position and their own responsibility for the proper exercise of transferred competences. The EU example shows that specific legal rules and principles have been adopted within this supranational grouping with priority given above the national (internal) legal orders of the member states.

Another feature typical for the European integration are common institutions (organs) entitled to prepare and adopt supranational legal rules, where such institutions themselves represent the driving power in order to deepen and promote the integration process.

The majority of regional groups across the developing world continue to stay at intergovernmental level, as their member states are not willing to share a part of their sovereignty with regional groups. The principal reason is that many states in Asia and Africa regard membership in regional organizations as an instrument to reinforce their sovereignty (*sovereignty-reinforced regionalism*). This approach then puts no pressure on building relevant structures of regional organizations, which (if ever in existence) does not represent an effective instrument for promoting and enhancing the integration processes.

Many non-European regional groups have, however, been inspired by the experience that European integration has had mainly in the area of institutional structure. Various organs copying the EU model are characteristic of every regional organization within the institutional area, i.e. the Commission or Secretariat, the Council (consisting of heads of states or Ministers), the regional Parliamentary Assembly, the regional Court of Justice and other organs depending on the scope of the regional agenda, e.g. economic and social issues; regional, central or development banks.

However, in reality such organs do not automatically copy the competences of such bodies within the European model because the need to respect the sovereignty of member states is strongly prioritized. For instance, the establishment of regional Commissions (following the European Commission model) makes it impossible to propose regional legislation; this results in states still having control over regional legislation or sanctions imposed due to breach of agreed rules being subject to the unanimous consent of the member states, etc.

A main obstacle in preventing the developing regional groups from coming closer to the European integration model is, therefore, a difference in understanding the place and importance of sovereignty of a member state within the integration processes, resulting in restricting the development and deepening of the integration process.

For specific historical, political and different economic conditions, the regional groupings within the developing world are not willing to assign a more important role to the regional groups in furthering the development and deepening of the integration process.

Regionalism and regional organizations are suitable also for the application of the rule of law, and thus contributing to the development and enhancement of regional processes and structures within a specific legal framework including legal stability and application of relevant legal guarantees. The rule of law within regional cooperation between the states is significantly affected by the principle of equality between the states when creating and applying the rules of international normativity, as well as the principle of the state's sovereignty. Such features affect the universal application of regional law with regard to all the member states within the regional organization which are supposed to be legally equal. Equality, however, should be maintained not only when applying the legal norms, but when creating regional normativity, too.

Regional organizations have set up different mechanisms and bodies to promote the rule of law, including legal cooperation (interregionalism or treaty regionalism), technical support, exchange of information and good practice as well as initiatives to ensure accountability (institutional regionalism).

The regional organizations obviously have their own systems for the settlement of different disputes, e.g. resulting from different interpretation or application of the organization's legal order or constituent treaty from member states, its practical activities, including financial matters, application of sanctions and many other problems. The number of disputes in international organizations varies, though we can say that it is rather higher in active organizations with a wider scope of competences. Experience within the international organizations in this area confirms that the parties of a dispute in the first stage try to avoid more formal administrative and judicial means and seek less formal procedures, such as meetings, investigations and consultation. This is also the main reason why international organizations devote special attention to consultations and meetings in their constituent instruments.

Similarly, in the settlement of disputes before the international judicial organs of general competences, the regional parties in a dispute can turn to the specialized courts of the international organizations after having used all the moderate and less painful methods of settlement. It is understandable because in having to refer the case to the judicial organs, the parties lose their control over the dispute. Consequently, the member states of international organizations do not seek the services of international courts very often—the European Court of Justice and the Court of Justice of the Andean Community being the exceptions. These proceedings, however, fully respect the principle of specialization of international organizations, since their bodies deal with disputes concerning only the activities of the organization and its member states laid down in its constituent instrument. As with states, the international organizations also have their own sanction regimes which are applicable to the member states for failure to carry out obligations arising from their membership. Even though they differ from the sanctions of the states, they have some features in common.

The organizations are entitled to apply them as a last possible remedy after having applied a softer coercive approach in order to make state parties to comply with their obligations of membership. Similarly to sanctions applied among states, when applying sanctions to international organizations a principle of proportionality and temporariness must be respected as well. Unlike individual sanctions applied by the states, the sanctions of international organizations have a centralized form with a greater political and moral importance, thus creating more pressure on the subject. Because they are adopted on the decision of the organization's body, they must be well reasoned and applied only if the unlawful behaviour or acts of the member state are duly confirmed. In this respect they differ from the individual countermeasures of the states in general international law, because the conditions for their application are subject to the individual assessment of a concerned state. On the other hand, it is possible to identify some common features through the system of collective sanctions of the UN (the decision of the Security Council, collective assessment of the conditions for application of the international sanctions). The current practice of international organizations confirms three main objectives to be pursued by the system of regional sanctions: namely, to ensure the proper institutional functioning of the regional organizations, the guarantees of the constitutional and democratic nature of the member states and effective implementation of the judgments of regional courts.

With respect to the efforts of regional organizations to guarantee the uniform interpretation and application of regional treaties, the analysis of the preliminary rulings proceedings confirms different approaches of regional organizations to this legal measure needed for the effective functioning of concrete regional organization. Within the organizations characterized by the compulsory model of the preliminary rulings procedure, the needs to guarantee effectiveness and the main goals of the organization prevent the possibility of individual different and/or erroneous interpretations of regional treaties or legal rules of internal legal orders by the domestic courts of member states. On the other hand, international organizations having the optional procedure of preliminary ruling procedures does not insist on the crucial role of the obligatory uniform interpretation of regional rules for the effective functioning of regional organization. This is, however, not detrimental to the eventual application of other proceedings dealing with the legal consequences of non-application of preliminary ruling procedures in the circumstances of a concrete case and concrete international organization.

The consequences of the institutionalization of international law in the late 20th century represents the advisory jurisdiction of judicial bodies of regional organizations from different geographical areas. Unlike the preliminary rulings procedure, advisory opinions of non-binding nature concern either the legal problems and/or questions regardless of their rising within legal disputes or not and may be generally characterized as qualified legal advice needed for the proper interpretation and application of regional law. The comparison of preliminary rulings procedures and advisory jurisdiction at the same time confirms that some of regional judicial bodies (ECHR, COMESA Court of Justice, Caribbean Court of Justice) provided both kinds of these proceedings for the need of different subjects. With respect to their legal relevance it is generally recognized that advisory opinions are authoritative, but non-binding statements on interpretation of regional law by an judicial tribunal, having the "soft law" nature and "less controversial" character being compared with binding judgments, compel states to behave in a certain manner. It is, however, worth noting that their non-binding nature is without prejudice to their undoubted importance for clarifying the relevant provision(s) of regional treaties through their authoritative interpretation.

Within the evolution of new regionalism since the 1990s the growing trend of the both regional human rights systems and regional human rights institutional structures may be identified. Regional mechanisms of human rights today cover five parties of the world: namely, Africa, the Americas, Europe, Arab countries and Asia-Pacific. They naturally differ in the reasons of their origin, resulting in the different concepts of human rights the need of interested states to establish a regional framework for human rights protection and the complexity of relevant regulations. As regards their effectiveness as a whole and the degree of their practical "everyday" efficiency for the protection of human rights, they may be briefly structured as follows:

Europe and the Americas—Advanced regional systems of human rights protection. These systems have a whole set of regional human rights treaties with respective supervisory, expert and judicial systems. The Inter-American system followed to large extent the European system although some problems still prevent its future development because the system is not universal due to absence of the USA as a state party to the Inter-American Convention of Human Rights, and the lack of direct access of individuals to the Inter-American Court of Human Rights (obligatory through the Commission on Human Rights).

Africa—An emerging regional system requiring further consolidation. The great problems consist of the absence of political will of some states to fully cooperate and participate in the regional system, the structural "overlapping" between pan-African and subregional courts, the lack of the direct access of individuals to regional judicial bodies, resistant objections against the supranational nature of regional judicial bodies, etc.

Arab countries—An emerging regional system *in statu nascendi* with respect to the initial stage of standards setting and implementation machinery, lack of institutional practice and operational human rights regional court, the inconsistency of regional human rights documents with respect to international human rights standards, etc.

Asia-Pacific—A region without an effective regional institutional structure of human rights protection. Taking into account the great cultural and political diversities among states, their lack of homogeneity today prevents any idea of a regional integration project. Subregional human rights mechanisms seem therefore more realistic.

Their analysis clearly confirms uneven level and complexity of regional human rights systems in different parts of the world. Their particularities result from a set of various factors having historical, religious, ethnic and other natures. A specific factor represents the "strict" concept of sovereignty, preventing external control of the human rights aspect before a regional judicial body on the basis of an individual complaint of a concerned person. This is one of the main reasons for different approaches to the regional human rights structures excluding direct access of individuals to a regional judicial body. Among them, one can mention the optional (non-compulsory jurisdiction) of the regional judicial body, the preventive "filtering" systems before non-judicial bodies (commissions) combined with their right to bring the case before a judicial body, systems in which different entities are entitled to bring the case before a judicial body but the individual has no such right, etc.

Although the regional organizations were emerging more or less spontaneously during the second half of the 20th century, this fact has never precluded their mutual relations and various forms of cooperation. Even though the intensity and form, as well as legal regulation, differed throughout various periods of the development of regionalism, the literature generally refers to this type of mutual relation as interregionalism. This is not a completely new phenomenon, since it emerged along with the first regional organizations in the second half of the 20th century as their associate segment, and it has been growing into a general phenomenon within current global international relations.

The interregional relations are carried out and developed in specific international forums, which represents a certain novelty within international relations and international law, since they are called for the purposes of interregional cooperation and, in some cases, we can already notice slight features of an emerging institutionalism (e.g. in the form of permanent secretariats).

Considering the specifications of old and new regionalism, the interregional relations appearing in the old regionalism may be called the old interregionalism, while those arising later and being connected with new regionalism are called the new interregionalism, both of them differing in character.

The old interregionalism was typical for having a dominant position in the European Community (EC), which entered into relations based on dialogue and cooperation both with the regional organizations and with the groups of states as well or with individual states, while also maintaining its exclusive position as the most developed regional organization (*the hub and spokes model*).

The EC within the interregional relations featured various characteristics at that time. The European communities, especially in their external relations, took advantage of mainly interregional cooperation mechanisms as a means to make the integration relations stronger and advanced within other regional groups, to strengthen their own international position and, finally, to ensure international regional security, stability and prosperity outside their own borders, too.

At the time of old regionalism, the interregional relations had been developing between the regional groups mainly in trade and economics and had been geographically limited due to the existence of the world colonial system. The development of interregional relations between political and security regional groupings was slowed down by being oriented internally and by the Cold War atmosphere, too.

However, after the Cold War ended and new regionalism started, the new interregionalism began to develop under more favourable conditions because the obstacles connected with the superpowers' policy, spheres of influence and the closed character of regional organizations had been removed. New interregionalism extended its scope geographically because new regional organizations in other parts of the world started to join the interregional relationship.

New interregionalism is now producing new types of relations (even if not having equal levels and intensity) which are becoming institutionalized, which is a new phenomenon in terms of international relations.

Ultimately, the interregional relations reflect the rules and principles typical for regional groups in different parts of the world. As a result, the regional organizations in the developing world promote the rather flexible and informal character of their interregional relationships, with no strong institutional structure and with rather informal systems of consultations and exchange of opinions. In contrast, the EU approach is affected by attempts to formalize and institutionalize the interregional relations at the higher level, which is enhanced by its significant position and growing intensity and complexity of such relations.

Considering the forms of current interregionalism, one can say that treaty interregionalism laid down the rights and obligations of the subjects of interregional relations through rules of international law. Currently it concerns a set of treaties of the EC-EU with other regional organizations, as well as with individual states and groups of states from different parts of the world. In brief, we can highlight the different content and institutional variety as well as uneven complexity of interregional treaties, reflecting different levels of relations and cooperation their parties have, on the one side, and the willingness of the parties to regulate such relations by means of international treaties on the other. In this respect we can speak about the individualization of the interregional treaty regulations.

Another feature the interregional treaties have in common is their institutional element, as there is a rule that those with a more complex character and higher level of cooperation (association agreements, partnership agreements) also bring a more complex institutional structure.

Within its framework, along with common bodies with general competence, there are also bodies of specialized nature for purposes of cooperation in specific areas, which implies an element of specialization. The existence of more or less developed and specialized institutional bodies thus allows describing the current treaty interregionalism as an institutional one. One can therefore infer that basic condition of the current treaty interregionalism represents institutional regionalism whose organizations are competent to conclude treaties with third subjects.

Even though the international treaties the EC-EU concluded within the framework of its interregional relations regulate mainly various types and forms of trade, economic and development cooperation, their impact on the general international law is indubitable. This is based especially on the fact that the essential element of such treaties constitutes an obligation of the parties to respect the democratic principles of international law and fundamental human rights (with reference to the Universal Declaration of Human Rights), as well as to the rule of law that the internal and external policies of the parties should be based on. Considering the significant (still more or less dominant) position of the EU within such relations, one can see it seeks to ensure respect for general values and principles of international law also in terms of interregional relations with third countries or their groups, as well as in terms of international regional organizations in various parts of the world. In the context of the treaty interregionalism, this respect is the basis and essential assumption for purposes of successful cooperation between the parties. Monitoring and ensuring that they are complied with in the process of the treaties' application is enhanced by the different institutional structure of treaties, political dialogue between the parties and the agreed consultations regime. The specific sanction systems are, however, not typical for interregional treaties.

Another feature of the interregional treaties lies in their provisions concerning political dialogue, the scope of which regularly goes beyond the interregional framework. This is so because the subject matter might be any issue concerning international policy constituting a matter of joint interest of the parties. A political dialogue might result in the coordination of procedures and positions between the parties at international conferences, within the UN, the World Trade Organization or any other international organization. In this respect it should be noted that interregionalism might bring impulses, proposals or recommendations made by the regional parties to deal with current issues of global international policy in the area of international conferences or within universal international organizations.

Finally, with respect to the democratization of international law, here, the contribution of interregional treaties is not limited to official bodies of international organizations or to the representatives of states. There is a tendency to also involve other structures and entities such as informal associations of civil society representatives, entrepreneurial circles, social and trade union partners and non-governmental organizations, providing them with the possibility to formulate their own views, positions or recommendations. The aforesaid is relevant not only in respect to the development of interregional relations themselves, but these entities in developing countries apply those provisions to enforce their legitimacy and importance within domestic civil society and in a wider context have a democratizing nature.

From the viewpoint of general international law, there are two more facts that should be mentioned in relation to treaty interregionalism. The first relates to the impact interregional treaties have on the treaty-making power of member states within regional organizations. For example, within the areas where the regional organizations have been authorized by their member states to conclude treaties with third parties, they substitute (fully or partially) the treaty-making capacity of member states. This generally results in limiting the subjects with treaty-making power in general international law. The second is the subject matter of interregional treaties containing common regional principles and values instead of individual values typical for international treaties concluded between states.

As regards other aspects of the relationship between the regionalism and general international law, history confirms that regional organizations were not established inside an international legal vacuum, but in the "background" of general international law, with which they entered into certain relations. The aforementioned applies to regional treaty-making organizations because the legal rules contained in it might have a larger or smaller impact on general international law, too. It is like this because general international law has no rule that would restrict the scope and content of regional law-making to matters related only to the regional organization and the subject of its activities.

Similarly, the process and the law-making of general rules of international law do not preclude the regional rule at the beginning of their creation if the content and significance of such rule exceeds the regional scope and interests, and a wider international community of states regards it as useful.

As a result, treaties adopted at a regional level might not only confirm or develop existing rules of general international law, but they might become initiators of its new rules, too. If the originally regional rules of regional law overlap in general international law, they can lose their regional character and can be regarded as contributing for the purposes of the development of the general international law. It is, therefore, possible that regional rules might gain the character of general rules in the future, provided that they reflect not only the particularity and specification of relations within a regional group, but also that the scope and application within the international group is wider. Third and non-member states can become familiar with them through custom or a treaty.

The aforesaid proves that currently there are no strict dividing lines between the regional treaty systems and general international law but the impact they have on each other might have different forms, extent or intensity in various periods.

To sum up, regional organizations' law-making can contribute to the confirmation of the rules of general international law, to their development among the members of the regional group or trigger the process of the creation of a new rule of general international law.

Finally, the aforesaid is not to the detriment of the "*soft law*" rules accepted and applied within the regional organizations through recommendations, resolutions, opinions, codes of conduct, etc., which, despite having legally unbinding character, may have a real impact on the conduct of the member states of the regional organization. This impact is apparent when these rules have been adopted in a transparent and democratic way and when their content is useful and practical. Such soft rules of the organization are currently recognized not only as useful for the organizations themselves but can play a role in the process of rising regional treaties and the customary rules. It should also be added that international organizations are, in certain areas, subject also to internal legal orders of their "host" states to such a scope and manner as compatible with their privileges and immunities.

With respect to general international law governing activities of international organizations, it should be pointed out that their dynamic growth in the post-war period meant that the legal rules of regional character were not sufficient enough to regulate all aspects of their activities. In the second half of the 20th century the rules of general international law were gradually completed in implementation. Therefore, the complex legal basis of regional organizations today consists not only of their constituent acts and their own legal orders, but also the relevant rules of general international law.

The International Law Commission was charged with the preparation of codification conventions in the 1970s and 1980s, regulating the uniformity of some activities of international organizations. Its character is not concerned with the specific activities of individual international organizations, but concerns activities common to international organizations regardless of their variety and number of member states (universal and regional).

Including the codification matters related to international organizations in the working programme of the International Law Commission was not a problem since the aim, according to its Statute, is to promote the progressive development of international law and its codification, and the Commission is entitled to carry out this function both in the fields of public international law and private international law. Because the codification and the progressive development of international law is not restricted only with respect to states and among states, the working programme of the Commission can include the rules concerning international organizations for the purposes of their codification and/or progressive development.

As with codification issues related to the states, the international organizations also contained the elements of codification and its progressive development to a different degree. Although some codification drafts could have been based on a more or less stable practice of international organizations, emphasizing the traditional codification aspect (representation of states in international organizations, conclusion of international treaties between the international organizations and the states or the international organizations themselves), the regulation of further matters was based on the relatively weak practice of international organizations (responsibility of international organizations for international unlawful conduct).

The codification outputs carried out by the Commission up to now include four international conventions, one draft of articles and one Guide to Practice on Reservations to Treaties, namely: the Vienna Convention on the Law of Treaties of 1969, the Vienna Convention on the Representation of States in their Relations with International Organizations of a Universal Character of 1975, the Vienna Convention on Succession of States in respect of Treaties of 1978, the Vienna Convention on the Law of Treaties between States and International Organizations or between International Organizations of 1986, the Draft Articles on the Responsibility of International Organizations of 2011 and the Guide to Practice on Reservations to Treaties of 2011.

Although the codification of topics related to international organizations taking place after a similar topic concerning the states had been completed, it had an impact on the Commission's work relating to international organizations. The results of the Commission's work confirm that in preparing some drafts, the Commission was more or less inspired by previous works, for example, within the preparation of the draft Convention on the Law of Treaties between States and International Organizations or between International Organizations or the Draft Articles on the Responsibility of International Organizations.

The outcome of the Commission's work was, despite diversity of international organizations, the unified rules of general international law in specific areas of their activities. As a practical consequence in these areas the organization's own rules apply only to a limited extent and in cases expressly laid down in codification treaties. It should be noted that the dominant position of the organization's own rules was confirmed in the Vienna Convention on the Law of Treaties of 1969 (Article 5), the Vienna Convention on Succession of States in respect of Treaties of 1978 (Article 4), the Vienna Convention on the Law of Treaties between States and International Organizations or between International Organizations of 1986 (Article 6), as well as in the Draft Articles on the Responsibility of International Organizations of 2011 (Article 64). This approach, fixing the scope of application of internal rules of organization vis á vis codified rules of international law, provides a legal guarantee for the proper application of relevant legal rules.

Regarding the difficulties of general international law arising due to lawmaking activities of international organizations, this matter was included in the International Law Commission's programme concerning the fragmentation of international law in 2002. The Commission's output is the Report of the Study Group.

According to the Study Group, international law is fragmented as a consequence of its development and diversification, with various sets of specialized and relatively autonomous groups of legal rules (commercial law, human rights law, environmental law) with their own institutions and principles. They are autonomous with respect to each other and so they relate also to general international law. These sets of rules (including regional character) do not necessarily comply with the general rules of international law, and if their deviations become more significant and their occurrence more frequent, it would harm the unity of general international law.

When analysing this aspect of fragmentation, the Study Group of the Commission concluded that the Vienna Convention on the Law of Treaties of 1969 is suitable for dealing with these problems upon application of the relevant principles of treaty law, namely, *lex specialis derogat legi generali*, the systemic interpretation of international treaties in accordance with Article 31 Section 3(c) of the Vienna Convention on the Law of Treaties, the *lex posterior derogat legi priori* principle and Article 103 of the UN Charter.

The Study Group at the same time also pointed out that the institutional scope of fragmentation was based on the parallel existence of two or more international judicial bodies having competing jurisdiction and the problems related to this procedural aspect of fragmentation. It was, however, decided to leave this issue aside as, according to the Study Group, it was best dealt with by the international courts themselves in their procedural codes.

Bibliography

Acharya, A.: Comparative Regionalism: A Field Whose Time Has Come? In: Fioramonti, L. (ed.): *Regionalism in a Changing World: Comparative Perspective in the New Global Order*. London and New York: Routledge, 2012, pp. 3–15.

Acharya, A.: Regionalism and Emerging (Intrusive) World Order: Sovereignty, Autonomy, Identity. In: *Paper for Conference on "After the Global Crisis: What Next for Regionalism?"*. Toronto: University of Warwick, 1999, pp. 2–30. Available at: www2.warwick.ac.uk/fac/soc/csgr/events/conferences/1999_conferences/3rdannualconference/papers/acharya.pdf

Afrika, J.-G.K., Ajumbo, G.: Informal Cross Border Trade in Africa: Implications and Policy Recommendations. In: *Africa Economic Brief*, Vol. 3, No. 10, 2012. Available at: www.afdb.org/fileadmin/uploads/afdb/Documents/Publications/Economic%20Brief%20-%20Informal%20Cross%20Border%20Trade%20in%20Africa%20Implications%20and%20Policy%20Recommendations%20-%20Volume%203.pdf

Al-Midani, M.A.: The League of Arab States and the Arab Charter on Human Rights. Available at: www.acihl.org/articles.htm?article_id=6

Alter, K.J.: The Global Spread of European Style International Courts. In: *West European Politics*, Vol. 35, No. 1, 2012, pp. 135–154.

Alter, K.J.: The New International Courts. In: *iCourts Working Paper Series*, No. 2, 2013, pp. 1–54. Available at: http://jura.ku.dk/icourts/research-resources/working-papers/

Alter, K.J., Hooghe, L.: Regional Dispute Settlement. In: Börzel, T.A., Risse, T. (eds.): *The Oxford Handbook of Comparative Regionalism*. Oxford: Oxford University Press, 2016, pp. 538–559.

Alvarez, J.E.: The New Dispute Settlers: (Half) Trust and Consequences. In: *Texas International Law Journal*, Vol. 38, 2003, pp. 405, 427.

Archer, C.: *International Organizations*. London: Routledge, 1992.

Baudenbacher, C.: Judicialization: Can the European Model Be Exported to Other Parts of the World? In: *Texas International Law Journal*, Vol. 39, 2003 pp. 381–400.

Berkofsky, A.: Comparing EU and Asian Integration Processes – The EU a Role Model for Asia? European Policy Centre (EPC), 2002. Available at: www.epc.eu/documents/uploads/606968147_EPC%20Issue%20Paper%2023%20EU%20Asian%20Integration.pdf

Berridge, G., Lloyd, L.: *The Palgrave Macmillan Dictionary of Diplomacy*. London, UK: Palgrave Macmillan, 2012, 401 p.

Bøås, M.: Regions and Regionalisation: A Heretic's View. In: *Regionalism and Regional Integration in Africa*. Uppsala: Nordiska Afrikainstitutet, 2001, Discussion Paper 11, pp. 27–39. Available at: www.files.ethz.ch/isn/102627/11.pdf

Börzel, T.A., Risse, T.: Diffusing (Inter-) Regionalism: The EU as a Model of Regional Integration. In: *KFG Working Paper Series* (The Transformative Power of Europe), No. 7, 2009, p. 23. Available at: http://userpage.fu-berlin.de/kfgeu/kfgwp/wpseries/WorkingPaperKFG_7.pdf

Brölmann, C.: Deterritorialization in International Law: Moving Away From the Divide Between National and International Law. In: Nijman, J., Nollkaemper, A. (eds.): *New Perspectives on the Divide Between National and International Law*. Oxford: Oxford University Press, 2007, pp. 84–109.

Brownlie, I.: *Principles of Public International Law*, 6th Edition. Oxford: Oxford University Press, 2003, 784 p.

Caflisch, L.: The Reform of the European Court of Human Rights: Protocol No. 14 and Beyond. In: *Human Rights Law Review*, Vol. 6, No. 2, 2006, pp. 403–415.

Chevalier, B.: Les nouveaux développements de la procédure préjudicielle dans le domaine de l'espace judiciare européen: la procédure préjudicielle d'urgence et les réformes principales prévues par le Traité de Lisbonne. In: *ERA Forum*, Vol. 9, No. 4, 2009, pp. 591–607.

Clapham, C.: Review Article Africa's International Relations. In: *African Affairs*, Vol. 86, No. 345, October 1987, pp. 575–584.

Danilenko, G.M.: The Economic Court of the Commonwealth of Independent States. In: *International Law and Politics*, Vol. 31, 1999, pp. 893–918.

De Chazournes, L.B.: Changing Roles of International Organizations: Global Administrative Law and the Interplay of Legitimacies. In: *International Organizations Law Review*, Vol. 6, 2009, pp. 655–666.

De Lombaerde, P.: How to "Connect" Micro-Regions With Macro-Regions? A Note. In: *Perspectives on Federalism*, Vol. 3, 2010, pp. E29–E37.

De Lombaerde, P., Söderbaum, F., Van Langenhove, L., Baert, F.: The Problems of Comparison in Comparative Regionalism. In: *Jean Monet/Robert Schuman Paper Series*, Vol. 9, No. 7, April 2009, pp. 1–22.

Dolzer, R., Schreuer, C.: *Principles of International Investment Law*, 2nd Edition. Oxford: Oxford University Press, 2012, 456 p.

Draper, P.: Breaking Free From Europe: Why Africa Needs Another Model of Regional Integration? In: Fioramonti, L. (ed.): *Regionalism in a Changing World: Comparative Perspective in the New Global Order*. London and New York: Routledge, 2013, pp. 67–82.

Elbert, L.: Regionalism and International Organizations. In: Klucka, J., Elbert, L. (eds.): *Regionalism and Its Contribution to General International Law*. Kosice: P.J. Šafarik University in Košice, 2015, 236 p.

Eliantonio, M., Roer-Eide, H.: Regional Courts and *locus standi* for Private Parties: Can the CJEU Learn Something From the Others? In: *The Law & Practice of International Courts and Tribunals*, Vol. 13, No. 1, 2014, pp. 27–53.

Fabbrini, S.: European Regionalism in Comparative Perspective: Features and Limits of the New Medievals Approach to World Order. In: *Paper Submitted at the 3rd Pan Helenic Conference on International Political Economy*, University of Athens, May 16–18, 2008, pp. 2–33. Available at: http://aei.pitt.edu/14996/1/EurReg.pdf

Fagbayibo, B.: Common Problems Affecting Supranational Attempts in Africa: An Analytical Overview. In: *Potchefstroom Electronic Law Journal*, Vol. 16, No. 1, 2013, pp. 35–69.

Falk, R.: The Post-Westphalia Enigma. In: Hettne, B., Odén, B. (eds.): *Global Governance in the 21st Century: Alternative Perspective on World Order*. Stockholm: Almkvist & Wiksell, 2002, 204 p.

Fanenbruck, C., Meisner, L.: Supranational Courts as Engines for Regional Integration? A Comparative Study of the Southern African Development Community Tribunal, the European Court of Justice and the Andean Court of Justice. In: *KFG Working Paper Series* (The Transformative Power of Europe), No. 66, 2015, FUB, pp. 6–27. Available at: www.polsoz.fu-berlin.de/en/v/transformeurope/publications/working_paper/wp/wp66/WP-66-Fanenbruck_Meissner_WEB.pdf

Fawcett, L.: Exploring Regional Domains: A Comparative History of Regionalism. In: *International Affairs*, Vol. 80, No. 3, 2004, pp. 429–446.

Fawcett, L.: The History and Concept of Regionalism. In: *UNU-CRIS Working Paper*, W-2013/5, pp. 3–18.

Fawcett, L., Hurrell, A.: *Regionalism in World Politics: Regional Organizations and International Order*. Oxford: Oxford University Press, 1995, 342 p.

Fedder, E.H.: The Functional Basis of International Privileges and Immunities: A New Concept in International Law and Organizations. In: *American University Law Review*, Vol. 9, 1960, pp. 60–69.

Fioramonti, L.: The Evolution of Supranational Regionalism: From Top-Down Regulatory Governance to Sustainability Regions? In: *UNU-CRIS Working Paper*, W-2014/2, pp. 2–26.

Fischer-Lescano, A., Teubner, G.: Regime-Collisions: The Vain Search for Legal Unity in the Fragmentation of Global Law. In: *Michigan Journal of International Law*, Vol. 25, No. 4, 2004, pp. 999–1045.

Franke, B.K.: Competing Regionalism in Africa and the Continent's Emerging Security Architecture. In: *African Studies Quarterly*, Vol. 9, No. 3, 2007, pp. 31–64.

Gilson, J.: New Interregionalism? The EU and East Asia. In: *Journal of European Integration*, Vol. 27, No. 3, 2005, pp. 307–326.

Hänggi, H.: Interregionalism: Empirical and Theoretical Perspectives. Paper Prepared for the Workshop: *Dollars, Democary and Trade: External Influence on Economic Integration in Americas*. Los Angeles, May 18, 2000, 14 p. Available at: www.cap.lmu.de/transatlantic/download/Haenggi.PDF

Hänggi, H.: Interregionalism as a Multifaceted Phenomenon (In Search of a Typology). In: Hänggi, H., Roloff, R., Rüland, J. (eds.): *Interregionalism and International Relations*. London and New York: Routledge, 2006, pp. 31–61.

Helfer, L.R.: Redesigning the European Court of Human Rights: Embeddedness as a Deep Structural Principle of the European Human Rights Regime. In: *The European Journal of International Law*, Vol. 19, No. 1, 2008, pp. 125–159.

Hellquist, E.: Regional Organizations and Sanctions Against Members: Explaining the Different Trajectories of the African Union, the League of Arab States and the Association of Southeast Asian Nations. In: *KFG Working Paper Series* (The Transformative Power of Europe) No. 59, 2014, 46 p. Available at: http://userpage.fu-berlin.de/kfgeu/kfgwp/wpseries/WorkingPaperKFG_59.pdf

Hettne, B.: Globalization and the New Regionalism: The Second Great Transformation. In: Hettne, B., Inotai, A., Sunkel, O. (eds.): *Globalism and the New Regionalism*. New York: St. Martin Press, 1999, pp. 1–24.
Hettne, B.: The New Regionalism Revisited. In: Söderbaum, F., Shaw, T. (eds.): *Theories of New Regionalism (A Palgrave Macmillan Reader)*. Basingstoke, UK: Palgrave Macmillan, 2003, pp. 22–42.
Hettne, B., Inotai, A.: The New Regionalism: Implications for the Global Development and International Security. In: *UN University: The Research for Action*, UN, 1994, 103 p. Available at: www.wider.unu.edu/sites/default/files/RFA14.pdf
Heyns, C.H., Padilla, D., Zwaak, L.: A Schematic Comparison of Regional Human Rights Systems: An Update. In: *African Human Rights Law Journal*, Vol. 5, No. 2, 2005, pp. 308–320.
Irwin, D.A.: Multilateral and Bilateral Trade Policies in the World Trading System: An Historical Perspective. In: De Melo, J., Panagariya, A. (eds.): *New Dimension in Regional Integration*. New York: Cambridge University Press, 1993, p. 97.
Jennings, R.Y.: *Collected Writings of Sir Robert Jennings*. Hague: Kluwer Law International, 1998, 1484 p.
Jetschke, A., Murray, P.: Diffusing Regional Integration: The EU and Southeast Asia. In: *West European Politics*, Vol. 35, No. 1, 2012, pp. 174–191.
Kaufmann-Kohler, G.: Interpretive Powers of the Free Trade Commission and the Rule of Law. In: *Fifteen Years of NAFTA Chapter 11 Arbitration*, Juris Net, LLC 2011, pp. 186–187. Available at: www.arbitration-icca.org/media/1/13571335953400/interpretive_powers_of_the_free_trade_commission_and_the_rule_of_law_kaufmann-kohler.pdf
Keller, H., Grover, L.: General Comments of the Human Rights Committee and their Legitimacy. In: Keller, H., Ulfstein, G. (eds.): *UN Human Rights Treaty Bodies: Law and Legitimacy*. Cambridge: Cambridge University Press, 2012, pp. 116–198.
Kelley, J.: The Role of Membership Rules in Regional Organizations. In: *ADB Working Paper Series on Regional Economic Integration*, No. 53, 2010, 53 p. Available at: www.adb.org/sites/default/files/publication/28527/wp53-membership-rules.pdf
Killander, M.: Legal Harmonisation in Africa: Taking Stock and Moving Forward. In: Fioramonti, L. (ed.): *Regionalism in a Changing World: Comparative Perspective in the New Global Order*. London and New York: Routledge, 2013, pp. 83–96.
Kim, J.: Development of Regional Human Rights Regime: Prospects for and Implications to Asia. Available at: www.tokyofoundation.org/sylff/wp-content/uploads/2009/03/sylff_p57-1022.pdf
Kingah, S.: Regional Courts and Human Rights in the Developing World. In: *UNU-CRIS Working Paper*, W-2013/11, 27 p.
Klabbers, J.: *An Introduction to International Institutional Law*, 2nd Edition. Cambridge: Cambridge University Press, 2009, 393 p.
Kühnhardt, L.: African Regional Integration and the Role of the European Union, 42 p. Available at: www.files.ethz.ch/isn/55859/Africa_Reg_Integration.pdf
Kunz, J.L.: Privileges and Immunities of International Organizations. In: *American Journal of International Law*, Vol. 41, No. 4, 1947, pp. 828–862.
Lenaerts, K., Arts, D., Maselis, I.: *Procedural Law of the European Union*. Thompson: Sweet and Maxwell, 2006, 1026 p.

Lenz, T.: External Influences on Regionalism: Studying EU Diffusion and Its Limits. In: *E-International Relations*, 2013, pp. 1–5. Available at: www.e-ir.info/2013/07/17/external-influences-on-regionalism-studying-eu-diffusion-and-its-limits/

Malamud, A., Gardini, G.L.: Has Regionalism Peaked? The Latin American Quagmire and Its Lessons. In: Fioramonti, L. (ed.): *Regionalism in a Changing World: Comparative Perspective in the New Global Order*. London and New York: Routledge, 2013, pp. 116–133.

Mansfield, E.D., Milner, H.V.: The New Wave of Regionalism. In: *International Organizations*, Vol. 53, No. 3, 1999, pp. 589–627.

Maull, H.W., Okfen, N.: Comparing Interregionalism: The Asia-Pacific Economic Cooperation (APEC) and the Asia-Europe Meeting (ASEM). In: Hänggi, H., Roloff, R., Rüland, J. (eds.): *Interregionalism and International Relations*. London and New York: Routledge, 2006, pp. 217–233.

Mbazira, C.H.: Enforcing the Economic, Social and Cultural Rights in the African Charter on Human and Peoples' Rights: Twenty Years of Redundancy, Progression and Significant Strides. In: *African Human Rights Law Journal*, Vol. 6, No. 2, 2006, pp. 358–381.

Mechlem, K.: Treaty Bodies and the Interpretation of Human Rights. In: *Vanderbilt Journal of Transnational Law*, Vol. 42, 2009, pp. 905–947.

Mols, M.: Cooperation With ASEAN: A Success Story. In: Edwards, G., Regelsberger, E. (eds.): *Europe's Global Links: The European Community and Inter-Regional Cooperation*. London: Pinter Publishers, 1990, pp. 143–160.

Mosler, H.: The International Society as Legal Community. In: *Collected Courses of the Hague Academy of International Law*, Vol. 140, No. IV, 1974, pp. 1–320.

Musungu, S.F.: Economic Integration and Human Rights in Africa: A Comment on Conceptual Linkage. In: *African Human Rights Law Journal*, Vol. 3, No. 1, 2003, pp. 88–96.

Narine, S.: Asia, ASEAN and the Question of Sovereignty: The Persistence of Non-Intervention in the Asia Pacific. In: Beeson, M., Stubbs, R. (eds.): *Routledge Handbook of Asian Regionalism*. New York: Routledge, 2012, pp. 155–165.

Ndiaye, T.: Case Story on Gender Dimension of Aid for Trade, ITC, UNIFEM, New York. Available at: www.intracen.org/uploadedFiles/intracenorg/Content/About_ITC/Where_are_we_working/Multi-country_programmes/Women_and_trade/Women%20Informal%20Traders%20Transcending%20African%20Borders.pdf

Nijman, J.E., Nollkaemper, P.A.: *New Perspectives on the Divide Between National and International Law*. Oxford: Oxford University Press, 2007, 416 p.

Njiwa, D.: Tackling Informal Cross-Border Trade in Southern Africa. In: *Bridges Africa*, Vol. 2, No. 1, 2013, pp. 1–3.

Nye, J.S. (ed.): *International Regionalism: Readings*. Boston, MA: Little, Brown & Co., 1968.

Odinkalu, C.A.: Contemporarity, Competition or Contradiction: The Relationship Between the African Court on Human and Peoples' Rights and Regional Economic Courts in East and South Africa. In: *Paper Presented at a Conference of East and Southern States*, Botswana, 2003, 21 p.

Oellers-Frahm, K.: Lawmaking Through Advisory Opinions? In: *German Law Journal*, Vol. 12, No. 5, 2011, pp. 1033–1055.

Osiander, A.: *The States System of Europe, 1640–1990: Peacemaking and the Conditions of International Stability.* Oxford: Clarendon Press, 1994, 368 p.

Oving, A.K.: The Effectiveness of the Enforcement Procedure in the European Community, Lund, 2008. Available at: http://lup.lub.lu.se/luur/download?func=downloadFile&recordOId=1563347&fileOId=1566255

Pasqualucci, J.M.: Advisory Practice of the Inter-American Court of Human Rights: Contributing to the Evolution of International Human Rights Law. In: *Stanford Journal of International Law*, Vol. 38, No. 2, 2002, pp. 241–288.

Pronto, A., Wood, M.: *The International Law Commission 1999–2009 (Volume IV: Treaties, Final Draft Articles, and Other Materials).* Oxford: Oxford University Press, 2010, 890 p.

Prost, M., Clark, P.K.: Unity, Diversity and the Fragmentation of International Law: How Much Does the Multiplication of International Organizations Really Matter? In: *Chinese Journal of International Law*, Vol. 5, No. 2, 2006, pp. 341–370.

Reinch, P.S.: International Unions and their Administration. In: *American Journal of International Law*, Vol. I, No. 3, 1907, pp. 579–623.

Reiterer, M.: Interregionalism as a New Diplomatic Tool: The EU and East Asia. In: *European Foreign Affairs Review*, Vol. 11, 2006, pp. 223–243.

Revauger, J.-P.: Regional Integration in the Commnonwealth Caribbean and the Impact of the European Union. In: *The Round Table: The Commonwealth Journal of International Affairs*, Vol. 97, No. 399, 2008, pp. 857–869.

Robertson, A.H.: *Human Rights in the World: An Introduction to the Study of the International Protection of Human Rights.* Manchester: Manchester University Press (MUP), 1982, 243 p.

Rodley, N.: The Role and Impact of Treaty Bodies. In: Shelton, D. (ed.): *Oxford Handbook of International Human Rights.* Oxford: Oxford University Press, 2013, pp. 621–648.

Romano, C.P.R.: The Proliferation of International Judicial Bodies: The Pieces of the Puzzle. In: *New York University Journal of International Law & Politics*, Vol. 31, No. 4, Summer 1999, pp. 709–751.

Rueda-Junquera, F.: European Integration Model: Lessons for the Central American Common Market. In: *Jean Monnet/Robert Schuman Paper Series*, Vol. 6, No. 4, 2006, 23 p. Available at: www6.miami.edu/eucenter/ruedafinal.pdf

Sadlier, G.: The ECHR – A Victim of Its Own Success. In: *Cork Online Law Review*, No. 7, 2007, pp. 65–85. Available at: http://corkonlinelawreview.com/editions/2007/COLR%202007%207%20Sadlier.pdf

Schmitz, T.: The ASEAN Economic Community and the Rule of Law, 2014. Available at: http://home.lu.lv/~tschmit1/Downloads/BDHK-Workshop_15-12-2014_Schmitz.pdf

Shany, Y.: No Longer a Weak Department of Power? Reflections on the Emergence of a New International Judiciary. In: *The European Journal of International Law*, Vol. 20, No. 1, 2009, pp. 73–91.

Söderbaum, F., Sbragia, A.: EU Studies and the "New Regionalism": What Can Be Gained From Dialogue? In: *Journal of European Integration*, Vol. 32, No. 6, 2010, pp. 563–582.

Stork, J.: New Arab Human Rights Court Is Doomed From the Start. In: *International Business Time*, Human Rights Watch, November 2014, pp. 1–5. Available at: www.hrw.org/news/2014/11/26/new-arab-human-rights-court-doomed-start

Šturma, P.: Drawing a Line Between the Responsibility of an International Organization and Its Member States Under International Law. In: *Czech Yearbook of Public & Private International Law*, Vol. 2, 2011, pp. 3–19.

Tan, M.: Member State Compliance With the Judgments of the Inter-American Court of Human Rights. In: *International Journal of Legal Information*, Vol. 33, No. 3, 2005. Available at: http://scholarship.law.cornell.edu/ijli/vol33/iss3/4/

Teló, M.: *European Union and New Regionalism: Regional Actors and Global Governance in a Post-Hegemonic Era*. Aldershot: Ashgate Publishing 2007, 406 p.

Teló, M.: Introduction: Globalization, New Regionalism and the Role of the EU. In: Teló, M. (ed.): *European Union and New Regionalism: Regional Actors and Global Governance in a Post-Hegemonic Era*. Aldershot: Ashgate Publishing, 2007, pp. 1–18.

Tomuschat, C.H.: International Courts and Tribunals With Regionally Restricted and/or Specialized Jurisdiction. In: *Judicial Settlement of International Disputes: International Court of Justice, Other Courts and Tribunals, Arbitration and Conciliation: An International Symposium*. Berlin: Springer, 1987, pp. 285–416.

Tussie, D.: Latin America: Contrasting Motivations for Regional Projects. In: *Review of International Studies*, Vol. 35, No. S1, 2009, pp. 169–188.

Ulfstein, G.: Individual Complaints. In: Keller, H., Ulfstein, G. (eds.): *UN Human Rights Treaty Bodies: Law and Legitimacy*. Cambridge: Cambridge University Press, 2012, pp. 73–115.

Valle, V.M.: Interregionalism: A Case Study of the European Union and Mercosur. In: *GARNET Working Paper*, No. 51, 2008, pp. 1–27.

Van Dijk, P., Van Hoof, F., Van Rijn, Zwaak, L. (eds.): *Theory and Practice of the European Convention on Human Rights*. Oxford: Intersentia, 2006, 1190 p.

Van Langenhove, L.: Regionalism as a Political Vision. In: *UNU-CRIS Occasional Paper*, No. O-2005/15. Paper Has Been Presented at the International Conference: "New Regionalism From Global and European Perspective", Prague, 2005, pp. 1–14.

Van Langenhove, L., Costea, A.-C.: The EU as Global Actor and the Emergence of "Third Generation" Regionalism. In: *UNU-CRIS Occasional Papers*, No. O-2005-14, p. 15. Available at: www.academia.edu/15719480/The_EU_as_a_Global_Actor_and_the_Emergence_of_Third_Generation_Regionalism

Väyrynen, R.: Regionalism: Old and New. In: *International Studies Review*, Vol. 5, No. 1, 2003, pp. 25–51.

Vicuna, F.O., Pinto, C.: The Peaceful Settlement of Disputes: Prospect for the Twenty-First Century. *Preliminary Report Prepared for the 1999 Centennial of the First International Peace Conference*. Council of Europe, Doc. CAHDI, 1998.

Virzo, R.: The Preliminary Ruling Procedures at International Regional Courts and Tribunals. In: *The Law & Practice of International Courts and Tribunals*, Vol. 10, No. 2, 2011, pp. 285–313.

Voitovich, S.A.: *International Economic Organizations in the International Legal Process*. London: Martinus Nijhoff Publishers, 1995, 199 p.

Yeo, L.H.: Institutional Regionalism Versus Networked Regionalism: Europe and Asia Compared. In: *International Politics*, Vol. 47, No. 3/4, 2010, pp. 324–337.

Yerima, T.F.: Comparative Evaluation of the Challenges of African Regional Human Rights Courts. In: *Journal of Politics and Law*, Vol. 4, No. 2, 2011, pp. 120–127.

Wahyuningrum, Y.: The ASEAN Intergovernmental Commission on Human Rights: Origins, Evolution and the Way Forward. In: *International Institute for Democracy and Electoral Assistance (IDEA)*, Stockholm, 2014. Available at: www.idea.int/sites/default/files/publications/the-asean-intergovernmental-commission-on-human-rights-origins-evolution-and-the-way-forward.pdf

Warleigh-Lack, A.W., Robinson, N., Rosamond, B. (eds.): *New Regionalism and the European Union: Dialogues, Comparisons and New Research Directions.* London: Routledge, 2011, 296 p.

Watts, A. (ed.): *The International Law Commission 1949–1998*, Vol. II. Oxford: Oxford University Press, 1999, xvi+609–1644 p.

Weiler, J.: The Community System: The Dual Character of Supranationalism. In: *Yearbook of European Law*, Vol. 1, No. 1, 1981, pp. 267–306.

Weiler, J.: *The Constitution of Europe: Do the New Clothes Have an Emperor? And Other Essays on European Integration.* Cambridge: Cambridge University Press, 1999, 364 p.

Wouters, J., De Man, P.: International Organizations as Law-Makers. In: *Leuven Centre for Global Governance Studies*, Working Paper No. 21, 2009, pp. 1–33. Available at: https://ghum.kuleuven.be/ggs/publications/working_papers/new_series/wp21-30/wp21.pdf

Wouters, J., Odermatt, J.: Are All International Organizations Created Equal? Reflections on the ILC's Draft Articles of Responsibility of International Organizations. In: *Global Governance Opinions*, 2012, pp. 2–10. Available at: https://ghum.kuleuven.be/ggs/publications/opinions/opinions13-wouters-odermatt.pdf

International Treaties

African Charter of Human Rights. Available at: www.achpr.org/files/instruments/achpr/banjul_charter.pdf

Agreement Between the EFTA States on the Establishment of a Surveillance Authority and a Court of Justice. Available at: www.efta.int/sites/default/files/documents/legal-texts/the-surveillance-and-court-agreement/Surveillance-and-Court-Agreement-consolidated.pdf

Agreement Establishing an Association Between Central America on the One Hand and the EU and Its Member States on the Other on June 29, 2012. Available at: http://eur-lex.europa.eu/legalcontent/EN/AUTO/?uri=uriserv:OJ.L_.2012.346.01.0001.01.ENG#L_2012346EN.01000301

Agreement Establishing the Caribbean Court of Justice. Available at: www.caribbeancourtofjustice.org/wp-content/uploads/2011/09/ccj_agreement.pdf

American Convention on Human Rights "Pact of San José, Costarica" on November 22, 1969. Available at: www.refworld.org/docid/3ae6b36510.html

Arab Charter on Human Rights. Available at: http://www.humanrights.se/wp-content/uploads/2012/01/Arab-Charter-on-Human-Rights.pdf

Arrangements for Effective Cooperation With Other Intergovernmental Organizations-Relations Between the WTO and United Nations. Available at: www.wto.org/english/thewto_e/coher_e/wto_un_e.htm

ASEAN Charter. Available at: www.asean.org/wp-content/uploads/2012/05/11.-October-2015-The-ASEAN-Charter-18th-Reprint-Amended-updated-on-05_-April-2016-IJP.pdf

ASEAN Free Trade Area. Available at: www.asean.org/communities/asean-economic-community/category/asean-free-trade-area-afta-council

ASEAN Treaties/Agreements and Ratification as of September 30, 2009. Available at: www.asean.org/archive/documents/ASCC-ASEAN-Agreements-and-treaties-090930.pdf

CEMAC Treaty: Central African Economic and Monetary Community, 1994 (Revised 2008). Available at: www.internationaldemocracywatch.org/attachments/173_CEMAC%20Treaty%20(French).pdf

Charter of the Association of Southeast Asian Nations. Available at: www.asean.org/asean/asean-charter/asean-charter

Charter of the Organization of American States. Available at: www.oas.org/dil/treaties_A4_Charter_of_the_Organization_of_AmericanaeStates.htm

Constitutive Act of the African Union. Available at: www.achpr.org/files/instruments/au-constitutive-act/au_act_2000_eng.pdf

Convention on International Civil Aviation, 1944. Available at: www.icao.int/publications/Pages/doc7300.aspx

Cooperation Agreement Between the European Community and Its Members States and the States of the Gulf, 1988. Available at: http://trade.ec.europa.eu/doclib/docs/2008/september/tradoc_140300.pdf

Cooperation Agreement Between the European Economic Community of the One Part and the Cartagena Agreement and the Member Countries Thereof- Bolivia, Colombia, Ecuador, Peru and Venezuela- of the Other Part on December 17, 1983, Official Journal of EC, L 157, June 24, 1988.

Cooperation Agreement Between Member Countries of ASEAN and European Community- Kuala Lumpur, March 7, 1980. Available at: http://asean.org/?static_post=external-relations-european-union-nuremberg-declaration-on-an-eu-asean-enhanced-partnership-nuremberg-germany-15-march-2007

Council Regulation (EEC) No 1591/84 of 4 June 1984 Concerning the Conclusion Cooperation Agreement Between the European Economic Community of the One Part and the Cartagena Agreement and the Member Countries Thereof- Bolivia, Colombia, Ecuador, Peru and Venezuela-of the Other Part on December 17, 1983.

East African Community Treaty (1967 EAC Treaty). Available at: www.eac.int/sites/default/files/docs/treaty_eac_amended-2006_1999.pdf

ECOWAS-Revised Treaty of the Economic Community of West African States. Available at: www.ecowas.int/wp-content/uploads/2015/01/Revised-treaty.pdf

EEC-Greece Association Agreement. Available at: www.cvce.eu/en/education/unit-content/-/unit/02bb76df-d066-4c08-a58a-d4686a3e68ff/1039c1de-c68c-43a2-a45a-66aef48c5c6f#ea36b530-f7ee-46f3-a26b-5dc4ea1a5508_en&overlay

Europe Agreement Establishing an Association Between the European Communities and their Member States, of the One Part, and the Slovak Republic, of the Other Part, OJ of 31.12.94 No L 359: 2–201. Available at: http://eur-lex.europa.eu/LexUriServ/LexUriServ.do?uri=CELEX:21994A1231%2830%29:EN:HTML

European Convention on Human Rights, 1950. Available at: www.echr.coe.int/Documents/Convention_ENG.pdf

European Convention on Nationality, 1997. Available at: http://conventions.coe.int/Treaty/Commun/QueVoulezVous.asp?CL=ENG&NT=166

European Convention on Transfrontier Television, 1989. Available at: https://rm.coe.int/168007b03

Framework Agreement on Cooperation Between the European Economic Community and the Cartagena Agreement and Its Member Countries, Namely the Republic of Bolivia, the Republic of Colombia, the Republic of Ecuador, the Republic of Peru and the Republic of Venezuela on April 23, 1992. Available at: http://ec.europa.eu/world/agreements/downloadFile.do?fullText=yes&treatyTransId=864

Free Trade Agreement Between the European Community and the Overseas Countries and Territories (OCT) (Council Decision 2013/755/EU of 25 November 2013 on the Association of the Overseas Countries and Territories With the European Union ("Overseas Association Decision").

International Agreement on Olive Oil and Table Olives, 1986. Available at: https://treaties.un.org/pages/ViewDetails.aspx?src=TREATY&mtdsg_no=XIX-30&chapter=19&lang=en

International Coffee Agreement, 1983. Available at: https://treaties.un.org/doc/Publication/UNTS/Volume%201333/volume-1333-I-22376-English.pdf

International Monetary Fund Agreement, 1996. Available at: www.imf.org/external/pubs/ft/aa/pdf/aa.pdf

Interregional Framework Cooperation Agreement Between the European Community and Its Member States, of One Part and the Southern Common Market and Its Party States of the Other Part on December 15, 1995. Available at: www.sice.oas.org/TPD/MER_EU/negotiations/Framework1995_e.pdf

The Kyoto Protocol to the Frame Convention on Climate Change of 1997. Available at: www.kyotoprotocol.com/resource/kpeng.pdf

Marrakesh Agreement Establishing the World Trade Organization, April 15, 1994. Available at: www.wto.org/english/docs_e/legal_e/04-wto.pdf

OHADA Treaty on the Establishment of the Organisation for the Harmonization of Business Law in Africa, 1993. Available at: www.google.sk/search?q=g&rlz=1C1CHZL_skSK695SK695&oq=g&aqs=chrome. .69i60l5j69i57.2856j0j7&sourceid=chrome&ie=UTF-8#q=ohad

Olivos Protocol. Available at: www.mercosur.int/innovaportal/v/4054/4/innova.front/textos_fundacionales

Partnership Agreement Between the Members of the African, Caribbean and Pacific Group of States on the One Part and the European Community and Its Member States on the Other Part on June 23, 2000 (Cotonou Agreement), Revised in Luxembourg on June 25, 1995 and Ougadougou on June 22, 2010. Available at: www.europarl.europa.eu/intcoop/acp/03_01/pdf/cotonou_2006_en.pdf

Political Dialogue and Cooperation Agreement Between the European Community and Its Member States of the One Part, and the Andean Community and Its Member Countries, (Bolivia, Colombia, Ecuador, Peru and Venezuela) of Other Part on December 15, 2003. Available at: http://eur-lex.europa.eu/legal-content/EN/TXT/?uri=CELEX:52003PC0695(01)

Protocol (A/P.I/7/91) on the Community Court of Justice of July 6, 1991. Available at: www.courtecowas.org/site2012/pdf_files/protocol.pdf

Protocol No. 2 to the Convention on Human Rights and Fundamental Freedoms. Available at: www.echr.coe.int/Documents/Library_Collection_P2_ETS044E_ENG.pdf

Protocol No. 11 to the Convention on the Protection of Human Rights and Fundamental Freedoms. Available at: https://rm.coe.int/1680084821

Protocol No. 16 to the Convention on the Protection of Human Rights and Fundamental Freedoms, Strasbourg 2013, Council of Europe Treaty Series, No. 124.

Protocol of the Court of Justice of the African Union. Available at: www.peaceau.org/uploads/protocol-court-of-justice-of-the-au-en.pdf

Protocol on the Statute of the African Court of Justice and Human Rights. Available at: www.peaceau.org/uploads/protocol-statute-african-court-justice-and-human-rights-en.pdf

Protocol to the African Charter on Human and Peoples Rights on an Establishment of an African Court of Human and Peoples Rights of June 9, 1988. Available at: www.achpr.org/instruments/court-establishment/

Rome Statute of International Criminal Court (1998). Available at: www.icc-cpi.int/nr/rdonlyres/ea9aeff7-5752-4f84-be94-0a655eb30e16/0/rome_statute_english.pdf

Southern African Customs Union (2002 SACU Agreement). Available at: https://wits.worldbank.org/GPTAD/PDF/archive/SACU.pdf

Treaty Establishing a Common Market for Eastern and Southern Africa (COMESA) of November 11, 1993. Available at: www.comesacompetition.org/wp-content/uploads/2016/03/COMESA_Treaty.pdf

Treaty of Lisbon Amending the Treaty on European Union and the Treaty Establishing the European Community, Signed at Lisbon, December 13, 2007. Available at: http://publications.europa.eu/resource/cellar/688a7a98-3110-4ffe-a6b3-8972d8445325.0007.01/DOC_19

Vienna Convention on the Law of Treaties, 1969. Available at: https://treaties.un.org/doc/Publication/UNTS/Volume%201155/volume-1155-I-18232-English.pdf

Vienna Convention on the Law of Treaties between States and International Organizations or between International Organizations, 1986 (A/Conf.129/15). Available at: http://untreaty.un.org/cod/avl/pdf/ha/vcltsio/vcltsio-e.pdf

Vienna Convention on the Protection of the Ozone Layer of 1985. Available at: http://ozone.unep.org/sites/ozone/files/Publications/Handbooks/VC-Handbook-2016-English.pdf

Vienna Convention on the Representation of States in their Relations With International Organizations of a Universal Character, 1975 (A/Conf.67/16). Available at: http://treaties.un.org/pages/ViewDetails.aspx?src=TREATY&mtdsg_no=III-11&chapter=3&lang=en

Vienna Convention on Succession of States in Respect of Treaties, 1978. Available at: http://legal.un.org/ilc/texts/instruments/english/conventions/3_2_1978.pdf

WAEMU Treaty on the West African Economic and Monetary Union, 1994. Available at: www.wipo.int/wipolex/en/other_treaties/details.jsp?treaty_id=313

Other International Documents

Annual Report of the ECJ, 2013, Council of Europe, European Court of Human Rights, 2013. Available at: http://curia.europa.eu/jcms/upload/docs/application/pdf/2014-06/qdag14001enc.pdf

Annual Report of the ECJ, 2017, Council of Europe, European Court of Human Rights, 2017, p. 7. Available at: www.echr.coe.int/Documents/Annual_report_2016_ENG.pdf

The ASEAN Intergovernmental Commission on Human Rights (Terms of Reference), ASEAN Secretariat, Djakarta, 2009.

Draft Articles on the Effect of Armed Conflicts on Treaties With Commentaries, UN 2011. Available at: http://untreaty.un.org/ilc/texts/instruments/english/commentaries/1_10_2. pdf

Draft Articles on the Representation of States in their Relations With International Organizations (With Commentaries) Yearbook of ILC, 1971. Available at: http://untreaty.un.org/ilc/texts/instruments/english/commentaries/5_1_1971.pdf

Draft Articles on the Responsibility of International Organizations With Commentaries, (DARIO), doc. A/66/10, 2011, General Commentary. Available at: http://legal.un.org/ilc/texts/instruments/english/commentaries/9_11_2011.pdf

English Version of the Statute of the Arab Court of Human Rights. Available at: www.acihl.org/texts.htm?article_id=44&lang=en-GB

Explanatory Report to Protocol No. 14 to the Convention for the Protection of Human Rights and Fundamental Freedoms Amending the Control System of the Convention. Available at: https://rm.coe.int/CoERMPublicCommonSearchServices/DisplayDCTMContent?documentId=09000016800d380f

Guide to Practice on Reservations to Treaties (Report of the ILC, GA, Official Records, Supplement No. 10 (Doc. A/66/10)).

ILC: Fragmentation of International Law: Difficulties Arising From the Diversification and Expansion of International Law: Report of the Study Group of the ILC (M. Koskenniemi), Geneve, 2006 (Doc. A/CN.4/L.702). Available at: www.repositoriocdpd.net:8080/bitstream/handle/123456789/676/Inf_KoskenniemiM_FragmentationInternationalLaw_2006.pdf?sequence=1

Joint Declaration on the Establishment of Official Relations Between the European Economic Community and the Council for the Mutual Economic Assistance on June 25, 1988.

Joint Declaration on Political Dialogue Between the European Union and Mercosur on December 1995. Available at: www.sice.oas.org/TPD/MER_EU/negotiations/ministerial_october2004_e.pdf

Official Records of the UN Conference on the Representation of States in their Relations With International Organizations, Vol. II, UN Publication. Available at: http://untreaty.un.org/cod/diplomaticconferences/repofstates_intlorgs-1975/docs/english/vol2/a_conf_67_index.pdf

Report of the Group of Wise Persons to the Committee of Ministers, Doc. CM (2006) 203. Available at: https://search.coe.int/cm/Pages/result_details.aspx?ObjectID=09000016805d7893

Report of ICL on the Work of 52nd Session (2000). Supplement No. 10 (UN Doc. A/55/10). Available at: http://untreaty.un.org/ilc/reports/english/a_55_10.pdf

Report of ILC on the Work of 54th Session (2002), par. 470. Available at: http://untreaty.un.org/ilc/reports/2002/2002report.htm

Report of the Secretary-General's High-Level Panel on Threats, Challenges and Change (2004): "A More Secure World: Our Shared Responsibility United Nations," 2004. Available at: https://documents-dds-ny.un.org/doc/UNDOC/GEN/N04/602/31/PDF/N0460231.pdf?OpenElement

Responsibility of International Organizations (Doc.A/66/10). Available at: http://untreaty.un.org/ilc/reports/2011/2011report.htm

The Rome Declaration-Declaration of the Leaders of 27 Member States and of the European Council, the European Parliament and the European Commission, March 25, 2017. Available at: www.consilium.europa.eu/en/press/press-releases/2017/03/25-rome-declaration/

Rule of Law and Constitution Building: The Role of Regional Organizations. International Institute for Democracy and Electoral Assistance, Stockholm, 2014. Available at: www.idea.int/sites/default/files/publications/rule-of-law-and-constitution-building.pdf

The Statute of the International Law Commission (UN GA Res. 174 (II) (21 November 1947): Establishment of an International Law Commission. Available at: www.worldlii.org/int/other/UNGARsn/1947/75.pdf

Yearbook of the International Law Commission 1981, Vol. II, Part Two. Available at: http://legal.un.org/ilc/publications/yearbooks/english/ilc_1981_v2_p2.pdf

Yearbook of the International Law Commission 2011, Vol. II, Part Two. Available at: http://untreaty.un.org/ilc/reports/2011/2011report.htm

Index